The Demanded Self

The Demanded Self

Levinasian Ethics and Identity in Psychology

David M. Goodman

DUQUESNE UNIVERSITY PRESS
Pittsburgh, Pennsylvania

Copyright © 2012 Duquesne University Press
All Rights Reserved

Published in the United States of America
by
DUQUESNE UNIVERSITY PRESS
600 Forbes Avenue
Pittsburgh, Pennsylvania 15282

No part of this book may be used or reproduced,
in any manner or form whatsoever,
without written permission from the publisher,
except in the case of short quotations
in critical articles or reviews.

Library of Congress Cataloging-in-Publication Data

Goodman, David M.
  The demanded self : Levinasian ethics and identity in psychology / David M. Goodman.
    p. cm.
  Includes bibliographical references and index.
  Summary: "Goodman demonstrates how the ethical dimension of human experience has too frequently been neglected within psychology's present constructs of the self and argues that the philosophical work of Emmanuel Levinas, whose work establishes an originary ethical attunement to the other person, can provide a radical corrective to such morally anemic definitions of the modern self. Includes clinical examples"—Provided by publisher.
  ISBN 978-0-8207-0449-4 (pbk. : alk. paper)
  1. Psychology—Moral and ethical aspects. 2. Levinas, Emmanuel—Ethics. I. Title.
  BF76.4.G65 2012

∞ Printed on acid-free paper

Dedicated to my Prisca

Contents

Acknowledgments xi

1 • An Introduction:
The Self Out of Which We Live 1
   The Self Out of Which We Live 4
      Narrowly Lived Self 5
      Science: A Parentified Child 6
      Scientific Reformation of the Self 7
      Forgetting the Other: Ethics Excluded 10
      Forgetting Ethics: The Other Excluded 12
      Ethics "Defined" 16
   Conclusion 18

Part One
Levinas's Project: Love of Wisdom ≠ Wisdom of Love

2 • Jewgreek.Greekjew:
A Translation of Hebrew into Greek 25
   Background on Levinas: Essential Influences 26
      Levinas the Jew (The Jerusalem Pole) 27
      Levinas the Philosopher (The Athens Pole) 30
      Levinas and the Holocaust 31
   Levinas as Jewish Philosopher? 34
   Levinas as Postsecular 37
   Levinas and Translation 40
      Torah and Translation 40
      Levinas's Translation Project 44
   Psychology as Greek 50
   Conclusion 52

3 • The Idol of Reason: From a Disengaged Self
to a Dis-interested Ethics 55
   Western Self: A Gyges Complex 57

Levinas's Critique of Detached Reason:
　The "Temptation of Temptation" 62
The Reasoned Therapist and Rational Patient 66
　Faceless Theories and Reasoned Therapists 66
　Rational Patients 69
Conclusion 70

**4 • The Normal Bell-Shaped Self:
From Immanentization of Knowledge
to Transcendence of the Other** 73
　The Ego Called Forth: The Ennui of Egoism 74
　The Powerful Powerlessness of the Face 77
　Immanent Psychologies: Science, History, and the
　　Plastic Face 81
　　The Normal Bell-Shaped Self 82
　　Levinas's Critique of Scientific Theory 84
　　Reforming Science 88
　Conclusion 91

**5 • The Buffered Self: From the Individual Subject
to a Subjected Individual** 95
　Idolatry: The Narcissistic Self of the
　　Present Order 96
　"Conatus Amandi" Rather than "Conatus Essendi" ... 100
　Individual Uniqueness as Noninterchangeable
　　Responsibility 103
　Egological Psychology: Sameness without Exit 107
　　Alienation of the "Masterfully Bounded" Self 107
　　Countercultural Therapy and a Demanded Self 112
　Conclusion 115

Part Two
The Demanded Self: Clinical Applications

**6 • *Hineni* and Transference: The Remembering
and Forgetting of the Other** 119
　My Brother's Keeper? 121
　Self Lived as *Hineni* 123

	Forgetting *Hineni*	129
	Conceptual Case Study: Transference	131
	Psychotherapy as Remembering	137
	Systematizing Levinas? The Clinical Conundrum and "Idea of Possibility"	141
	Conclusion	143
7 •	**Hearing "Thou Shalt Not Kill": Psychoanalysis, Enactment, and Levinasian Ethics**	145
	Enactment in Psychological Perspective: Relationship and Repetition	147
	Levinas and Enactment: Violence and Expiation	151
	Conclusion	154
8 •	**The Psyche Awakened: The Other as a "Trauma Which Heals"**	159
	The Assault of the Other	161
	Traumatizing the Traumatized: A Nucleus Fortified	164
	Case Example: Jill	165
	Insomnia: Self Lived with Windows and Doors Open	168
	Conclusion	171
CONCLUSION •	**The Demanded Self: Horizons More Vast Than History**	173
	Levinas as a Prophetic Voice	173
	Parting Statements: The Demanded Self	180
Notes		181
References		205
Index		225

Acknowledgments

When writing a book one draws dangerously close to the edge of utter absorption. And, ironically, while writing a work whose primary goal is to challenge the self-centering orientation of Western paradigms, I must admit that the writing process did little to dislocate me from myself. Rather, it ratcheted up my anxiety and self-referential thoughts in ways that I never thought imaginable. I am thankful to the community of persons, colleagues, and family around me that both tolerated me amidst this writing process and tethered me to the love of which I speak in the following pages. I am thankful for the warmth of loved ones around me, many not directly acknowledged here.

First, I wish to thank my wife, Priscilla, who has borne the burden of my stress, insecurities, and obsession with this project with graciousness, support, and encouragement. She represented for me a Levinasian self beyond what my abstractions allow me to express in the following pages. She will forever be my most precious Other.

Second, I am indebted to my mentor and friend, Al Dueck, who embodies Levinas's "wisdom of love" and sensibility of justice, responsibility, and ethics. It is rare that a student is blessed by a relationship to an advisor so formative both intellectually and personally, introducing me to Levinas's work and reminding me of the depths of my Jewish heritage. I appreciate his patience during my dark periods and his encouraging reminders and admonitions.

Third, I wish to thank Jim Brenneman, whose passion for Hebrew thought, pacifist ethics, and guidance have had great effect, even from a distance. The rigor of his research inspired and challenged this project. Fourth, I am grateful for Susannah Heschel's willing dedication to this project, for the depth of her scholarship, for generously sharing her time, for the warmth of our exchanges, and for the seemingly endless connections that she graciously offered. She brought her father's work to life for me, giving further inspiration to the following pages.

Fifth, I am very thankful for Linda Wagener and her passion for the practical while traversing the most abstract terrain, her stunning cross-disciplinary knowledge, and her encouraging playfulness.

Sixth, I could not have accomplished this project without my best friend, Brian Becker, part brother, part sparring partner. His encouragement, readings, wisdom, and friendship have inspired and shaped my thought.

My grandfather, who died shortly before I began this project, was, without comparison, my biggest fan. He wanted to know everything about what I was doing, what I was reading, and what my future held. Memory of his welcoming eyes and waving hands enlivened me with passion and excitement about this work.

Emmanuel Levinas, the primary thinker behind these pages, represents a "scream in the night" (to use Heschel's words about the prophets). I am thankful for the power of his voice and the incisiveness of his thought. He awakened an "otherwise than being" that will forever challenge my thought and practices within psychology. For his courage, I am grateful.

Likewise, the life and work of Abraham Joshua Heschel is spread throughout the footnotes of this book, both literally and figuratively. His work, like Levinas's, is an inspiring reminder of a different way of being and a calling toward "moral grandeur and spiritual audacity," his life lived as *hineni*, a life lived for justice and love.

I am deeply indebted to Derek George and Heather Macdonald for their thoughtful, thorough, and provocative edits and responses. Likewise, rich conversations with Philip Cushman, Frank Richardson, Marie Hoffman, Mark Freeman, Stuart Pizer, Linda Luz-Alterman, Jack Beinashowitz, Rebecca Drill, Heather Thompson-Brenner, Anne Thompson, Kenneth Reich, and George Kunz were sources of life-giving conversation and meaning in this process.

Several contexts and spheres have also been an incredible source of community and assistance: First, my research group at Fuller, particularly Scott Grover, Julia Langdal, Steven Huett, Adam Ghali, Sabrina Abney, Paul Jones, and Elizabeth Welsh, have given their time, wisdom, and friendship throughout this project. Second, at the

Danielsen Institute at Boston University, my research opportunities, clinical experiences, and incredible dialogues helped keep this project vital. Brian McCorkle, James Burns, and George Stavros were generous with time and financial resources. Enriching conversations with Carol Wintermyer, Miriam Bronstein, David Rupert, Christopher O'Rourke, Lauren Kehoe, Sarah Hassen, Denisa Husarova, Brian Grady, and Tony Gross enlivened this period of writing. My research assistants, Adriana Marcelli and Katie Howe, painstakingly brought clarity and organization to this work where there was little before hand. Katie's questions about and engagement with the text brought excitement to the process. Yearly involvement in the Psychology for the Other conference, Theoretical and Philosophical Psychology (APA Division 24) events, and Psychoanalysis (APA Division 39) gatherings have created spaces for intense learning, scholarly interchange, and support. Finally, my patients at the Danielsen Institute at Boston University and Cambridge Hospital/Harvard Medical School have been a source of amazing and humbling growth.

There are, of course, many others that participated in making this work possible. They are too numerous to list. Please accept my most deeply felt gratitude.

1
An Introduction
The Self Out of Which We Live

In a museum housed in Prague's Jewish Quarter, I stumbled upon an ancient tome inscribed with a definition of Judaism that frames the heart and intent of the following pages: "Judaism is a reminder to the world to awaken from moral slumber."

Elie Wiesel claims that it is our moral obligation to remember (Wiesel et al. 1990); we must look back upon Auschwitz, Dachau, and Treblinka as a means of interrupting the complacency of human consciousness. So quickly, we anesthetize ourselves to the demand made upon us by our lived experience of others, to others' suffering and needs. Wiesel argues that humanity must continuously awaken itself via the alarm of its violent history, littered with horrifying markers of our moral torpor, from *Shoah* to pograms to slavery.

Additionally, less overtly egregious and more subtle violences play out through more insidious and desensitizing influences. In the modern West, one such influence is the preponderant self-orienting and self-referential configuration of human subjectivity. Emmanuel Levinas, a twentieth century Jewish philosopher, argues that in the contemporary Euro-American world, the modern self is such that persons live "anonymous[ly]" alongside other persons. He writes that people "find themselves side by side rather than face to face" (Levinas 1989, 212). He states that the self is largely lived "for-itself." His words point to the fundamental ethical impoverishment of the Western self.

There is a complex genealogy to the development of the egoist self in modern history (some of which is addressed in the following chapters), but the primary focus in this work is psychology and its relation to this anesthetization. As a clinical psychologist, I am profoundly aware of the ways that the discourses, definitions, and constructs of the human self in modern psychology often represent and propagate a way of being that gives primacy to the self and subsequently muffles the other. Like individual consciousness, psychology must be awakened from its moral slumber. My hope is to contribute to a remembering and awakening in a professional community implicated in our present way of experiencing ourselves and others but also carrying the wonderful potential of being anarchic and countercultural in our effect on persons and society.

This book asks the following questions: Do our understandings of the self promote justice? Are the languages used to define human identity and selfhood conducive to ethically lived relationships? Do the selves that modern psychology propagates with its research and clinical practices help to orient persons toward greater moral recognition of and ethical responsibility for the other? How does psychology attend to the question of "goodness"?

More specifically, what if the paradigms of science and its modern history have produced a construct of the self that is severely truncated? What if the self-contained and universally discernable self is merely the derivative of a democratizing language game whose rules have led to myopic conceptions of human identity? What if science, in overextending itself, has left out significant elements that have profoundly destructive repercussions? What if the self is not truly "a being concerned for its own being" (Levinas 2004, 77)? What if the self is only a self "insofar as the self is for-the-other" (Cohen 2002, 42)? That is, what if there is an inexhaustible and unavoidable demand placed upon the self in relationship to others that is fundamental to selfhood? Abraham Joshua Heschel (1963), the beloved twentieth century rabbi and theologian, expresses this sensibility poignantly when he writes, "A person is he of whom demands can be made, who has the capacity to respond to what is required, not only to satisfy his needs and desires. Only a human being is said to be responsible. Responsibility is not something man imputes to himself; he is a self by virtue of his capacity for responsibility, and he would cease to be a self if he were to be deprived of responsibility" (106).

This book challenges the assumptions behind the naturalized, rationalized, and supposedly amoral versions of the modern self and proposes a viable alternative; creating a picture of an ethically constituted self emerging out of conversation with a Jewish philosophical tradition. Scattered throughout the text, I will explore the historical, sociopolitical and economic antecedents to the modern self by investigating the context out of which modern science arose and its subsequent assumptions and uses in psychological theories and practices. Examining the progression of modern psychology toward an emphasis upon egological discourses (centered on the rational and self-preserving faculties of the individual subject) will set the stage for a critique of dominant constructs of the self within it. I argue that modern psychology's starting point in the given order (i.e., what *is*) has limited the questions asked and the means to answering these questions. Their overextended and reductive scientific horizons have constricted their perspectives.

To this end, a Jewish philosophical perspective, as represented by Emmanuel Levinas, will be advanced as a radical corrective to the morally anemic definitions of the modern self. I argue for a version of the self that is inherently demanded. In this version of the self, moral demandedness constitutes self/identity before and more prominently than natural and discoverable processes. The self is most free, most alive, and most awake when exposed to and called forward in responsibility to the other. Applying this Jewish philosophical critique to reigning paradigms of self, an "other-centered" psychology emerges; a psychology that promotes self-emptying, kenosis, and a laying down of one's life for the other (for both the therapist and patient). Freedom is not merely about unencumbered self-expression, actualization, or being fully "functional." And living out the fundamental responsibility for the other promotes a substantive freedom frequently unknown in contemporary contexts (Levinas 1968/1994).

Psychology must remember something more original than its empiricism and normative models allow. Its language still reflects an autonomous, rational self inherent in our historical era, rather than something that precedes and anachronously arrests history—what

Levinas referred to as an *anarchic self* and what I describe as a *demanded self*.

The Self Out of Which We Live

We become what we think of ourselves. (Heschel 1963, 7)

Constructs of the self are not merely detached formulations that remain abstract and objective. These constructs become optics that mediate experience and exist as powerful determinants of persons, cultures, and societies. Definitions of the self set the stage for determining what the self's responsibility is to itself and to others. Some constructs of self sensitize persons to the needs of others and empower them toward social action. However, other constructs of the self permeate a culture with an anesthetizing and deadening way of being, where the self no longer recognizes the other person in a socially responsible and ethical way. That is, there are constructs of self that foster justice and others that foster injustice. The feminist tradition and feminist therapists have long understood that psychological systems and therapy are part of either maintaining the status quo or calling for social change and cultural subversion (Benjamin 1998; Brown 1997, 2004). More recently, crosscultural and multicultural accounts of psychology have brought new levels and dimensions to this challenge (Enriquez 1993; Gergen et al. 1996).

After Foucault, we recognize that discourses and definitions are not "an innocent affair" (Kepnes, Ochs, and Gibbs 1998, 17; see also Foucault 1977). They emerge from existing constellations of power and powerfully shape perception. Language, politics, economics, and social practices coalesce into a discourse through which the self is defined (Prilleltensky 1994; Walzer 1994). Constructs of the self do not emerge from a value-neutral, ahistorical, or apolitical context (Cushman 1995); they are derivative of a sociopolitical, cultural, historical, and economic order.

Furthermore, these definitions and constructs become the *self out of which we live*. Definitions construct human experience. These regulative constructs out of which the self lives are not formulated and conscious, but rather lay at the foundation of our formulations and consciousness (Taylor 1989). They are lived out unreflectively and are "embedded in practices" of everyday life (204). The shape of this self forms our reality—what is given attention, what is considered good, what constitutes the object of focus, and what is the nature of the other in relationship to this self.[1] The self's shape provides the territory, geography, topography, and terrain upon which experience walks.

Narrowly Lived Self

If the self is a living discourse that emerges from the stories (economic, political, religious, social, etc.) that a society tells itself, then (like any story) there are overarching themes, particular parameters as to how "reality" is defined, a system of references, and normative rules of engagement. Cushman (1995) writes, "Each era has a predominant configuration of the self, a particular foundational set of beliefs about what it means to be human. Each particular configuration of the self brings with it characteristic illnesses, local healers, and local healing technologies" (3).[2] Stern (2003) describes this as being part and parcel of being "narrative creatures" whose stories and implicit self-constituting discourses allow for coherency, security, and shared understanding. However, Stern explains, "Telling one story means not telling another. The world is heterogeneous, and any account of it, or of its parts, appears orderly, regular, and seamless only at the cost of excluding from consideration other, conflicting ways of seeing and understanding. Narrative coherence is the result of invisible underlying assumptions that shear off some parts of life and corral others" (144). To tell ourselves one story of selfhood is to exclude and be blind to alternatives.[3] In short, the contours of the self both allow for and limit the types of experience possible and the ways in which one experiences. As it has been extensively argued elsewhere (Cohen 2002; Richardson, Fowers, and Guignon 1999; Shuman and Meador 2003), modern science and its more recent offspring, the psychological discipline, function as powerful and dominant authorities and sources through which the self is given definition within twenty-first century American culture.

A first step in the process of unpacking what is included and excluded in the *self out of which we live* is considering what contextual and historical guides have configured the preponderant definitions of the self. Understanding the heuristic by which we construe our selves and others requires something of a genealogy, an uncovering of the systemic underpinnings.

Science: A Parentified Child

Many scholars have narrated how the "timbers of Modernity" (Toulmin 1990) erected the edifice of science that remodeled the European intellectual landscape over the last several centuries (Danziger 1990, 1997; Leahey 2004; MacIntyre 1990, 1998; Toulmin 1990). The story illuminates how the historical, theological, political, and economic contexts of Europe during the sixteenth century and following created a significant shift in ethics, reason, and human identity.

In short, modern history ushered in a large-scale shift wherein scientific epistemology became the dominant means of knowing and living in the world (Critchley 2001). Science was propelled into authoritative status as an arbiter of warring factions and traditions in postfeudal and war torn Europe (Toulmin 1990). It was tasked with the formation of a discourse about reality that could be democratically agreed upon across all rational beings, regardless of tradition or historical context; it was charged to bring stability and peace. Asked to be free of ideology, science attempted to democratize and universalize all knowledge, to discern the truths that lie beyond perspective and era. It was to be a secular truth, using a language that transcended particular discourses—a *lingua franca* (Dueck and Reimer 2009). This commission warped science's development and, like a parentified child, its identity was lost in the context of the family system. Homeostasis—stability and order—was its priority and the inherent limitations in its methodology were ignored for the sake of function (to be addressed more fully in chapter 4). Science ultimately trumped and consumed philosophy and theology in order to establish a foundational epistemology to which all rational persons could agree (Danziger 1990). This "quest for certainty" (Toulmin 1990, 55–56)—of which modern science was a significant part—obfuscated and made inconsequential all things that lay outside of the natural, rational, measurable, and observable present order. Anything that could not be classified or quantified became nonscientific and irrelevant. Cohen (1994) writes,

In straining to establish and maintain the rights of its universality, knowledge insists on its autonomy as well, building for itself the protective hegemony of a paradigm or ideology. It resolutely remains within itself by transforming every other into "the same," from one end of its universe to the other. Such is the *empire of the empirical*. But the strain of establishing and maintaining its internal security and equilibrium shows. It inevitably excommunicates (as "subjective," "primitive," "infantile," "stupid," or "mad") the claims and orientations it can never comfortably make its own. Outside of science we are but fools and madmen. (xiii)[4]

In the vacuum of any "unity system of common belief," the "task of organizing personality in the West" (Rieff 1987, 2) became a fundamental concern. Modern psychology became the organizer.[5] However, modern psychology was born into a context that espoused the universalizing and democratizing sensibilities of the Enlightenment project. This was a setting wherein certainty was sought, governing principles were intoxicating, and universal truths were deemed discernable through scientific methodology. And, with an empirical epistemology at the helm, the visible, measurable, and observable given order was understood to be all there is in the equation of identity. The implications of this on how the self encounters, responds to, and understands the other are tremendous.

Scientific Reformation of the Self

> *The masterful, bounded self of today, with few allegiances and many subjective 'inner feelings,' is a relatively new player on the historical stage.* (Cushman 1995, 357)

John Locke was one of the earliest to perceive the anthropological gap left open in modernity. As a successor and radicalizer of Cartesian thought, Locke recognized that the implications of this epistemological shift must inevitably reach into our understanding of the human self and identity. He was among the first of the modern philosophers to venture into what he called a "reformation" of the self (Cushman 1995, 378).[6] Locke, and those who followed after him, were concerned with establishing a construct of the self—a self out of which people might live—derived from the "methodological application of scientific discipline" and not the "bonds of tradition and authority"

(377). Descartes's concern for autonomous reason was applied, by Locke, to the definition of the human self. Scientific methodology, then, became the epistemological source for understanding human identity and interhuman relations.[7]

By the nineteenth century, beginning with psychophysics and structuralism, psychological methodologies began utilizing scientific discourse as the primary language and heuristic for the human self. Quantification and measurement allowed psychology to be considered an "exact science" and to distinguish itself from philosophy, spiritualism, and theology (Danziger 1990, 147). In the process of "deconversion" (Rieff 1987, 2) and "disenchantment" of the material world (Weber 1994), the "sanctity and status of the church" was given over to secular enterprises (Cushman and Gilford 2000, 993). Psychology adopted the methodology of the natural sciences, seeking an observable, replicable, and explicable order for its definitions of identity. The formation of common discourse and approaches to understanding the human self lent legitimacy and prestige to psychology's claims as it appeared to promise the same reliability and verifiability as the natural sciences. Despite the opposition of particular modernist thinkers who decried the formation of a psychological science (e.g., Hume and Kant),[8] psychology was inducted into the hall of modern sciences and served a particular and local purpose in Western history (Gergen 2000). Rieff (1987) contends that the yearning for a "post-communal faith" ultimately paved the road for a parade of modern psychological theories.

Psychology[9] in its many modern forms became the discipline that a secularizing society would entrust with the task of defining the human person. The secularizing language of modern psychology, with its inherent values, assumptions, vocabulary, and limitations, was passed along, constructing the next generation's language and reality. As Lyotard (1984) writes, science became the "metanarrative" through which the parameters of meaning were determined. Critchley (2001), commenting on the permeation and domination of scientific epistemology, observes,

> As we are all acutely aware, we live in a scientific world, a world where we are expected to provide empirical evidence for our claims or find those claims rightly rejected. The scientific conception of the world, which dates back to the early decades of the seventeenth century in

England and France, dominates the way we see things and, perhaps even more importantly, the way we *expect* to see things. We expect to see things somewhat like spectators in a theatre where we can inspect them theoretically—the Greek word for a theatre spectator is a *theoros*. Things are present as objects that are empirically and immediately given in the form of sensations or representations. Science gives us knowledge of the nature of such things. These things are then called "facts." (4)

Universal and transhistorical facts were central to the advancement of a new organization of the self and personality. The modern scientific gaze—fixated on rational measurement of the natural (immanent) order—set the basis for the psychological sciences to represent selfhood in a generic form, with attributes, characteristics, drives, adaptation-based functions, and a complex intrapsychic topography. Now, in the beginning of the twenty-first century, we have sophisticated nosologies and vocabularies for diagnoses, personality types, and the specific effect sizes for particular types of treatment orientations as they relate to specific personality characteristics and diagnostic profiles. We have tools that measure personality differences across categorical and dimensional scales. Nearly a century and a half from their inception, the psychological sciences have established themselves as an economic, political, and academic force. The influence of the psychological discipline stretches from individual treatment in hospital settings to pop culture exposure on TV shows and best selling, self-help books that populate entire sections in Barnes & Noble. It exists as an accepted and sought-out source of discourse. The language, concepts, and practices surrounding the Euro-American, psychologized self have had enormous repercussions on intrapsychic, interpersonal, societal, economic, and political life.

Modern psychology has helped form the story out of which the Western self lives. Human persons are now what Philip Rieff (1987) calls "psychological men" and the psychotherapist a "secular spiritual guide" (25). The language of "mental health"—adaptation, coping, needs, ego, and so forth—are common place, the public language for the self. Depression, anxiety, psychosis, dissociation, and somatization are now household descriptors for describing problematic function.[10] Modern psychology has created systems of meaning that are familiar and assumed. These psychological discourses have, over time, contributed significantly to the constructed horizons of human experience, and thus have supremely influenced the possibilities and limitations of our thought and actions. The human person is understood through these discourses by default; a product of its preponderant use in our contemporary context.

If, as described above, the *self out of which we live* is a story told to the exclusion of others, then what remains unformulated within our story? What is not given space? What is lobbed off in our historical situatedness and our derivative consciousness? Defined primarily through scientific paradigms, what is concealed in the modern "psychological" self?

Forgetting the Other: Ethics Excluded

> *Narrative coherence may foreclose an ethical resource.* (Butler 2005)

Heidegger critiques Greek and Enlightenment philosophies for "a forgetfulness of Being," but it may be better understood as a "forgetfulness of the other" (Critchley 2002, 19). Taylor (1989) argues that Western theories have "read so many goods out of our official story, we have buried their power so deep beneath layers of philosophical rationale, that they are in danger of stifling" (520). For a variety of reasons, the emergent self within modern history became a self lived "for-itself." It existed as a self defined in isolation, based on rational and empirical principles and detached from relationship. Individuals were construed within a monadic discourse and understood in relationship to principles and quantifiable measurements (Danziger 1990, 1997). Firm, "non-porous" boundaries between the self and other provided clear demarcations between individual identities (Cushman 1995). Chapters three through five will chronicle the ways in which this has contributed to a normative narcissism out of which many live.

In response to the modern self and its codification in Euro-American philosophy and psychology, there have been increasing pockets of discontent. In *The Covenanted Self,* Walter Brueggeman (1999) points to a remarkable couple of years in the first quarter of the twentieth century when four disparate thinkers—Buber, Rosenzweig, Ebner, and Marcel—challenged the autonomous and agentic ego and suggested the interhuman and "restless, unsettleable relation" to be a location of more profound meaning when discussing human identity (1).

For a variety of reasons, some of which involve the desire to maintain parity with medical professions in order to bill for services, modern psychologies have been slow to recognize and internalize these critiques and alternatives (Clegg and Slife 2005; Cushman and Gilford 2000). Mainstream psychological theory and practice continues to push toward empirically based practices/treatments, seen in the growing popularity of cognitive behavior models and manualized treatment regimens. Essentialist and universalizing language has infused the psychological sciences far more than other social sciences (Gantt and Williams 2002). Many modern psychologies remain deeply entrenched within a monadic and individualistic paradigm, and the Enlightenment self continues to survive and thrive in psychological theory and practice.

Contrarily, much of contemporary philosophy has dispelled the decrepit myths of the modern self. In the place of a unified, monadic self with universal drives and normative adaptive characteristics, there is a growing consensus that humans are inherently interdependent and social, linguistically bound, and political. The intersubjective space between persons has become a profoundly rich locale for new research and for creative engagement with new models of understanding the self as constituted in a relational nexus. These are beneficial steps that will, hopefully, provide further movement away from the reified, "richly furnished interior" (to use Foucault's words) of the modern self that has hampered our ethical sensibilities and tolerances.

There are kindred movements within particular camps of the psychological literature where one can witness a growing awareness of the monadic and acontextual skew of constructs of self, along with the alienation, isolation, and disconnection that they produce phenomenologically and sociologically. Attachment literature, object relations theory, community psychology, crosscultural and multicultural psychologies, intersubjectivity theory, particular neurobiological research, feminist thought, narrative theory, and relational psychoanalysis are just a few examples of the shifting of psychological paradigms to be more inclusive of the other in how the self is defined. Hermeneutical and social constructivist philosophies have contributed greatly to these challenges to the mainstream: mutuality, reciprocity, and relationality have become buzz words and popular correctives to the individualism latent in modern psychological paradigms.

This book also moves toward a greater relational understanding of the self, but challenges its shape and trajectory. The laudable move from monadic individual to socially constituted subject often retains a version of the self that is essentially distanced from ethical relation. The Western self, even in its more relational forms, is a narrowly lived self that excludes a substantively ethical mode of relating and way of perceiving. The goal here is to bring ethics out from underneath its suppression in philosophical and psychological discourse (Robbins 1991).

The work of Emmanuel Levinas provides a helpful means of navigating this issue. His project specifically considers the relationship between the ethical and the psyche, and his primary focus is on how the self encounters the other. Levinas's thought will be the primary engine by which the modern, Euro-American self is called into question throughout the following chapters. His admonition that "ethics is first philosophy" is a radical alternative to the logocentrism and empiricism that has provided the bedrock for modern philosophies and psychologies. His starting point, a Jewish philosophy, is profoundly different from the preponderant paradigms.

Forgetting Ethics: The Other Excluded

When one reads about "ethics" in the psychological literature, one generally encounters "ethical codes" prescribed for professional practice.[11] These codes, such as those published under the American Psychological Association (1992), are centered around reducing possible harm to patients and research participants and/or protecting professionals against the risk of legal and financial liabilities and infractions (Birrell 2006).[12] Largely preventative, these ethics subscribe to the "lowest common denominator" of ethical meaning (Brown 1997, 58) and are often conflated with risk management (Birrell, 95). It is significant to remember that the APA did not even develop a code of ethics until 1953, largely as a response to the "Nuremberg war crimes trials, when it became clear that principles of science and good research methodologies could also yield the horrors of fascism and the experiments of the Nazi doctors" (Brown, 52).

In general, however, modern psychology does not consider the realm of ethics when addressing definitions of the self. As long as it remains "scientific," the field trusts that it is engaging in the betterment of humanity. Brown (1997) explains,

> Among the underlying problematic assumptions of dominant ethical codes in psychology, one is particularly thorny: the assumption that what psychologists do as researchers, clinicians, teachers, supervisors and consultants is basically benign and inherently of value because it is based on "science," and that it will remain good only so long as it is firmly anchored in "science." This assumption defines "science" as knowledge derived from logical positivist "proof through disproof" controlled experimentation. It is voiced most strongly in the APA code's most recent revision, in which the opening sentences of the preamble replace a primary allegiance to human welfare with a hymn to "a valid and reliable body of scientific knowledge based on research" [APA, 1992: 1599]. (Brown, 53–54)

Little attention, however, is paid to more implicit social and cultural attitudes and values. Brown wrote, "They emphasize the avoidance of overt 'sins,' but pay little attention to errors of omission or covert expressions of damaging attitudes and values" (52).[13] Ethics, from this stance, has little to do with the very constitution, definition, and normalization of persons. "[T]here is very little emphasis in the psychological literature on the ethics of relationships and how ethical rules play themselves out (or fail to) in living relationships...or how we are or are not present with the human being facing us" (Birrell 2006, 97–98).

Modern psychologies, riding the crest of naturalistic sciences and its claims of neutrality, have often decentered and displaced morality and ethics from their descriptions of the self. Gantt and Williams (2002) argue this clearly: "In adopting the methods and philosophical justifications of a positivist, naturalistic science of human behavior, most psychologists have felt it necessary to abandon questions about morality and ethical obligation" (1). Modern psychologies have either left morality out of the purview of their constructs or assumed that morality emerges from what is discerned to be most natural, normative, and functional. In the latter approach (arguably the most common in reigning psychological paradigms), thoughts, feelings, and behaviors deemed adaptive or "normal" are implicitly coequated with what is "good" and "right" for the individual. The repeatable, verifiable, and measurable focus of the psychological sciences has limited its scope of study to the description of what *is* (i.e., an empirically deduced human "nature"). Human nature then, applied prescriptively, becomes the basis of morality and ethics.

Furthermore, particularly in modernity, morality has either been located internally as an attribute or characteristic of the rational thought of the Cartesian subject (e.g., moral reasoning, moral consciousness, etc.) or has been located externally as the outgrowth of social contract and societal requirements that allow for the maximization of pleasure for the majority of persons and allow for the possibility of social order (e.g., Mill, Paine, Hobbes). Part of the brilliance of Freudian theory was the collapsing of both paradigms into one metatheory of personality. Freud's treatment of morality epitomized the modern shift in moral discourse that had preceded him and set the stage for the theories and practices of modern psychology that were to follow. His "exile" of morality to the superego was representative of the prevailing trends in how morality and the self were understood to be related (Doherty 1995), illustrative of the distancing of morality from the self. Morality became a subtype of reasoning and a form of rational consciousness.[14] Taylor (1989) observes, "It is not essential to the Ego that it orient itself in a space of questions about the good, that it stand somewhere on these questions. Rather the reverse. The Freudian Ego is at its freest, is most capable of exercising control, when it has the maximal margin of manoeuvre in relation to the imperious demands of the Superego as well as in the face of the urgings of the Id. The ideally free Ego would be a lucid calculator of pay-offs" (33). Ethics was exiled from the ego, located in an often "tyrannical" superego that had been internalized and imposed from surrounding civilization (Doherty 1995, 9; see also Freud 1930/1961b), derivative of external strictures borne out of tradition and social contract. In Freud's model, morality was often antithetical to nature. And, with nature as the fundamental subject of the psychological sciences, morality was ostracized from modern constructs of self.[15]

The self out of which we live, storied in the scientific world within which we live,[16] formed around a new language that removed morality even further from the definitions of being human, at the very least making morality derivative of the universalized principles of human nature. "Mental hygiene" supplanted "goodness" (Rieff 2006, xxiv). Doherty (1995) writes, "A cornerstone of all the mainstream models of psychotherapy since Freud has been the substitution of scientific and clinical ideas for moral ideas" (9). The language and ideas of right and wrong, good and bad, and just and unjust, for many within psychology, became a relic of religious oppression, a neurosis inducing system of dogma that created ego-dystonic irrationality (Ellis and Blau 1998; Freud 1927/1961a). What is good, what is right, and what is holy are subsumed into the describable realm of functionality (Rieff 2006). The parameters of scientific inquiry dislocated morality and ethics from its definitions of the human self.

Thus, the "language game" of modern psychological tradition cannot speak substantively about or engage meaningfully with morality, obligation, and ethics. These desacralizations within Euro-American language have been prominently featured in the expanding and imperializing progression of scientific thought in the modern, industrializing world (Berger 1970). Because of the "unfortunate adoption of scientific epistemology, coupled with an unyielding theoretical commitment to reductive causal explanations, contemporary psychology is singularly ill equipped to account for human action in any manner that might preserve its essentially moral character" (Gantt and Williams 2002, 10–11). Modern psychological constructs of the self and human identity are purportedly amoral, neutral, and nonevaluative, with the language of ethical experience, demand, obedience, and obligation left out of normative discourse regarding selfhood.

Particular postmodern thinkers have worked to restore an understanding of the person as a moral and ethical being. Beyond the argument that the self is situated, contextual, embedded, local, historical, and traditioned, they remind us that every configuration of the self bears particular "moral ideas" and a "moral topography" (Taylor 1989). Furthermore, thought is always mixed with questions of value, priority, and goodness. The self is engaged in perpetual moral reasoning and encounter, whether or not it is aware of it. Cushman (2007) argues, "The good, according to this interpretation, encompasses much of what current therapists refer to as character structure, object relations, self-state regulation, identity, Jungian complexes, the subject positions of gender, race, and class.... Understandings of the good may differ in content, but not in location: they are central to human being. Traditions about the good are not clothing we take on or off. They come to constitute us" (78).

Ethics, for Levinas, is disturbing and existentially dislocating. Though helpful and a step in the right direction, the representations of "ethics" made by Cushman, Taylor, and others need to be more radical.[17] The "goods" of the self that Taylor speaks of within particular moral topographies, moral space, and moral ontologies are not what Levinas meant by ethics. Ethics, in his view, is not a set of principles, capacities, or judgments, not a type of consciousness, a series of attributes, or ascribing to a registry of goods. Ethics is not a philosophical subdiscipline or a regulatory set of rules and laws. Kant's "categorical imperative" or Rawls's consensus-based ethics is a wholly different type of ethics than Levinas's. His definition, born from his Jewish heritage, was more specifically visceral, lived, interpersonal, and phenomenological.

Ethics "Defined"

What is meant by "ethics" from a Levinasian perspective? Defining this term is a complicated venture. Levinas, despite his frequent use of the term "ethics," clarified many times that his work was not an "ethics" in any doctrinal, normative, or principled form. When asked "What is the ethical?" Levinas (2004) responds, "It is the recognition of holiness." He explains further: "*The concern for the other breaches concern for the self.* This is what I call holiness. Our humanity consists in being able to recognize this priority of the other" (235, *italics mine*). Ethics, for Levinas, is a specific and interhuman ethical response to the other's needs. It is taking responsibility for the needs of the other, and putting him or her before oneself.

What has goodness to do with the human self? According to Levinas, goodness is the wellspring of the self. For Levinas, the "ethical" is the necessary condition for the self. There can be no self without recognition of the other person and an ethical responsibility for him or her. The self cannot be defined without the other and it is in ethical relationship to this other that the self is bestowed. He explains, "Thus ethics is no longer a simple moralism of rules which decree what is virtuous. It is the original awakening of an I responsible for the other; the accession of my person to the uniqueness of the I called and elected to responsibility for the other" (Levinas and Robbins 2001, 182).

With Levinas at the helm, I argue for a radically different understanding of an ethical self, invoking Levinas's definition of the ethical as holiness and goodness.[18] This self is a demanded self. Ethics is moral attunement to the other, the radical exposure of the self to the needs, calling, and demand of the other. It is a posturing of the self toward the outside of the self, always at its own edges and beyond.

Ethics and selfhood, instead of being ontologically construed, interrupt nature, history, and essences, disturbing the complacency of our definitions and calling us beyond the status quo. Ethics is found in relationship to what transcends the self, calls it into question, and calls it toward love. Ethics is a story of the self that perpetually exceeds the history, situatedness, embeddedness, locality, history, normality, and contemporary tradition of the self. Simply stated, it challenges our normative depictions of and discourses about selfhood, particularly those that emphasize autonomous selfhood. It is a countercultural version of the self, not allowing nature and the immanent to define that which is, at least in part, transcendent (always beyond and in excess of). Ethics, in this sense, cannot be constructed. It constructs us.

The "recognition of this priority of the other" is too frequently omitted from the way that modern psychology conceptualizes the self. Morality and ethics are largely ignored in discussions about human identity, or, at most, when morality and ethics are discussed, they are not understood to mean the same thing as the "holiness" alluded to above.[19] Levinas (1961/1969) argues that modern psychologies are "deaf to exteriority" (291), thus forging constructs of selfhood that work to reduce difference and otherness and make persons intelligible through categories of sameness. Subsequently, we become subjects who are deafened to otherness, and with it, ethical relation.

Thus the scientific inception of modern psychology, in setting the scope and limiting the prevailing constructs of the self and their derivative "technologies of healing," thereby incapacitate ethics from defining human identity. These psychologies form a generic shape of the human self lacking in moral richness. Levinas's Jewish philosophy will be used in the pages that follow as a prophetic corrective to the reigning constructs of self that undergird Western civilization, and more specifically, as a corrective to certain forms of modern psychology and their theories and clinical practices.[20] Williams (2007) states, "The result of all of this is a new perspective on, or, better perhaps, confrontation with, ethics and a new root metaphor for human being and for personality. Rather than being a subset of the contemporary epistemological and the ontological projects, ethics is moved to the center of all considerations of being and thus all psychological understanding. This ethical perspective lies at the heart of psychology and psychoanalysis insofar as they deal with questions of who we are, who we ought to be, and how we ought to be with each other. To the extent psychology does not deal with just these questions it is irrelevant to the human condition" (692).

Conclusion

My hope is that persons interested in clinical work, social sciences, theoretical and philosophical psychology, contemporary continental philosophy, psychoanalysis, intersubjectivity theories, and psychological, anthropological, and sociological research can use this text to enter into some of the conversations taking place at the intersection of Levinas's ethical theory, psychology, psychoanalysis, religion, and philosophy. The conversation questions the complacency of a self lived "for-itself" and looks at a countercultural version of the self that lives in ethical responsiveness to others along with corollary therapeutic practices that engender this sensibility.

Taylor (1989) states, "We have to fight uphill to rediscover the obvious, to counteract the layers of suppression of modern moral consciousness" (90). In contemporary psychological work, a profession-wide dissociative amnesia allowed a scientific "narrative rigidity" (Stern 2003, 132) to develop. In clinical psychology, it is generally understood that as patients learn about their history, assumptions, and contexts, they can begin to ask themselves hard questions and engage in the arduous process of change and growth. Similarly, psychology should learn from its history, honestly consider its assumptions, and diligently explore its role within society (concurrently shaping and being shaped by its context). It is of considerable interest, however, that for a discipline that emphasizes the need for discerning sources and seeking etiological nuance, modern psychology often sleepwalks through its own assumptions about the human self. Questions about what underlies our definitions of the human self, what philosophical systems are drawn from, and what greater contextual elements are involved in the formation of the self out of which we live, are largely ignored in mainstream psychological literature. For a variety of reasons, modern psychologies have reflected and propagated versions of the self that are valorized as ahistorical and without need of critical examination (Cushman 1995).

There is no shortage of critiques of modern psychology and psychotherapy. The origins and shortcomings of the "masterfully bounded self" have been elaborated upon by many. A growing number of scholars and clinicians have decried psychology's culpability in the moral condition of Western society. Doherty (1995) admonishes his colleagues by stating, "We can no longer hide behind the wizard's veil of clinical objectivity and moral neutrality. The culture we helped to shape for a hundred years is in crisis, partly because people believe what we told them about the good life" (20). Richardson, Fowers, and Guignon (1999) remark that "thoughtful critics...express concern that a certain one-sided individualistic outlook is built into the very fabric of therapy and practice, making it likely that modern psychotherapy helps perpetuate a way of life that gives rise to many of the problems in living that therapy itself is intended to ameliorate" (239). The status quo of the "sovereign" self within our society, a self that has been both worshipped and "defamed" by its primacy (Heschel 1963), is guarded and maintained by many facets of the psychological profession. Many psychologies have reflected the cultural terrain of "self-worship" and have been the primary educators and justifiers of this as a social norm (Vitz 1977).

During the twentieth century, the work of Erich Fromm provided a prophetic voice that critiqued the normative order as being an inappropriate measure of human identity.[21] Fromm (1955) argues that psychology became an "apologist for the status quo" (73) and contends that we have come to define maturity and health "as adjustment to our society, without ever raising the question whether this adjustment is to a healthy or a pathological way of conducting one's life" (74).[22] Fromm (1947) further reminds us, "The great humanistic ethical thinkers of the past... were philosophers *and* psychologists; they believed that the understanding of human nature and the understanding of values and norms for his life were interdependent" (viii). Echoing much of what will be fleshed out in the following chapters, he suggested, "Psychoanalysis, in an attempt to establish psychology as a natural science, made the mistake of divorcing psychology from problems of philosophy and ethics" (6).

Aligning with a variety of contemporary critics of mainstream, modern psychology (Cohen 2002; Cushman 1995; Gantt and Williams 2002; Prilleltensky 1994; Richardson, Fowers, and Guignon 1999; Slife and Wendt 2006; Williams and Gantt 1998), I suggest a moral discourse regarding the self that allows for calling into question or fissuring the given order. Modern pictures of the autonomous, agentic self are held suspect across a variety of disciplines, but in modern psychology, it remains the dominant heuristic. A reassessment of our understanding of the self is necessary. Locke understood that based on the changing zeitgeist, there needed to be a fundamental shift in the way that the world understood the self; the same reappraisal and reformation is needed in the present, though in a fundamentally different direction than he would have suggested.

Derrida (1978) is accurate when he argues that the language for the *self out of which we live*, the common sense through which we experience, is a form of "autistic" discourse where the other is lost, and our ethical obligations to him or her are muted. It is a "societal pathology" (Fromm 1955): the story of the self that we tell ourselves, reflected in psychological practices, deafens us to a substantive sense of moral demandedness in our self-definition and experience. Throughout this work, I argue that the ethical dimension of human experience is too frequently forgotten, neglected, and unattended within present constructs of the self and their parent discipline, modern psychology. The scientific imperative to secularize and democratize meaning has reduced conceptual possibilities and, with them, the possibility of an ethical or demanded self.

If, as argued in this chapter, the self out of which we live is an optics—a way of seeing and experiencing—then how can the self become an ethical optics (Levinas 1985); an optics both shaped by ethical relationship and attuned to the other? This concern is similarly voiced by Cushman (1995) when he asks: "Are there not new configurations of the self that we could develop, new ways of being human, that could help us live in a different terrain, a terrain that might allow new moral understandings of ourselves and others to emerge?" (355). Might psychotherapy become a practice that values this process of finding "new ways of being human," particularly as it relates to the paucity of moral attunement present in the current self out of which we live? Might psychotherapy be a process whereby our patients'[23] moral attunements in relationship to others are enriched and enlivened?

As psychologists, we have an obligation to consider the goodness of our constructs. A prophetic challenge—a calling from beyond the status quo—is needed; for of its own resources, science cannot move beyond it. From whence does a voice come to dislodge us from our blinded and constricted common sense? How can we judge the validity, goodness, and appropriateness of the self out of which we live? If this self is largely a normative phenomenon that is socially constructed and lived out, then from where do alternative possibilities come other than through the dialectic of history?[24]

In response to some of these questions, the following section will more fully delineate the unique quality of Levinas's thought in order to lay the basis for his prophetic model of dialogical ethics, using his admonishment of Western philosophy, history, subjectivity, and morality to explore and constructively challenge contemporary psychological constructs of the self.

Part One

Levinas's Project:
Love of Wisdom ≠ Wisdom of Love

2

Jewgreek.Greekjew

A Translation of Hebrew into Greek

In the foreword to Wiesel's *Night* (1960/1990), the French Catholic writer and Nobel Laureate François Mauriac exclaims, "I believe that on that day I touched for the first time upon the mystery of iniquity whose revelation was to mark the end of one era and the beginning of another. The dream which Western man conceived in the eighteenth century, whose dawn he thought he saw in 1789, and which, until August 2, 1914, had grown stronger with the progress of enlightenment and the discoveries of science—this dream vanished finally for me before those trainloads of little children" (8).

During an interview, Levinas questioned how the Western world could speak about morality after Auschwitz.[1] Western systems of morality, in his eyes, had failed. MacIntyre (1984) similarly describes moral discourse within contemporary culture as being in shambles. Taylor (1989, 2007) observes that modern thought and culture was largely detached from any deep moral sources. Critchley (2007) argues that the context of disappointment, failure, and lack that pervaded the formation of modern philosophy led to a severe deficit in the development of a meaningful "theory of the ethical subject" (39).

In part, the overextension of science within modernity, and its radical implications concerning how the self is understood and lived, produced this moral failure. The scientific gaze is incapable of defining the human person without severe truncation. Mining history for its meaning, science has no access to "horizons more vast"

(Levinas 1961/1969) than the given sociopolitical, economic, and natural order. Reason and history have failed as an approach to persons. Psychological theories and practices have failed as well.

The work of Levinas represents an alternative course. Levinas is a prominent, relatively recent philosophical voice in the conversation about the moral condition of the *self out of which we live*. Levinas's most fundamental concern is how ethical relation to the other was lost in Western thought and discourse. He attempts to bring ethics out of dormancy and suppression, into human experience (Cohen 1994; Robbins 1991). His "ethics as first philosophy"[2] offers a trenchant critique of the trajectory of Western thought from its Hellenistic roots through its more contemporary versions in Husserl and Heidegger.

Though Levinas made few explicit references to psychology, he critiqued the many Western philosophical wells from which modern psychologies drink. There has been considerable recent interest in the application of Levinas's philosophy to clinical psychology.[3] His philosophy is a powerful avenue through which these psychologies can consider the ethical implications of their definitions, constructs, and practices.

This chapter begins with a brief sketch of three primary influences upon Levinas's life, providing a context for understanding his work and showing his unique ability to create dialogue between disparate epistemologies and languages. Second, I suggest that Levinas's overarching project is one of *translation,* expressing his Hebrew sensibilities in and through the "Greek" academy. I describe the importance of this translation to the process of introducing new possibilities and challenges into the status quo and the self out of which we live. This chapter will set the stage for the following chapters that consider how Hebrew sensibilities might infuse, challenge, and shape the normative practices and constructs of the self within Euro-American psychological thought and the work of therapy.

BACKGROUND ON LEVINAS: ESSENTIAL INFLUENCES

Levinas is often read without sufficient attention to the essential tension and dialectic between "Hebraic" thought and the dominant vein of Western ("Greek") philosophy.[4] Levinas "moves constantly between the poles Jerusalem and Athens, or between prophecy and philosophy"⁵ (Burggraeve 2007, 21). However, the "Jerusalem pole" is often omitted in expositions and applications of his thoughts, and with it, the prophetic and more radical nature of his work.⁶ Gibbs (1992) writes, "Levinas has been read as a philosopher, while the Jewish dimension of his thought has largely been ignored, or honored by a mention and then ignored" (10). This is particularly true in recent scholarship that relates Levinas's thinking to psychological theories and practice,⁷ leading to a domestication and, often, misunderstanding of the prophetic nature of his work.

Levinas's frequent allusions to Scripture and religious terminology require a religious literacy without which his thought loses some of its dimension. For instance, his concepts of "glory," "substitution," "expiation," "election," and even his central argument for ethics (holiness) and responsibility cannot be duly considered without understanding the Jewish history, beliefs, and practices that undergird their application.⁸ Cohen (1994) explained, "One way to characterize the 'Jewishness' of Levinas's thought at the broadest level is to see its opposition to philosophy as the most recent avatar of the ancient and perhaps eternal opposition between Jerusalem and Athens, the Bible and Homer, Jew versus Greek" (127).⁹ Throughout Levinas's work, as Gibbs (1992) writes, he argued that "philosophy stands in greatest need of its other, of an ethics that breaks in upon the ontological pursuit of identity and autonomy. The yearning for transcendence, radical transcendence, for a relationship to an other that does not admit of assimilation, that yearning is philosophical to the core, but Levinas contrasts that desire for alterity with the dominant philosophical tradition, which reigns complacently from Parmenides to Heidegger. Levinas claims that philosophy can be renovated, reoriented in pursuit of radical transcendence, in the service of ethics" (23).

*Levinas the Jew (The Jerusalem Pole)*¹⁰

Three formative influences upon Levinas's life and their subsequent impact upon his philosophical and confessional work include his Lithuanian Jewish heritage[11]; Western philosophical tradition, particularly his phenomenological training with Husserl and Heidegger; and the Holocaust.[12]

Levinas was born in Kaunas (a.k.a. Kovno), Lithuania in 1906 to a moderately well-off, traditional, Orthodox Jewish family. From birth, Levinas was surrounded by Jewish culture, "like the very air one breathes" (Cohen 1994, 114). Before WWII, one quarter of Kaunas's population was Jewish, and the city was known for its prestigious yeshivas and Jewish cultural institutions. Vilna, the capital of Lithuania (not very far from Kaunas), was commonly referred to as the "Jerusalem of the East" (Malka 2002/2006, 3). Levinas's family also interacted with contemporary liberal culture.[13] His parents spoke Yiddish to one another, though Russian was the primary language used in their home. Starting at age six, Levinas learned Hebrew. He was constantly exposed to a variety of ideas and cultures, particularly from 1915–1919, when his family was expelled from Lithuania due to pogroms and German invasion and resituated in the Ukraine.

Kaunas was an "inexhaustible reservoir of rabbis, of Talmudists and educators" (Malka 2002/2006, 15). It was a style of Yeshiva learning whose methods of study were highly sophisticated and whose emphasis upon scholarship remains prominent to this day.[14] Furthermore, it espoused a particular form of Judaism, reacting to the shifting landscape of European Judaism following the beginnings of Hasidism in the eighteenth century. The Litvak culture that developed dominated Lithuanian Jewry, forming a union against the Hasidic Judaism that had been established to its east in the Ukraine and Belarus. Hasidism was less concerned about intellectual rigor, placing greater value on the immediate experience of God, God's love, and "being in God" (Burggraeve 2007, 23), as opposed to the Litvak "love of knowledge" and "familiarity with texts" (Malka 2002/2006, 11), which adamantly opposed the pietism, emotivism, and mysticism of Hasidic practice.[15] Lithuanian Jews, largely "Enlightened Jews," highly involved in the academy and higher education, regarded Hasidic Jews as less rational and inordinately emotional. Lithuanian Judaism wanted to remain in perpetual dialogue with the reason of the Greeks and the wisdom of the Torah (Nadler 1997). Its form of Orthodox Judaism saw its task as the universalization of Judaism, engaging the Torah in the present world, actively shaping and translating surrounding culture and thought.

These sensibilities remain clear and powerful influences on Levinas's decisions in life and the nature of his work. His discomfort with the primacy of the subject's experience and his critiques of mysticism and its emphasis on the presence of God and union bear considerable weight throughout his philosophical system, where he largely eschews the language of experience and relationality involving fusion, preferring instead separation and the "atheistic" self (Levinas 1961/1969; see also Horner 2001 and Putnam 2002).

Additionally, Levinas's drive to make the particularity of Jewish ethics a universal challenge to human persons emerges from a long tradition within Judaism that spans back to Philo[16] and was a prominent feature of European Jewry. For Levinas, it was a critical project wherein justice might be reintroduced to the world order. His Judaism, oriented toward the relevant and essential vitalization of an ethical civilization, lays the foundation for his "translation" work.

Another facet of Levinas's Lithuanian Judaism (though less distinct from other forms of Judaism) was its sensitivity to idolatry. Levinas remained ever vigilant and sensitive in his work to the human propensity to idolatry. He viewed ontology, egology, many versions of metaphysics, and Western notions of knowledge, from pre-Socratics to Heidegger, as strewn with idolatrous conceptualizations and practices. Levinas presses hard against these systems.

The obtuseness and complexity of his work can be explained, in part, by his battle against intellectual reification—another form of idolatry.[17] Levinas's writing style has been compared to the elliptical and nonlinear genres of the Midrash and Talmud (Aronowicz 1994). Critchley (2007) refers to Levinas's work as *"structurally Judaic"* (50). Behind this is a recognition that truth is formed in living relationship, ethical relationship, and thus cannot be captured in propositions. Truth is conversational. His constant desire to unsay everything that he said aimed to make his text, as he put it, "uninhabitable" (ctd. in Malka 2002/2006, 286). He did not want his thought to become a philosophical system or series of tenets. If anything, one of his major philosophical contributions is showing that systems and tenets cannot contain the contents of ethical interchange nor found forms of rationality. Moral systems and propositional laws were, for Levinas, derivative of an unsystematizable, ethical responsibility. In this way, he believed he would keep even ethics from becoming an idol. Challenging society and persons to veer away from feeling "at home" in themselves or a particular, static system of thought, his goal was to perpetually disorient and disturb complacency. Thematization and totalization were, for Levinas, synonymous with the formation of idols if unconditioned by the infinite, primordial, ethical relation.

Another trait within Levinas's Judaism is its perpetual insistence upon "service to God" through submission to the Torah and the following of commandments (Malka 2002/2006, 16). Ethics was the central and foundational element in this form (and many forms) of Judaism, ethics or the pursuit of holiness fundamental to every facet of human life. Life lived in submission to the Torah is freedom birthed from responsibilities (Levinas 1968/1994). Whereas the majority of Western thought had esteemed reason, ontology, egology, epistemology, and/or metaphysics as the first philosophy, Levinas argues that ethics is more original than any other part of human experience, consciousness, or being (1989). The Torah and its commandments, encountered in the face of the other, are the wellspring of Levinas's corpus. "Here the face of the other speaks God's word and reveals the law to me. Levinas radicalizes a certain relationship to the law in Judaism" (Robbins 1991, 143).[18]

Levinas the Philosopher (The Athens Pole)

From an early age, Levinas was versed in classic literature. He cut his teeth on the great Russian novelists (Dostoyevsky, his favorite, and Tolstoy's death, his first reported memory!). In 1923, Levinas traveled to France to begin his philosophical studies at Strasbourg University. In 1928, he went to Freiburg University in Germany to study phenomenology under Edmund Husserl. He developed a close working relationship with Husserl and was highly influenced by phenomenology, from that point on, employing it in his philosophical discourse. When Levinas returned to France, he translated some of Husserl's work, making him the first to introduce Husserlian phenomenology into the French academy and bringing him into the philosophical limelight. His commentary on Husserl remains one of the definitive works to this day. Jean-Paul Sartre and Maurice Merleau-Ponty were both introduced to phenomenology through Levinas's writings.

In Freiburg, he also studied under Heidegger, whose existential extension of phenomenological method and picture of a sensate being living in the world had a significant impact on Levinas's thought. Though Levinas quickly became embittered toward Heidegger because of his affiliation with Nazism, Levinas always saw *Being and*

Time as a basic prerequisite for any thinker in Western philosophy.[19] Much of *Totality and Infinity* was a response to and critique of Heideggerian philosophy.

Levinas wrote extensively on subjectivity, consciousness, egology, metaphysics, ethical theory, the interhuman, sociality, sensate experience, death, time, *Dasein*, being, otherness, and myriad other topics that were and are central to continental philosophical conversations. To Levinas, Husserl and Heidegger's thoughts on consciousness, history, ontology, and metaphysics represent the greater Western philosophical tradition he wished to engage and challenge. His dialogue with Plato, Descartes, Kant, and Hegel can be seen throughout his more specific conversations with these more contemporary, influential twentieth century philosophers—his teachers.

Levinas taught in the prestigious philosophy departments at the University of Poitiers, University of Nanterre, and University of Sorbonne. Such thinkers as Blanchot, Derrida, Merleau-Ponty, Sartre, Lyotard, and Ricoeur are just a few of the many significant figures within Western thought that came under Levinas's influence. The list continues to grow.[20]

Levinas and the Holocaust

Though Levinas had already served his required term in the French military early in the 1930s, during World War II, he was drafted once again. While serving as a French translator, he was captured at Rennes, along with the entire French Tenth Army, as the German army poured into France. Under the terms of Geneva Convention, Levinas's status as a soldier protected him from the common fate of a Jew during Nazi occupation. He lived in a POW camp in Hanover, Germany, forced into hard labor for nearly five years (1940–45). His father, mother, and two brothers were killed by Nazi soldiers. His wife and daughter, hidden in a monastery with the assistance of Maurice Blanchot, survived.

Levinas witnessed the mass dehumanization that took place in the middle of twentieth century Europe, from the pograms of Czarist Russia that affected generations of his family to his personal losses in the *Shoah* (Burggraeve 2007). He witnessed the collusion of particular Christian communities, Western philosophers (e.g., Heidegger), and even the French government (Vichy) with Nazism (Levinas

1976/1990b; 1988/2007b; see also Ericksen and Heschel 1999). The *Shoah* (Holocaust) remained forever in his memory as a "tumor that cannot be cured" (Malka 2002/2006, 80). Levinas's (1974/1998c) second main philosophical treatise entitled, *Otherwise than Being or Beyond Essence,* was dedicated "To the memory of those who were closest among the six million assassinated by the National Socialists, and of the millions on millions of all confessions and all nations, victims of the same hatred of the other man, the same anti-semitism." The Hebrew text below this dedication that most assume is merely a Hebrew rendering of the same quote actually, far more personally, translates: "To remember the soul of my father, my teacher, Rabbi Yechiel, the son of Rabbi Abraham Halevi; my mother, my teacher, Deborah, the daughter of Rabbi Mosche; my brothers, Dov, the son of Rabbi Yechiel Halevi, Aminadab, the son of Rabbi Yechiel Halevi; and my father-in-law, Rabbi Shmuel, the son of Rabbi Gerschon Halevi, and my mother-in-law, Malcha, the daughter of Rabbi Haim. May their souls be bound" (ctd. in Smith 2005, 117).

Though Levinas rarely referenced these atrocities in his philosophical works, the remainder of his philosophical and confessional work bore the stamp of this devastating period and Levinas's many losses. His biographer, Salomon Malka (2002/2006), wrote that Levinas's experiences during WWII "became unspoken elements, negatives, but precisely as such, elements surviving in his philosophy. The heroic effort that demanded a repudiation of fatalism would, in a sense, remain the silent source of everything else" (64). Levinas stated that his life was "dominated by the presentiment and the memory of the Nazi horror" (qtd. in Malka 2002/2006, xiv). Underneath Levinas's ethical philosophy is "the ever present sense of imminent catastrophe" (Smith 2005, 113). Without this recognition, it is difficult to be sensitive to the meaning of Levinas's words. This is partly why he is too quickly written off as hyperbolistic by some scholars.

Levinas's work is a perpetual application of his Jewish sensibilities—a desire to challenge the world to justice and holiness—to the philosophical systems of Europe. He explains, "My critique of totality has come in fact after a political experience that we have not yet forgotten" (1985, 79). Grounded in Greek-European philosophy, particularly Heidegger's thought, Levinas viewed Nazi totalitarianism as an extension of the philosophical primacy of ontology. He often argued that justice is made impossible in such systems. He viewed Western notions of detached rationality, ontological systems, constituting consciousnesses, and notions of freedom and humanism as precursors to the eschewing of ethical responsibility. He saw egology as logically extending into a morally anemic and totalitarian version of selfhood. His sensibilities and ethical theory reflected his response to a trajectory of Western thought that led to eugenics, genocide, human experimentation, and what he refers to as the violent "reduction" of the other. In one of his first articles, entitled "Reflections on the Philosophy of Hitlerism," Levinas (1934/1990a) writes, "This article stems from the conviction that the source of the bloody barbarism of National Socialism lies not in some contingent anomaly within human reasoning, nor in some accidental ideological misunderstanding... [but] from the essential possibility of *elemental Evil* into which we can be led by logic and against which Western philosophy has not sufficiently insured itself" (63). Malka (2002/2006) writes, "Levinas said so himself: it is the Shoah that revealed, through the absurd, the emptiness of a merely 'humanist' Western culture" (xi).

This is the world and lineage of thought to which Levinas was responding. In the beginning of *Otherwise than Being, or Beyond Essence,* Levinas (1974/1998c) describes persons as "allergic egoisms which are at war with one another" (4) and the world as a game "without responsibility, where everything possible is permitted" (6). It is a world that has to be reminded to state "After you, sir," to see something other than the sameness of oneself when looking at another person, to not turn other persons' bodies into bars of soap. Levinas's aim was to remind the world that its history, systems, and totalizations cannot capture an infinity that indwells, transcends, disturbs, and disorients the natural and the banal. He wanted to challenge the violence-making of Western thought and rekindle the phenomenology of the self's ethical responsibility to the other. "The whole of Levinas' thinking," Burggraeve states,

> can be interpreted as an immense effort to bring to light the roots of violence and racism, and as an attempt to overcome this in principle by *thinking otherwise*. This 'thinking otherwise' is developed from the beginning as a thinking about the 'other,' since according to Levinas

the other is precisely that which is denied in racism. For him, evil lies in 'being' in so far as the being—expressed eminently in his or her effort to be—absorbs the other into itself. It is this same evil, the evil of the 'reduction of the other to the same,' that Levinas discovers in anti-Semitism, as the radical intensification of racism. In anti-Semitism, hate is directed at the Jew as intolerable other. In racism, the enemy is the other as such. (2007, 28)

Cohen (1994) paints a broad picture of the influence the Holocaust had upon Levinas's subsequent thought:

> Then and henceforth Levinas would propound an ethical and dialogical metaphysical grounded in a careful phenomenological description of the human situation in both its individual and social moments. From the pain, horror, and confusion of political, social, and ethical upheavals on a scale unprecedented in European history, Levinas would forge a philosophy grounded in the highest demands of personal ethics and social justice. From the unparalleled extremity and incongruous juxtaposition of this historical and historic contrast of good and evil, war and peace, culture and barbarism, justice and injustice, Levinas created a philosophy infused with the highest moral teachings of Judaism. (119)

LEVINAS AS JEWISH PHILOSOPHER?

There has been contentious debate about the relationship of Levinas's philosophical thought to his Judaism. Some refer to Levinas as a continental philosopher who also wrote confessional works. Others argue that Levinas is a theologian versed in phenomenological methodology (Badiou 2002). Still others, like myself, recognize the significant interplay of Levinas's Judaism and his philosophical method and content (Cohen 1994, 2003b; Gibbs 1992, 2000; Putnam 2002).

The desire to maintain Levinas as "purely" a philosopher (separate from his theological assumptions) is a remnant of modernist sensibility that views religion and confessional thought as a move away from the purity of rationality. This is exactly what Levinas works against. Rational thought is not secular and pure. It is wrestled into existence in lived, ethical relationship. Ford (1999) writes that Levinas "grounds all the sciences in the ethical. He refuses them the sort of autonomy which might let them forget that the very rationality which allows them to develop is to be referred ultimately to the face to face and responsibility" (38). It is, for Levinas, the religious and unquantified facet of human experience and relationship that births reason, not a series of dictums and theorems one step removed. Love informs reason.

The relationship between Levinas's Judaism and his philosophy was, however, complicated. Levinas himself rejected the terms "Jewish philosopher" and "Jewish thinker." Throughout his lifetime, he segregated his philosophical and Jewish works, even using different publishers. He claimed that he would never use a biblical story or theological proposition to argue a particular philosophical point (Levinas 2004). He distrusted theology and vigilantly defended the philosophical rigor and foundation of his academic work.[21]

However, he was somewhat inconsistent on this point.[22] Known for advocating a "return to Judaism" (Herzog 2005), Levinas readily admitted that his project was one of translating "Hebrew" into "Greek," taking a biblical conception of the human person (2004) and translating it into the language of the academy. Cohen (2003b) writes, "Levinas acceded to the authority of Jewish tradition by creating original ethical philosophies in dialogue with western civilization as a whole...[giving] voice to the Hebrew spirit in Greek letters" (137; see also Malka 2002/2006, 279). As Halperin explains, his sensibilities were clearly forged in his strict talmudic and Jewish cultural and religious heritage.

> Various texts have appeared in different contexts that attempt to tell Levinas that he is a Jewish thinker. But he did not care very much for such etiquette, and he did not want to remain confined to a confessional thought. He wanted to be understood and perceived as a thinker, period. But he could not deny that his thinking, taken as a whole, was in reality often read as Jewish thinking. Because it was entirely inspired by this Jewish education, this ahavat Israel, this Jewish knowledge that he had always possessed. When you open *Totality and Infinity* or *Otherwise than Being* or *The Humanism of the Other*, you will find phrases or paragraphs without references and without footnotes, but which, while reading them, you can feel are fundamentally Jewish thoughts that are being presented by Levinas in his philosophical works. (ctd. in Malka 2002/2006, 139; see also Levinas 1988/2007b)

Levinas works with his Judaism in a "complex, peculiar, and mediated" manner (Robbins 1991, 129). For example, Levinas's thought ran parallel to particular postmodern modes of thinking, but maintained a unique trajectory that is consistent with his "Hebrew" sensibilities. For example, some movements in postmodern philosophy have severely wounded Enlightenment reductions of the self and other by increasingly recognizing the irreducibility (excess/transcendent quality) of the other that disallows reduction into categories. Many contemporary thinkers have challenged the hegemony of autonomous reason and its ahistorical and acontextual claims. Postmodernism, as a whole, is a heterogeneous movement whose shared sensibility (if that is even fair to say) denounces the epistemological hubris of the Enlightenment project. The other is held to have an "epistemic transcendence" within the growing lineage of postmodern thought (Westphal 2004, 180). It is not uncommon to place Levinas within this camp based on his assertions about the "irreducibility of the other" and the transcendence that the other represents. It is obvious "Levinas demands that thought be humble" (Cohen 1986, vii). But, so do Lyotard, MacIntyre, Kierkegaard, Pascal, Kuhn, Polyani, Gadamer, Heidegger, Derrida, and even Foucault. Epistemological humility is not what makes Levinas distinct. It is the radical, ethical nature of his philosophical system.

Levinas shares this postmodern sensibility of epistemic transcendence, but sees something different than most postmodern thinkers. In the infinite distance between my epistemological categories and the other is a trace of the divine. The irreducibility of the other does not merely call me to epistemological humility. Westphal (2004) writes, "Levinas is interested in the recovery of epistemic transcendence *for the sake of* ethical transcendence" (180). The other's unintelligibility is a calling, a demand, and a responsibility directed toward me as if from a "master" who "invest[s] and justif[ies] my freedom" (Levinas 1961/1969, 251). Also, it is an imperative as if from the poorest of the poor, the widow, orphan, stranger, and the alien to whom and for whom I am ethically responsible. He or she comes to me as a "glorious abasement" (251). Whereas most postmodern thinkers challenge our inability to attend to the excess of meaning, Levinas recognized holiness and demand in this situation. Levinas wished to restore not only a sensing or hearing of otherness, but also a sensing of the ethical demand inherent in this otherness.

This is one of the differences between secular postmodern depictions of transcendence and Levinas's "postsecular," ethical account. His Judaism—eschewing idols and emphasizing *mitzvot*—is unabashedly at work in his postmodern conversation.

Levinas's understanding of goodness also took a distinctively Jewish shape. Putnam (2002) named two essential truths in Hebrew Scripture: first, "that every human being should experience him/herself as *commanded* to be available to the neediness, the suffering, the vulnerability of the other person"; second, "One can—indeed, one must—*know* that this is commanded of one without a philosophical account of how this is possible" (48). It will become clearer throughout the following chapters that the Tanakh (Torah) is the source of Levinas's postsecular thought.

Levinas as Postsecular

> *Philosophy, I believe, is derived from religion. It is summoned by religion that is adrift, and religion is probably always adrift.* (Levinas, qtd. in Malka 2002/2006, 136)

Levinas straddled a space best understood as postsecular.[23] That is, his Judaism informed and shaped his philosophical inquiry. Levinas's grounding in his religious tradition, rather than natural scientific methodology or the rules of detached reason, is especially unique when put in conversation with psychology.

Postmodern philosophy widely contends that all interpretation and communication involves translation and that all translation is accomplished through a situated and traditioned heuristic (Gadamer 1975; Gibbs 2000; MacIntyre 1984). There is no unmediated, untranslated experience, an essential reminder that postmodernism gave to the West.

In its "quest for certainty" (Toulmin 1990), science gained power through attribution: through objective methodologies, it was believed that experience need not be mediated by human subjectivity, tradition, and community. Rather, a "reality" could be discovered and a certainty about this reality, achieved only through the removal of tradition and its "ideology," which forces a filtering translation. Reality was discoverable as long as reason was autonomous and unaffected. The view from this rebuilt tower of Babel allowed a comprehensive picture of all things. However—and this has been the postmodern critique—the picture generated from atop the tower was still being interpreted by historically situated, prejudging, and linguistically/ideologically loaded persons. From the start, its foundation determined the horizon and the panorama seen from the zenith. Simply put, science was and is a translation of experience, a particular tradition rendering experience into concepts. Modernity marked a period in which translation and tradition were denied and insidious, ever present but unrecognized. Susceptibility to idolatry became pandemic, as the definitions of selfhood emerging from this time attest.

Recent trends in postmodern thinking have battled against the false dichotomy between tradition and secular reason (Dueck 2002; Kepnes, Ochs, and Gibbs 1998; McClendon and Smith 1994; Milbank 2006; Smith 2004). They argue that there is no such thing as "secular reason" (Smith 2004), that reason, including that which is generated through scientific methods, is traditioned, particular, and grounded in a context, and that these roots should be made explicit. This form of rationality or reason is what is meant here by postsecular. Instead of assuming a homogenous form of rationality, scholars like Alasdair MacIntyre (1989) are asking, "Whose rationality?" Levinas's understanding of rationality, for example, was certainly quite different than that of Locke.

MacIntyre, among many others, sees within postmodernity an equalizing of the playing field. An increased recognition of reason's situatedness and science's nonexempt status calls into question the subordinate place of philosophy and religion to the institutions of science and its methodology. Science is a tradition, with its own presuppositions and horizons of meaning. J. K. Smith (2006a) states, "At the heart of the postmodern critique of modernity is an unveiling of the way that science—which is so critical of the 'fables' of narrative—is itself grounded in a narrative" (66). Modern science is a narrative that gives meaning to reality, but (as Lyotard suggested) also and uniquely is a metanarrative of "facts" and "findings" superior to the "beliefs" and "practices" of other narratives, even though it was "just another language game, albeit masquerading as the game above all games" (67). It viewed itself not as a tradition, but as the means of moving past traditions toward a view to which all rational persons could subscribe. It became the adjudicating tradition, muting all other traditions with disparate assumptions.

Though Levinas did not explicitly name his presuppositional framework as distinctively Jewish in his philosophical works, Dueck and Parsons (2007) capture Levinas's postsecular sensibility well when they state, "Contrary to the Enlightenment model, Levinas begins with the Other and the ethical demand he or she makes.... With Levinas, we hope to preserve the 'thick' texture of religious discourse while maintaining the benefits of a 'thin' ethical contribution to the larger public arena" (273).[24] Furthermore, in the introduction to Levinas's *Nine Talmudic Readings,* Aronowicz (1994) writes that Levinas's "aim remained an openness to the world at large and an integration into secular culture. However, in Levinas's eyes, this universality could not be accomplished without reentering into the particularity of the Jewish tradition" (xiv). Thus, Levinas's firm dichotomization of philosophical and confessional work was more a product of his modern context than an actual ideological demarcation.

The implications of using a postsecular approach within modern psychologies are enormous. Instead of merely reifying and objectifying depictions of the human person that are based on measures of norms and patterns of human "nature," there is the possibility of a starting point that can alter the trajectory of our constructs and interrupt their insidious relationship to the status quo. (The significance of this will become even clearer in chapters 3 and 4). Beginning with questions revolving around ethical considerations regarding the self tends to allow for greater potential of ethical answers (Cohen 1985). For Levinas, the question of selfhood begins with transcendence, which "designates a relation with a reality infinitely distant from my own reality, yet without this distance destroying this relation and without this relation destroying this distance, as would happen with relations within the same; this relation does not become an implantation in the other and a confusion with him, does not affect the very identity of the same, its ipseity, does not silence the apology, does not become apostasy and ecstasy" (1961/1969, 42). If the transcendent is excluded from our formulations, then the ethic that emerges will resemble social contract, normative maxims, and self-aggrandizement. Through postsecular constructs, the sacred order has the possibility of being reintroduced, and ethical responsibility has the possibility of being reinstituted within the very definition of persons.

This increasing openness to postsecular methods and constructs within philosophy allows for a radical challenge to the methodology, practices, and assumptions of modernity from the particularity of rich theological and cultural traditions. Though slow to recognize and implement these changes within the postmodern philosophical landscape, modern psychologies are now increasing space for new forms of dialogue that resituates science to its appropriate place (reducing its overextension into human identity).

LEVINAS AND TRANSLATION

As stated earlier, Levinas's "dialogical ethics" (Cohen 1994, 121) is a mode of dialogue between two languages—Hebrew and Greek—and is ultimately best understood as translation (Aronowicz 1994; Gibbs 1992, 2000; Robbins 1991).

Torah and Translation: Calling the Present into Question

The concept of translation, particularly Levinas's mode, is not a contemporary concoction, but a sacred ritual. It is not immersed in the "quest for certainty" (Toulmin 1990, 55–56), but rather in a history of worship and practice, of Torah and Talmud, whose aim is holiness, not rational propositions, rooting Levinas's methodology in millennia-long dialogue. It is not merely another theory, derived from a particular individual or historical movement, its adequacy assessed by the measurements of logic or Ockham's razor. Its language and method is Hebrew and ultimately profoundly other than Greek in authentification, legitimation, and purpose. Its difference from conventional ideology and methodology is part of what gives it the power to speak so prophetically today; it is an other that must be heard. This is a strength of postsecularism; listening to rooted and lived traditions allows those traditions to alter the banalities of the status quo, to disrupt given and situated reason. It is a gift from beyond ourselves.

Cushman (2007) refers to Jewish talmudic and midrashic practices as "a story about the indispensable nature of interpretive, compassionate moral engagement and political activism that demands, and finds, relationship" (64). In Judaism, the fact that all interpretation and communication involve translation is not only accepted, but is celebrated as the very place where goodness and truth emerge. Furthermore, within Judaism, not only is the Torah interpreted in community and relationship, the Torah itself is recognized as being a translation born from community and relationship (see Heschel 2006). The Midrash is an example of a process that pushes against the human tendency toward idolatry (Cushman 2007). It is a dialogue that "precludes any closure" (Malka 2002/2006, 126). It is forever alive, always avoiding over identification with the present; pulled forward through perpetual conversation. In this tradition, human relationship and covenant produce consciousness and reason. Translation is necessarily relational and intertextual. Intertextual, here, has two meanings. First, the Talmud and Midrash are both dialogical texts whose primary basis and content is an intertextual discussion. Second, this work suggests that each person is living out of a story or narrative of selfhood. They are a text whose dialogue with another is intertextual, and this dialogue "teaches" us and demands of us a responsibility, a responsibility that yields a freedom largely unknown to the Euro-American self (Levinas 1961/1969).

Autonomous reason and the formation of rational propositions from logic stand in opposition to the more primary interhuman and intertextual conversation out of which and through which God passes. God is not to be named, grasped, or possessed. In conversation, God is not understood; God is invited. Levinas often spoke of God as that which passes between persons living in ethical relationship. Similarly, Cushman (2007) writes, "Most important, one must come to understand that God is not only in the product, but also in the process; that it is in the space between persons, between persons and texts, between one text and another, between one word and another, that God resides; that the activity of engaged communal searching and study and care and critical thinking is, somehow, a way of relating to or being a partner with God.... In other words, participation in the activity of engaged, compassionate study and interpersonal interaction is a kind of relation with God" (68). Doctrinal purity is derivative of responsibility for one's neighbor, caring for the widow and the orphan. "To receive the gift of the Torah—a Law—is to fulfil it before consciously accepting it" (Levinas 1968/1994, 40).

In Hebrew thought, concepts do not precede experience, but rather the subject lives in relationship to an other and "concepts" become an intersubjective creation born out of lived illumination (revelation). This is an affected and ethically constituted beginning of consciousness. Levinas (1989) viewed the other as a revelation, a new encounter with the Torah, a teaching of the Law. The practices that surround the interpretation of the Torah, the Talmud, the Midrash, and the Mishnah are all conversational, dynamic, ethical and dialogical (Cushman 2007). Cushman writes that this form of dynamic and interpersonal interpretation allows for "both respecting and challenging a text, thereby simultaneously revering and yet continuously updating the tradition.... [T]hese interpretative practices seem...to embody the most important of all Jewish commitments: the fight against idolatry" (65–66).

Revelation, in Judaism, must be dialogued with and translated into the present consciousness, the current systems, and the current reason in order to truly be revealed and lived.[25] It is "simultaneously an attempt at letting the Jewish texts shed light on the problems facing us today and an attempt at letting modern problems shed light on the texts" (Levinas 1968/1994, ix). It is a "literally unending process of interpretation" (Putnam 2002, 46). Revelation is a dialogue between the present order and something beyond the order, and an ethical relationship that allows this dialogue to transpire. Revelation requires active and dynamic interpretation. It cannot be understood and then applied to the present; it must be understood through the present as something that cannot fit into the present. This dialogue changes the language of the present, alters the constructs through which the present is viewed, giving new meaning, an epiphany. Levinas (1982/2007a) states that "the Word of God can be maintained in the spoken language used by created beings amongst themselves. The marvellous contraction of the Infinite, the 'more' inhabiting the 'less'" (xiii). Within Judaism, there is a complex relationship between the law and reason, discerned in the practice of talmudic interpretation. In Hebrew thought, what is being commanded of us and the call to responsibility lay at the foundation of knowledge and being. The first questions asked of the Talmud are not the truth about the world, but rather the demand upon ourselves (Heschel 2006; see also Rabinowitz 1999). "Where else but in the Talmud do we encounter a language so devoted to finding justice in every mundane situation, so committed to finding out exactly what we are commanded to do in the face of others" (Stone 1998, 19)?

Revelation, in Judaism, is also a practice in remembering what is not otherwise present within the given order. Remembering is not merely the cognitive process of recollection, a conjuring up of memories. Rather, remembering is the aliveness of the past within the present, an interrupting, shaping, and conditioning of the present moment by a perpetual haunting of the past: "a past that is on the hither side of every present" (Levinas 1974/1998c, 12). It is the Exodus alive within my body, a push toward a deliverance constituted by justice. It is the Abrahamic journey from his home, resident in my psyche, a self unable to return to itself. Remembering is outside of history (of being) but is more truly real than the consciousness constituted by the conditions of time and context. The node of remembering, the connection of a noncognitive, alive past to the burgeoning present, is responsibility. The prophets of the Hebrew Scriptures provide a model of what Levinas is working to do; they did not come to debunk the religious enterprises and construct something new. Instead, they pointed back to what preceded their own history and formed the identity of the Jewish people. The prophets challenged the status quo in its disconnection from this immemorial past. They did not reject religion, but rather wanted it to be emptied of its pagan meaning and reinstilled with something more original.

Revelation is remembering the transcendent in the immanent. "[T]he Torah is not closed or settled," but rather, it is "a vigorous and imaginative re-remembering, that is, reinterpretation of Torah for a new time, place, and circumstance" (Brueggemann 1999, 27). The Torah is not to be engaged in abstract and detached thought; it is to be applied, translated, interpreted, and pulled into the present order—in practice and action, in conversation. It is a remembering not for the sake of increased conceptual clarity, but rather as an awakening from moral slumber. It is a memory that forever calls, demands, and obligates.

Furthermore, the purpose of this remembering is not for the sake of salvation for the ethnic Jew alone. It is about the redemption of humanity (Levinas 1976/1990b). It makes the teachings of the Torah, its life-giving goodness and reminders, a gift to all humankind (see Heschel 1962; 2006). Malka (2002/2006) states, "What it means, perhaps, is that one must 'talk about them' until one comes to talk about them in Greek, until one translates the teaching pointed to in Deuteronomy six into the language of philosophy, which is to say, essentially, until these teachings have been made accessible to everyone" (109). Taking the particular revelation and expressing it in our contemporary discourses[26] was Levinas's project. For Levinas, the term "Israel" ultimately meant "the humanity of the human" (1988/2007b).

Levinas's Translation Project

Levinas followed the ancient heuristic and dialogical style of speaking the Torah into the present by translating[27] it into twentieth century Western philosophy.[28] Levinas viewed his project as a continuation of the Septuagint, translating the Hebrew language into Greek (Levinas 1986a).[29] By "language," Levinas did not mean spoken tongue, but rather "modes of thought" and different wisdom traditions (Gibbs 1992, 157). Pitkin (2001) delineates the difference well: "Levinas maps these concerns onto the dual philosophical and linguistic categories of the 'Hebrew' and the 'Greek'. In this mapping, the 'Hebrew' tradition maintains the insistence on the primacy of the ethical, and indeed offers the paradigm for it—the paradigm of the nonegocentric self, which is endlessly opened, called out of itself by its responsiveness and responsibility for the other. The 'Greek', by contrast, represents the ontologically oriented aspect of the European phenomenological tradition" (236).[30] Levinas (1968/1994) viewed the present or given order as a Greek world and Greek the *lingua franca* or universal language of understanding within Western society. In addition to its historical lineage, Greek thought was an "attempt at utter intelligibility, at clarity, at an exposition that aims at every human being regardless of background or prior assumptions" (x). Greek connoted the universal and given order of reason and rationality. Levinas's focus on Husserl and Heidegger was but a particular manifestation of this general trend. Greek, particularly in Levinas's later work, was not a pejorative term, but rather the necessary place of shared language—normative language—that allowed discourse and meaning to arise. However, Levinas contends that this universal language and dominant rationality always needs a dialogue partner, an antithesis that called from beyond. The ethical encounter was the "beyond."

What is the purpose behind this translation? Gibbs (2000) argues, "Translation models ways to learn from others, to attend to the saying or the writing without subsuming or simply merging. In the process, the here is changed" (279). Once translation occurs, the present order is altered.

To translate the Torah, according to Levinas, the Hebrew language *needs* to be spoken through the Greek. It needs to be spoken through a world that has some affinity for the infinite and alterity, but ultimately is a totality that suppresses rather than addresses the other. Levinas was uniquely equipped for this practice as he has been referred to as a "doubled man" (Gibbs 1992, 22), fluent in both the Jewish, talmudic tradition and also the phenomenological tradition of Western philosophy. He embodied both Jerusalem and Athens, though Jerusalem is clearly his birthplace.

In Levinas's work, the process of dialogue, here described as translation, is best understood in terms of its positive and negative elements—where, respectively, Hebrew sensibilities can already be seen within Greek sensibilities and where it is utterly foreign and unformulated. Positively, the process of translation seeks to find within modern languages, traditions, and conceptions (i.e., Greek thought) shared sensibilities with ethically-infused ancient wisdom, languages, traditions, and conceptions (i.e., Hebrew thought). These shared correlates are shaped, honed, and emphasized as the locations within modern traditions that are already receptive to the meaning of what is being translated. Levinas affirms the philosophy of Plato and Descartes as a place where the "good beyond being" and the "idea of infinity" (respectively) are present. Levinas similarly references elements of Pascal and Kant's philosophy as places where the Hebrew can already be seen within the Greek. "A translator brings in what the foreign poet wants to say, but also brings in the INHERITANCE that lives in the foreign language" (Gibbs 2000, 295).

In psychology, the positive process of translation accesses those meeting places where Hebraic sensibilities shine through in particular dominant discourses. Recent movements that attend to the interhuman through intersubjective models, language such as "attunement to" and "recognition of the other" describing identity formation, and the emphasis on receptivity to intrapsychic and interpersonal versions of otherness are just a few of many places where Greek already speaks to the memory of the ethical condition of the self. In addition to clinical conceptual and therapeutic approaches that engender these sensibilities, many in psychology have been active in issues related to social justice (poverty, gender inequality, gay rights, and destigmatizing, to list only a few). This, too, represents a Hebrew sensibility that addresses the ethical. Positive translation recognizes, nourishes, and deepens these theoretical, clinical, and professional approaches.

Negatively, the process of translation recognizes where modern traditions (Greek thought) do not have the space upon their horizons to attend to a particular meaning or emphasis within the (Hebrew) tradition being translated. Much like constructs of the self, all conceptual frameworks are cohesive narratives whose stories necessarily exclude alternate conceptions. During translation, these excluded elements become more apparent. The Hebrew ushers in these elements so that modern frameworks can understand them.[31] As it then enters these elements into its framework, the Greek language (in the best case scenario) accommodates and changes.

In order to introduce new facets that could not be expressed in Greek ideology and Western philosophical language, Levinas scatters religious terminology and biblical illustrations throughout his philosophical writings. Oppenheim (2006) states that Levinas's work testified "to the superabundance that is religious language, which may both complement and interrogate contemporary philosophic narratives" (25). Modern psychologies' linguistic paucity for the self, due to its reliance on history and normativity, is in profound need of a language more abundant and demanding than the status quo permits. Election, expiation, substitution, revelation, and the trace of the Divine are all religiously infused terms that alter the receiving tradition as it assimilates their meaning. Gibbs (2000) suggests that translating Hebrew into Greek (conceptually) "cultivate[s] new possibilities" into the Greek that were not present beforehand (279). It is stretched and its horizon is altered. Modern languages must be renewed, "revealing possibilities that had previously not been available in that language" (294). Gibbs states that the aim is to "allow a new judgment of that civilization to be heard in its own language.

In Levinas's philosophical work, the Jewish saying clearly challenges and judges the modern Western philosophical tradition. But in order to make even that judgment intelligible, it is necessary to translate into that Western language...the translation project must preserve its sensitivity to the original language" (301).

In terms of modern psychology, the negative part of translation requires bearing witness to that which psychological theories, discourses, and methodologies cannot access. Clinical approaches that place a primacy on expressive individualism, symptom reduction, rationality, adaptation, individuation, and fulfillment create stultifying limits in the language they teach about selfhood. Furthermore, technician/expert style approaches to the therapeutic dyad often preclude clinical psychologists from working with a thick language for love, relationships, and ethics. In the negative frame of translation, dialogue and ongoing interchange can provide the possibility of recognition of what these discourses cannot allow for, the versions of self propagated (with their cultural/historical underpinnings), and their impact on surrounding culture and the therapeutic dyad. Through this dialogical process, new possibilities are given space to blossom. This process creates a "fusion of horizons" (as Gadamer puts it) that extends, expands, and challenges the limits of one's previous perspectival limits.

Translation is not conceptual colonization or an imperialistic overthrow. It is a mutually illuminating conversation. Levinas did not see Hebrew thought as a superior tradition meant to trump the Greek tradition. In fact, he contends that the Torah must stand the test of Greek reason (Gibbs 2000, 299). In Chaim Potok's (1975) novel *In the Beginning,* Rebbe Sharfman expresses this point to the main character, David Lurie. "Lurie, if the Torah cannot go out into your world of scholarship and return stronger, then we are all fools and charlatans. I have faith in the Torah" (435). Ultimately, the purpose of Hebrew thought is to take Greek reason where it cannot go on its own. Cohen (1994) writes, "Despite its rigorous standards and intellectual heights, and despite its bravest, Promethean struggles, philosophy by itself will never know its why or wherefore" (xvii). Levinas teaches "that with no less rigor one must learn from the language, insights, and lives of the prophets, sages, fathers, mothers, kings, judges, psalmists, and rabbis of Israel, as well as the wise men, philosophers, sophists, scientists, and artists of Greek pedigree. Athens is too proud by itself to turn to Jerusalem, but it must be turned to Jerusalem nonetheless, for all our sakes" (xvi).

In this process of translation, Levinas's Jewish heritage provides alternate epistemological and metaphysical emphases, a reorienting corrective to the constricted Greek horizon. Greek thought has become the common sense of the West, its dialogue partners often muted in the margins. Dialogue allows for the hegemony of dominant ideology to begin to recognize that to which it is unable to attune. The difficulty is finding a way to speak a Hebrew ethics "in the Greek language, a language which, as Derrida suggested, is characterized by a fundamental 'autism'" (Robbins 1991, 117). If the Greek has become "an absorption in the self-same, a withdrawal from and refusal of exteriority" (117), then how can the incommensurable Hebrew sensibility of other-centeredness and demandedness be translated in and through it? If the Greek language is the "language of a shut-in" (117), then how can that which is shut out be allowed back in? This is Levinas's prophetic challenge.

For Levinas, Judaism is a reminder in history that judges history (Levinas 1976/1990b; Burggraeve 2007). At a party marking his eightieth birthday, Levinas reflected "To be Jewish [is] an awareness of the extraordinary privilege of undoing the banality of existence" (qtd. in Malka 2002/2006, 84). It is an eternal dialogue partner whose purpose is "both to join and to judge" (Gibbs 2000, 302)—analogous to the positive and negative elements of translation described above. Cohen (1994) stated, "It is rather a perennial thinking...that must in each generation, and in each person, be reawakened, renewed, rethought, and refined in current idiom. It is a thinking captivated by responsibilities and obligations beyond those of pure thought.... It is truth beholden to goodness, as truth *should* be" (xii). History and reason cannot generate this prophetic reminder; it must be born from a living tradition, a dialogue and translation that takes us beyond ourselves. Idols take a new shape in each age, and with each age, a prophetic voice must work in new ways to name and dethrone these idols.

While Jerusalem, for Levinas, is not superior to Athens, it is definitely prior to and more original (Burggraeve 2007, 286; Levinas

1985). It is a past and future that must be brought into every present, and the Greek, the present order to which and within which the Hebrew finds its voice and speaks. Levinas (1982/2007a) writes, "Our great task is to express in Greek those principles about which Greece knew nothing.... Jewish peculiarity awaits its philosophy. The servile imitation of European models is no longer enough.... These texts, through their two-thousand-year-old commentaries, still have something else to say" (193). Ultimately, the particularity of Judaism must be spoken through a philosophy and a culture; Judaism is a memory that must forever be remembered in more universal contexts. Levinas (1985) states,

> I have never aimed explicitly to "harmonize" or "conciliate" both traditions. If they happened to be in harmony it is probably because every philosophical thought rests on pre-philosophical experiences, and because for me reading the Bible has belonged to these founding experiences. It has thus played an essential role—and in large part without my knowing it—in addressing all mankind.... At no moment did the Western philosophical tradition in my eyes lose its right to the last word; everything must, indeed, be expressed in its tongue; but perhaps it is not the place of the first meaning of beings, the place where meaning begins. (25)

This sensibility is captured best when Levinas (1976/1990b) states, "Judaism is the brother of the Socratic message" (233).

Thus, Levinas continued to speak the language of Greek within the philosophical academies, but forced a new meaning. Robbins (1991) writes, "He *reinscribes* the question of the ethical because in order to pose it he must (re)read and repeat a philosophical tradition that suppresses this question. In order to restore priority and fundamental sense to the question of the ethical, he must detach the question from the conventional senses with which the philosophical tradition covers up the question. Thus, in order to pose the question of the ethical anew, to repose the question, he must bring the question out of *its* repose and dormancy" (101).

However, Euro-American thought, in its current shape, cannot understand Levinas's critique of ontology and his assertions concerning ethical primacy. Cohen (1994) argues, "Because the West is essentially a scientific civilization, is determined by the will to truth, it leaves no room, as it were, for a criticism that strikes at the roots of critical thought. One cannot challenge the comprehensiveness of being, the totality of what is, the absolute, in other words, when there is no vantage point or place from which to make the challenge" (123). This means moving outside of existing parameters of meaning and comprehensibility[32] as Levinas's thought is nearly incomprehensible within contemporary paradigms. Substitution, expiation, and a subjectivity held hostage are not easily located within "Enlightenment syntax" (Dueck and Goodman 2007). Its narrative's meaning is truly other to the meaning of Western constructs of the self. However, Levinas worked to bridge this gap by playing within the rules of Western philosophy until they forced him toward a disingenuousness to his Hebrew core. At these places, philosophy is pulled forward—contorted—as it wrestles with what is other than and beyond it. Derrida (1978) explains that Levinas "lodges himself within a traditional conceptuality in order to destroy it" (111). Where the Hebrew cannot be understood from within the Greek, the Greek must accommodate (not merely assimilate). This marks "the way in which speaking Greek to say 'Hebrew,' applying a Greek language to a Hebrew experience that is incommensurable with it, does not happen without transforming the Greek language" (Robbins 1991, 124).

PSYCHOLOGY AS GREEK

> The ideas of the Enlightenment taught man that he could trust his own reason as a guide to establishing valid ethical norms and that he could rely on himself, needing neither revelation nor the authority of the church in order to know good and evil. The motto of the Enlightenment, "dare to know," implying "trust your knowledge," became the incentive for the efforts and achievements of modern man. The growing doubt of human autonomy and reason has created a state of moral confusion where man is left without the guidance of either revelation or reason. The result is the acceptance of a relativistic position which proposes that value judgments and ethical norms are exclusively matters of taste or arbitrary preference. (Fromm 1947, 5)

As modern psychologies have become the dominant arbiters of meaning concerning human identity, it is not a far stretch to see these psychologies fitting clearly within what Levinas meant by Greek. First, psychology is the Western academy's language for describing human persons and function. Second, it trades with definitions that are, by their nature, universalized and generalized. It is the Greek source by which the self out of which we live is shaped and lived. It is Greek both in its epistemological heritage (Western philosophy) and in its universalizing methods and near universal adherence within Western culture. Contemporary psychologies' roots lie in Hellenic thought (Faulconer and Williams 1985, 1990). Williams (2005) writes, "Science, as well as philosophy, was born in the confidence of the earliest pre-Socratics that a rational and serviceable account of the universe could be rendered relying on reason itself, without recourse to myth or tradition.... From these attempts grew our Western preoccupation with metaphysics and epistemology" (236).

The Greek epistemological heritage is inherently blind to Levinas's definition of ethics. Alford (2002) reminds us that Freud's "motto is that of the Greek Enlightenment: *gnothi sauton* (know thyself)" (538). In contrast, Gantt and Williams (2002) express the Hebrew sensibility when they write, "We believe [Levinas's] work alerts the entire discipline to some things of great import that it has forgotten—things which, if reunderstood, can significantly impact for good our intellectual efforts at understanding human beings, as well as our efforts to enhance the ethical tone and the abiding quality of our clients' lives" (24). Judaism put Levinas in touch with what was missing in the current *self out of which we live*. This religious sensibility can provide a prophetic eye whose lens is shaped by a lived ethic and shared practices—a place where revelation from outside of history is allowed to pass through. The formulas of logic and historical rules of reason are not worshipped in this place.

The constructs of the self conceptualized and practiced by modern psychologies need to be in dialogue with that which comes from "otherwise" than normative ideology and emergent notions within the status quo. "[I]n their purely non-political formulation, they must transcend the social, economic, juridical, and political forms which they receive, and even place them in question, so that the rights of the Other person can be taken to heart anew" (Burggraeve 2007, 186). Cushman (2007) challenges his readers: "Our job, as was the job of the rabbis who created midrash, is not to use a text unquestioningly, but instead to question, historically situate, critically appraise it" (71).

Likewise, as psychologists, the task involves more than the application of normative depictions of the human person and theoretical frameworks that have sprung from the treatment of this normative person. Rather, the constructs of self employed in clinical practice must be constantly called into question. This very process of critique is ethics (Critchley 2002).

Conclusion

> *Thus Levinas's entire philosophy can be understood as but another layer of meaning attached to Sinai, another interpretation—the priority of the other, conscientiousness before consciousness, ethics before reason—exalting and penetrating to the heart of one of the great moments in the religious history of the world.* (Cohen 1994, 127)

Modern psychology needs to begin to dismantle its collusive and corrosive alliance with the Cartesian subject and individualism. Its slowness to change is due, among many things, to its parasitic relationship to the natural sciences (Gantt and Williams 2002; Richardson, Fowers, and Guignon 1999). Additionally, modern psychology's long history of "physics envy" (Leahey 2004), desire for parity and societal legitimacy, and a myriad of other cultural and societal pressures feed into this rigidity and slow pace of change.

The focus of Levinas's work is on the interhuman, the relation between the self and the other. Here, within the ethical space of the dyad, a subversive and prophetic voice can begin to awaken the slumbering consciousness of the Western subject (Levinas 1968/1994). Because modern psychologies represent the philosophy of selfhood that is dominant within the present order, Levinas's work can serve as a prophetic voice in the midst of a Greek discipline. Levinas (2004) states, "It can also be considered from another perspective—the ethical or biblical perspective which transcends the Greek language of intelligibility—as a theme of justice and concern for the other as other, as a theme of love and desire which carries us beyond the finite Being of the world as presence" (72). After Levinas, psychologies should no longer assume that normality, adaptation, and even nature are appropriate measures of selfhood. The imperative for modern psychologies should be a subject whose psyche is demanded, obligated, and responsible. Alford (2007) writes, "Winnicott's land is Athens, the land of emerging individuality and creativity, where the self-conscious *psyche* (the Greek term we translate as 'self') first emerged. Levinas's land is Jerusalem, the land of prophecy, faith, and worship of a being so infinitely other that it is beyond being. Nevertheless, philosophers and prophets have spoken to each other before" (529).

The following chapters will narrow their focus and relate Levinas's Jewish philosophy and translation project to three trends that have profoundly influenced the assumptive sets of modern psychologies. Chapter 3 explores Levinas's response to the disengaged and autonomous reason of Greek thought (and modernity) with a picture of disinterested ethics, wherein the self cannot use rationality to gain immunity from responsibility for the other. In chapter 4, the immanent skew of modern thought is challenged by Levinas's depiction of a transcendent other whose impact upon the self reverses and interrupts the given (natural) order. In chapter 5, Levinas's emphasis on the ethically subjected individual calls into question modernity's emphasis upon the individual subject. Some implications for modern psychology are fleshed out in each chapter.

3

The Idol of Reason
From a Disengaged Self to a Dis-interested Ethics

> *Knowing is not due to coming upon something, naming and explaining it. Knowing is due to something forcing itself upon us.* (Heschel 1963, 109)
>
> *Philosophy is the wisdom of love in the service of love.* (Levinas 1974/1998c, 162)

In ancient Greece, truth, goodness, and beauty were qualities of the Divine and inexorably linked, mutually illuminating dimensions of life. Nonetheless, within Plato, Aristotle, and the traditions that followed, Western philosophy was frequently articulated as a "love of wisdom." Goodness and aesthetics were lived and interwoven into reason, but reason had subtle primacy. In modernity, truth—the seeking of conceptual clarity, universal principles, discernable patterns, order, and autonomous rationality—is triumphant, goodness and beauty clearly subservient to it (Cohen 1994). Reason has become hegemonic.

Embracing the mandates of scientific rationality, philosophy itself moved from questions of meaning and purpose to validation and logic (e.g., logical positivism). In modernity, with significant precursors in Greek epistemology, truth and goodness were divorced, with truth wanting its emancipation from goodness for the sake of "purity."[1] This divorce marked the beginning of a tenuous relationship between ethics and reason. Ethics became subservient to reason.

Hobbesian social contract theory, democratic assertions concerning individual rights, and the generic claims of value in human life were the products of an ethics starved of deeper rootedness (Taylor 1989). Linked to human history, human methodology, and human horizons of meaning, ethics became an afterthought, forced to play within the rules of a game that utterly altered it. The constructs of self that have emerged from this scientific worldview emphasize freedom as self-creation, autonomy, functionality, and rationality. In the West, modern psychology has become a systematized vehicle through which the modern self—rational, immanent, and internal—is still propagated.[2]

In a world where scientific method and practices have become the "neutral," universal language, most perceive truth and reason of greatest consequence, with goodness and beauty extraneous elements or compartmentalized as a part of one's religious ideology or personal choice (Bellah et al. 1985). Levinas understood and based his critique on the ramifications of this divorce between ethics and reason (and, ultimately, ethics and identity) and their profound bearing on the self's relationship to itself and the other.[3]

Obedience to reason has often laid the bases of discourses that exclude responsibility for the other. Subjection to reason has meant an eschewing of ethical subjection to the other. Impersonal maxims dictate identity, selfhood, and love more fundamentally than the live, interhuman dynamic and its calling upon the self. This is seen most clearly in the modern depictions of reason as disengaged, detached, objective, and capable of being "value-free" and "neutral."

Ironically, within modernity, this objectifying discourse was forged as a means of avoiding violence and providing the possibility of conversation in the heat of warring traditions (Toulmin 1990). For Levinas, however, autonomous and disengaged reason is a cardinal source of violence on the micro and macrolevels of Western civilization. It leads persons to live anonymously alongside one another and leads nations to totalitarian violence (Levinas 1989, 1976/1990b). The promise of unification under reason has, according to Levinas, been a false promise from which many of our ailments arise. It has been a "more subtle and sophisticated violence perpetuated intellectually and spiritually in the name of the abstract universal" (Cohen 2003b, 145). Burggraeve (2007) expressed this with great clarity:

> According to Levinas, left to itself, Greek thinking begins from the question of how to overcome the conflictual plurality and irrationality of 'Opinion,' or *doxa,* and passion. That is, it is animated by a desire for unity and autonomy. Furthermore, Greek thought has always held that the only way to achieve these things was obedience to Reason, which is general and all-encompassing. The vision of Reason can be found throughout western thinking.... This obedience to the will of Reason is also to resolve all violence, both subjective and interpersonal. After all, this obedience is based on the insight and evidence that it holds not only for me, but everyone and equally. Hence does the subject agree, submitting itself to the law of Reason, making it its own inner law (thus also defining humanity by the power of understanding). Hence, too, can many people, with their very plurality threatening to be in conflict, enter into mutual agreement but without compelling one another.... Fundamentally, the basis for this love of universal wisdom, including the general laws and structures of the 'polis,' is and remains (a self-interested desire for) autonomy. (186–87)

In this chapter, Levinas's critique of detached and autonomous reason is considered by employing the helpful heuristics of the Gyges's myth and Levinas's concept of the "temptation of temptation." Implications on the current frames of a rationality-oriented, modern psychology and clinical practice are considered.

WESTERN SELF: A GYGES COMPLEX

Levinas's critique of the Western self begins with his vehement concern about Western notions of rationality. Cohen (1994) writes, "Levinas's critical aim is to disturb and challenge rational thought. His terms and locutions are carefully chosen to upset reason at its most rational. They aim to upset reason in the way that the obligations of ethics upset the telos of reason—from outside and above" (122).

According to Levinas, the story of Western philosophy, as early as the pre-Socratics and increasingly pronounced after Descartes, is a tale privileging being, knowledge, rationality, existence, and the "sovereignty" of the constituting ego (egology). In this tale, consciousness begins with the immanent order, a historical and ontological account of the way things are. Knowledge is constructed from an agentic, active ego. The subject, or ego, gives an account of the world through the perceptual and constituting apparatuses with which the ego is endowed. With Husserl and Heidegger this was most clearly systematized through the concepts of intentionality, constitution, and horizonality. In their thought, the "intentional I" converts the data resident in an object or person (*intuition*) into an experiential phenomenon that can be known in consciousness (as *consciousness of*). The ego intends or constitutes the object in such a way as to allow it to become meaningfully present in its horizon of previous experience (*habitualities*) and conceptual categories. An object/person is perceived when it is cut to the size of the perceiving ego (Heschel 1963). That is, "the other is aimed at, invested and assembled by the ego (cogito) on terms laid down by the observing subject" (Smith 2006b). The ego is the arbiter of knowledge and the constituter of the other. This is the model of human subjectivity that is preponderant in Western philosophical and psychological theory. Levinas (1991/1998a) wrote,

> And, similarly, it would be a matter of understanding all alterity, which is brought together, received, and synchronized in presence within the *I think*, and which then is taken up in the identity of the *I*—*it* is a matter of understanding this alterity that has been taken up by the thought of the identical as *one's own* and, in so doing, of reducing one's *other* to the *same*. The other becomes the *I*'s very own in knowledge, which secures the marvel of immanence. Intentionality, in the aiming at and thematizing of being—that is, in presence—is a return to self as much as an issuing forth from self.... In thought understood as vision, knowledge, and intentionality, intelligibility thus signifies the reduction of the Other to the Same, synchrony as *being* in its egological gathering. The *known* expresses the unity of the transcendental apperception of the *cogito* or of the Kantian *I think*, the egology of presence affirmed from Descartes to Husserl, and even in Heidegger. (191)

To illustrate this version of subjectivity, Levinas uses the myth of the Gyges' ring, as found in Greek literature in a variety of forms.[4] For Levinas, the myth of Gyges, the shepherd who found a ring that made him invisible and visible at will, represented a self able to constitute its surroundings—make its world visible to itself through rational faculties—while remaining impervious to the gaze of others. Consciousness and the psyche, in this story, are equated with the intentionality of consciousness; reaching out and possessing experience (objectifying) without being called upon or possessed in the process.

The rational person sees things as they are, without any necessary claim upon his or her sense of identity. In other words, Levinas uses the myth of Gyges as an example of perceiving, experiencing, and constituting others without need of being present, responsible, and susceptible to their needs. In his book, *A Secular Age*, Taylor (2007) refers to this self as a "buffered self," that sees "itself as invulnerable, as master of the meanings of things" (38). He further describes it as a version of the self wherein "the possibility exists of taking a distance from, disengaging from everything outside the mind" (38).

The notions of visibility and invisibility are also addressed in Greek and Hebrew literature (Beals 2007). The Greek historian Herodotus begins *Histories* with the myth of Gyges. For the Greeks, Gyges' invisibility is ultimately rewarded; Gyges becomes king. He possesses what he desires and has the power to do so through his self-protected, invisible state. In the Hebrew tradition, Adam and Eve's attempt to hide from God—to become invisible—bore significant consequences, expulsion from the garden. Beals wrote, "The Hellenistic story is one of using invisibility to possess what one did not possess, while the Hebrew story is one of invisibility leading to a dispossession" (4).

Levinas's (1961/1969) Jewish sensibilities took precedence over the Greek as he suggests that this Gygean way of being is "the very condition of man, the possibility of injustice and radical egoism, the possibility of accepting the rules of the game, but *cheating*" (172–73, emphasis added). The invisibility of the self, for Levinas, was the beginning of violence. Barrett (1958) wrote, "Detachment was for the Hebrew an impermissible state of mind, a vice rather than a virtue; or rather it was something that Biblical man was not yet even able to conceive.... a pale shade of the actual existing human person" (76–78) whereas for the Greek, detachment was an ideal that paved the "path of wisdom" (77), creating an unaffected distance that allowed rationality to achieve its purest form.

Invisibility, for Levinas, can be equated with Locke's disengaged ego or with any form of cognition that provides the human person with the ability to engage "rationally" without any sociality or interhuman permeating and setting the basis for this rationality. Levinas (1989) viewed rationality not as a "light" that shines upon experiences bringing it into consciousness, but rather as derivative of ethical relationships. Rationality was not built out of detached theorems tapped into by human consciousness. As Peperzak (1995) writes, "Instead of seeing *theoria* as the ultimate level of human perfection, [Levinas] maintains that good practice—the practice of the good—transcends contemplation, and his proof consists in refined analyses of an undeniable, central but trivial fact: the fact of everybody's being faced by other humans" (xi).

Husserl and Heidegger are also critical of the Cartesian subject and Locke's "punctual self." Detached reason is, in Heidegger's eyes, not possible; consciousness is always situated and historically affected, and the practical activity and context out of which we are living is the very shape of our rationality. This is Heidegger's radical move and corrective. Levinas builds considerably from this point. With Heidegger, he recognizes that rationality cannot be detached and distanced. A positivist empiricism, particularly in regards to oneself, is an illusion. However, Levinas views situatedness and "conditioned" consciousness quite differently. Despite Heidegger's critique of the detached subject, it is evident that the human subject remains author of experience. Self-reflexivity, though not possible in a detached manner, remains the core faculty of the person. One's death conditions one's consciousnesss more than much of anything else. It is still a story about the human subject that is "for-itself." The self remains a form of private property, with thickened boundaries between "I" and "other."

For Levinas, consciousness is not merely situated in history and conditioned by context. Consciousness is situated in ethical relationship and bestowed and conditioned by an inexhaustible calling made upon it. Autonomous reason is not possible. Disengaged reason is possessive and violent to the other. Reason that does not lay claim upon the subject is a distortion and a truncation of the experience of the other.

Levinas radically revises Husserl's formulation of consciousness as the intentional activity of the mind by inverting the directional arrow of intentional activity. In Levinas's "inversion of intentionality" (1974/1998c, 47), the face of the other is not aimed at via consciousness, but rather aims at the exposed subject. That is, instead of the ego constituting and shaping the other, the other constitutes and shapes the ego. In Levinas's thought, the self is called into selfhood by the other, and (in proximity to the other) infinity "interrupts being's unrendable essence" (89); holding the self hostage to an infinite responsibility. The self is ethically transfixed.

The other's interruption of the ego's processes is thus a central characteristic and contention of Levinas's thought. The implications of this are vast. Marion referred to this "counter-intentionality" as a "revolution" and stated, "When it was declared that the ethical is the ultimate horizon of philosophy, a current was made to flow backwards" (qtd. in Malka 2002/2006, 276). From this perspective, autonomous reason is no longer a characteristic of an autonomous subject. Rather, reason is imbued with exposure and susceptibility to the other and responsibility dispels the illusion of the subject's self-generated freedom. According to Levinas, "the *for-the-other* in the approach to the face—a for-the-other older than *consciousness of…*—precedes, in its obedience, all *grasping*, and remains prior to the intentionality of the *I*-subject in its being-in-the-world…as if obedience were its very accession to hearing the prescription, as if the *I* obeyed before having heard, as if the intrigue of alterity were woven prior to knowledge" (1991/1998a, 166). How this inversion of intentionality is made possible is addressed in the following chapter where Levinas's concept of the "face" is explored.

The invisibility produced by the ring in the myth of Gyges—its pull toward power and the immunity it affords in the presence of others—is a powerful illustration of what Levinas contends to be the configuration of the Western ego. The ring bearer constructs his or her own meaning and sees without being seen, detached from the responsibility to anything outside of itself. This self is immune, unmoved, and unaffected by the other's demand.

Within modern philosophy and modern psychology, the self is author of its own reality and constructor of its meaning. It is a basic freedom and liberty that the individual is "afforded" in the modern world. Yalom (2000), in his book *Love's Executioner,* expressed this fundamental assumption: "Freedom means that one is responsible for one's own choices, actions, one's own life situation. Though the word *responsible* may be used in a variety of ways, I prefer Sartre's definition: to be responsible is to 'be author of,' each of us being thus the author of his or her own life design" (8). Self-construction is the existential and central feature of human existence. This epitomizes the monadic, constituting, rationally oriented, and individualistic representation of the self. In a multitude of forms, this is the story within Euro-American psychologies, a story adopted from Western history and its modern moorings.

The Gygean self is the normative, *self out of which we live*. It is a self that lives within the illusion of invisibility, an anesthetized way of being wherein one remains ethically immune to the other. "This myth captures the very ontological structure that Levinas seeks to overturn" (Beals 2007, 78). A self caught in the "Gyges Complex" is not disturbed by the face of the other, but rather defends against it, quantifying and possessing (Kunz 1998). This can be further seen in Levinas's description of the temptation of temptation.

Levinas's Critique of Detached Reason: The Temptation of Temptation

In *Nine Talmudic Readings,* one of Levinas's (1968/1994) explicitly confessional writings, he suggests that Western philosophies (and arguably modern psychologies as well) are caught up in the temptation of temptation. The temptation of temptation is his description of the dilapidated and detached "moral attitudes" of the Western self (32). According to Levinas, the temptation is to hear and feel the call of the other—experience one's responsibility for one's brother or sister—and then simply disregard and ignore it. Beyond this however, the temptation of temptation is to develop and live out of a way of being that no longer even allows the call of the other to be heard (Gibbs 1992). This is a meta-level, constitutional issue, a state in which a person's very mode of being and shape of self precludes it from recognizing the otherness of the other and the responsibility therein.

Speaking directly to the temptation of temptation resident in much Eurocentric philosophy and social and political theory, Levinas critiqued the conventional rationality that never led the self beyond itself. In the safety of thought, the self remains "for-itself." "It is as if rationality (that is, according to the Western understanding of it as the absorption of knowledge by being) were still an intoxication; as if, all erect in its vigilance as lucidity, the reason that identifies being slept on its feet or walked like a somnambulist, and were still dreaming, as if, in its sobriety, it still slept off the effect of some mysterious wine" (1982/1998b, 16). He further explains that the "temptation of temptation" is not for the kind of "pleasure over to which the one tempted risks to surrender himself, body and soul.... What is tempting here is the situation in which the self remains independent.... The temptation of temptation is philosophy...it takes off from a self which, in engagement, is assured a permanent disengagement. The self is perhaps nothing other than this" (qtd. in Robbins 1991, 112–13). Levinas is referring to a detached form of rationality in which one believes one can think, calculate, and reason through something without being already affected and involved. It manifests in the self's desire to remain independent, conserve its freedom, maintain its security, and sustain its self-referential status. It is the courage and freedom of a Sartrean (1943/2001) self-createdness. It is an immunity in life where one can first assess, discern, and view without being shaped, called, and demanded of. It is a self without reference to the other. Levinas (1982/1998b) wrote that this form of the self "shows itself concretely in the maintenance of its identity against all that would come to alter its sufficiency or its *for-itself*. It shows itself in humanity's refusal to undergo any cause exercised upon it without its consent. In all things one awaits from man a free and rational decision.... Nothing happens to man that might not be to some degree assumed, nothing could touch him without the mediation of reflection" (44).

However, Levinas recognized this self-protection and detachment as a distortion and truncation: "the knowledge which takes its distance, the knowledge without faith, is logically tortuous; examining prior to adherence—excluding adherence, indulging in temptation—is, above all a degeneration of reason, and only as a result of this, the corruption of morality" (Levinas 1968/1994, 48). In *Crime and Punishment,* Dostoyevsky's (1866/2008) character Razumikhin exclaimed, "Logic can anticipate three possibilities, but there are millions of them! Cut out all the millions and you bring it down to the question of comfort! A very easy solution of the problem! It is temptingly clear-cut, and there is no need to think! That is the main point—you needn't think. The wholly mystery of life can be put on two sheets of printed paper" (246). It is in this way that Levinas saw forms of knowledge and reason in Western philosophy as a "degeneration" of reason. If knowledge reduces to manageable truisms all experience—mediating and protecting us from encountering alterity—then there is no need to truly think and reason. Thought becomes a pulling from formulas, platitudes, past experiences, and thematized perceptions—a "comfortable enough" sameness. "From this," Levinas contends, "stems the inability to recognize the other person as other person, as outside all calculation, as neighbor, as first come" (35). The ego is "sovereign," leaving no room for alterity, and with no room for alterity, there is no room for ethical responsibility. The immanent order of *my* self, *my* organism, *my* status, and *my* heroism becomes the totality of my being. Heschel (1963) observes, "Examine an obtuse mind, and you will find that it is dominated by an effort to cut reality to the measure of the ego, as if the world existed for the sake of pleasing one's ego.... How rarely do we face a person as a person! We are all dominated by the desire to appropriate and to own" (61).

This disengaged, "autistic"[5] representation of the self has fallen into disrepute in much twentieth century philosophy. Levinas's critique is compelling primarily due to its radical ethical stance. "Ethics as first philosophy" means that reason is not detached, but rather bears in it a demand. Levinas (2004) writes, "And does not justification—in its semantic context of rightness and justice—thus go back to the responsibility for the other, that is, to the proximity of the neighbor—as to the very domain of intelligibility or original rationality where, on this side of every theoretical explanation, in the human, the being that until then is justified in its natural unfolding as being, and as giving itself out to be the beginning of all rationalization, is brusquely put into question in me and seeks for itself a pre-initial rightness?" (80).

Pitting modernity's "detached knowing" against Levinas's "dis-interested" knowing, provides further nuance to this issue. Descartes and Locke suggest a disengaged reason for the sake of rationality, whereas Levinas suggests a dis-interested ethics. That is, one's attention to another must not be loaded with the interest of one's needs. A dis-interested stance is necessary for the ego to be dislodged from its presumed centrality and immunity. Detached knowing is the modern belief that one can be disengaged and detached (able and obligated to objectify reality). Dis-interested knowing is Levinas's call for knowledge and experience to be dis-interested from its own egoism. Levinas (1961/1969) states, "We think that existence for itself is not the ultimate meaning of knowing, but rather the putting back into question of the self, the turning back to what is prior to oneself, in the presence of the Other" (88). It is a form of reason where the self *knows* through justice and ethical "optics" as opposed to self-interest and its singular identity (Levinas 1961/1969, 1974/1998c). Elsewhere Levinas (2004) writes, "When I talk about ethics as a disinterestedness, I do not mean that it is indifference; I simply mean that it is a form of vigilant passivity to the call of the other which precedes our interest in Being, our inter-esse as a being-in-the-world, attached to property and appropriating what is other than itself to itself" (80).

Levinas's description of the other person as radically other—a true alterity—is scandalous to the modern depictions of the self (Pitkin 2001).[6] Modernity espouses sameness, certainty, and detached reason, "the instrument by which an ego or society of egos makes same that which is different, possessing and domesticating it. Reason reduces the other, appropriates, disempowers, totalizes. The particular is placed under the general category. What is foreign, what is different, is subsumed within my system. It is made the same to remove its threat. All surprises prove to be just parts of the process, that is, not surprises at all. This is ontology" (Olthuis 1996, 140). Sameness, universality, homogeneity, and secular humanistic ideals are interrupted by his critique. Rubenstein (1992) argues, "The conception of humanity in general is a meaningless and tragic abstraction. As Hannah Arendt has shown, the process whereby Jews were turned into human beings in general, lacking all concrete legal, political, and national status, was the final preparatory step to turning them into superfluous people whose extermination was of no consequence to any existing political community" (238). Recognition of otherness, on the other hand, denies the power of systems and removes abstractions as a means of defining persons, forcing us beyond categories into an ethically based relation and justice-filled sociality that conditions and informs reason. Dueck and Parsons (2007) state that Levinas "critiques Enlightenment approaches because human existence cannot be constructed as a panoramic totality, on a foundation that is solid and self-evident. Science, rationality, and agency are derivative of the face-to-face relationship. Ethics is prior to cognition, sensibility, praxis, knowledge, and history" (276). This has direct implications for psychological theory and practice.

THE REASONED THERAPIST AND RATIONAL PATIENT

Faceless Theories and Reasoned Therapists

Modern psychology often works with a generalized version of the self. The individual subject becomes a particular representation of universally valid and rationally derived principles that are several steps removed from lived experience. "[T]he individual was regarded as a collection of discrete, stable, and general qualities. These qualities were thought of as being identical in kind from one individual to another, varying only in degree" (Danziger 1990, 157–58).[7] To accomplish this, normative measures or averages taken among groups provide a picture of regularity that is then translated into ontologies applicable to all individuals, preexisting dimensions where difference evaporates. Even in the study of individual differences, the distinction between persons is still situated in a general rubric or spectrum of sameness—e.g., introvert vs. extrovert (Gantt and Williams 2002). Burston and Frie (2006) point out that such "empirical generalizations" can help identify "overarching trends in human behavior but in the end they refer to a disembodied, ahistorical entity—a 'generalized other'" (3). And as Birrell (2006) states, "The generalized other is also a stereotyped other" (104).[8]

Psychological paradigms that relate patients—subjects—to generic models of humanity employ a thematizing and totalizing system that cannot attend to the difference, purpose, and morality inherent in being human. The patient can never be *other* in such a system. He or she is merely located within preconceived maps. On the normal bell-shaped curve that provides the scale and locale for comparative analysis, patients are located on the swell of historical and cultural sameness. Human beings are reduced to particular characteristics, rational properties, diagnostic categories, ego functioning, and behavioral patterns/repertoires.

The centrality of ethics for Levinas and the centrality of detached rational measurement in modern psychologies are clearly incompatible. These psychologies define psychic structures, categorize symptom clusters, designate cutoff points for degrees of functioning, and assume a nature behind which all thought, emotion, and behavior can be relegated. Foucault (2003) argues that in modern times each person can be described as a "case" (xxiv). That is, every individual becomes a singular representation of a particular place in a larger system of meaning; a place-card on a preset table, "plug and play" representations of a ready-made explanatory framework. In other words, modern psychologies embody the detached knowing and disengaged reasoning of which Levinas speaks. It is a "relationship of knowing in which everything is equalized" (Levinas 1989, 90).

Jean-Luc Marion (2005) provided a vivid illustration of how this happens when a person submits to medical treatment:

> [W]hen I find myself in a medicalized situation (e.g., admittance to the hospital, removal of clothing, transfer to surgery, the reading of test results, submission to treatment)...the hospital technology's inevitable hold of power over me eliminates in me anything that will not reduce to a medical object. Under the gaze of medical personnel, and very soon under my own gaze, the treatment of my sick body will lead to its interpretation according to the parameters of physical bodies (size, quantification, measurements, etc.), with the result that my living flesh will disappear. Soon I will no longer feel the fact that I feel myself: anesthesia will not only deliver me from my pain, but also from my suffering itself, and thus from my self's self-suffering. Next, every non-objective function will disappear from this self (me), and my flesh, or that which is animated within me, will become an animal-machine. This medical definition of my body as an object will also allow for the distinction of health from sickness in terms of norms. Thus is opened the fearful region in which man can make decisions about the normality, and thus the life and death, of other human beings—because these human beings have become simple human objects. (11–12)

Thus, diagnoses, formulations, and research findings construct and reduce to a faceless sameness the other that sits before me in the consulting room. Sterile descriptions derived from immanent processes and fixed intrapsychic apparatuses become not only admissible, but the norm in a scientifized world. "Neutral," "value-free," and democratic language is the scientific discourse of which modern psychologies consist. This is not meant to deny the importance of diagnoses, formulations, and research findings in clinical work,[9] which is exceptionally useful and potentially meaningful (both for therapist and patient) if held in nonreifying and nontotalizing ways. An important question is whether these diagnoses and formulations are born out of the lived experience of the particular person in front of me, or whether these preconceived categories and sophisticated formulations are an application of a system of thought to that person? Is "knowledge" used to illuminate the patient, or is relationship to the patient an illumination of dynamics, struggles, needs, and hopes that bear on the therapist's psyche and allow meaning and narrative to form?

In Levinas's system, generalities cannot capture selfhood. "For Levinas, the human psyche—ego, self, subjectivity, soul, I—is from the first not a scientific object, not even a failed or deferred scientific object, but a moral event, an event of sensibility deeper than rationality" (Cohen 2002, 41). The "subject" is always irreducible to the themes generated in history. If the self is reduced to these categories of being, then it is merely a "plastic image" of the self, a possessable version of selfhood that merely reflects an imposed order of being (Clegg and Slife 2005). It is a stripping of the face, leading to lives lived in relationship to *faceless* others. Levinas (1993/2000) writes that "the moment the other becomes material, he loses his face" (196). Ford (1999) suggests that "the Enlightenment and its aftermath tended toward a 'faceless self' and that many of the challenges to the Enlightenment suffer from the same defacing of people" (21–22). The person is a particular representation of a universal system: a faceless and abstract formulation. An empirical and positivist psychology can practice with little else. When rationality is put first and made primary, it yields access only to the quantifiable and discernible, mere truncations of human experience. This will be argued more extensively and carefully in the following chapter.

Over the years, most theoretical orientations have valorized the therapist's "neutral" and "objective" perspective. That is, the therapist needs distance, boundaries, lucidity and clarity, and cognitive resources to make sense of the patient's pathology, difficulties, and/or patterns. The therapist is relatively invisible, immune, and the observer so that the he or she can provide a reasoned approach. Though this "objectivity" and "neutrality" has increasingly come into a state of disrepute (within approaches informed by postmodern conversations), it has transformed into new forms. For instance, within many cognitive-behavioral approaches, the therapist uses a more technician-oriented repertoire, administering prescribed models, manualed interventions, and particular understandings of change and effectiveness. As such, the therapist sits in a Gygean stance, less affected while affecting the other.

Rational Patients

The repercussions of reducing others to a faceless generality are complex and unquantifiable. The Greek thought that "one's rational self is one's real self" (Barrett 1958, 89) has shaped Western consciousness and constructs of the self for the last two millennia. Modern psychologies often merely assume a traditional, rationalist paradigm (Burston and Frie 2006), "start[ing] with the proposition that human beings are possessed of a formidable array of attributes and abilities because they are a priori possessed of an active rationality capable of perceiving, understanding, intending, comprehending, and willing" (Williams 2007, 684).

This lineage of thought and its technologies of healing implicitly teach patients that rationality, knowledge, and understanding are the most fundamentally important attributes of the human subject. Levinas (1989) writes that "when asking about the meaning of this identity, we have the habit either of denouncing in it a reified substance, or of finding in it once again the for-itself of consciousness. In the traditional teaching…subject and consciousness are equivalent concepts" (92). As with Gyges and the temptation of temptation, the self becomes a knowing, possessing, constituting, intentional, agentic, and ethically immune perceiver. Psychological terms—including reality testing, disputation of belief, schemas, awareness, insight, mindfulness, lucidity, and rational decision making—from cognitive-behavioral traditions to constructivist models to psychoanalytic discourses reflect treatment technologies that emerge from dominant technologies of the self, with their "regimes" (as Foucault puts it) of a rational subject as the highest end of human functioning. Psychotherapy, working from within these technologies and their assumptions, provides language and "cheat sheets" for patients to define themselves and practice within more "rational," "regulated," and "functional" ways of being.

In mainstream models, where we continue to administer therapy principled by the Cartesian subject, where is a patient challenged to become more ethically attuned and emotionally available

(Orange 2009)? Often, the safety of individual identity is, in fact, bolstered through explanatory language and self-referential terminology, words that mediate experience and may further distance our patients from others. Our constructs of the self promote mastery, control, and greater self-certainty. Certainly, rationality, mastery, self-control, and a positive sense of self-worth are essential prerequisites for ethical attention and responsiveness, but rationality and functionality are often treated as the end game, limiting the parameters by which patients understand both their identity and their relationship to others. Levinas's work "resists the instrumentality of the scientific enterprise—the notion that science is primarily intended to be the instrument of the masterful, bounded self, the discoverer of techniques for controlling the other. The ethical relation rests, instead, on uncertainty and the perilous adventure of forever insufficient knowers sacrificing their certainty and even their control for understanding" (Clegg and Slife 2005, 69).

Relying on knowledge, perception, and rationality, there remains a buffer and non-porousness between the self and the other. Levinas (1985) writes, "The most audacious and remote knowledge does not put us in communion with the truly other; it does not take the place of sociality; it is still and always a solitude" (60). The emphasis upon autonomous reason within modern psychology has the effect of trickling down into a daily anonymity, alienation, and intrapsychic and interpersonal violence (Levinas 1989; 1976/1990b). Atkins (2005) states that "the cogito cannot be fundamentally involved in the world; it must always be an outsider, content to observe and never to participate. The latter is precisely the fate of the Cartesian subject. Once evicted, nothing will repatriate the metaphysical subject to the world, and the rest of the history of the philosophy of the subject is the history of the attempt to resolve the unbearable tensions of a subject in exile, either through the reintegration of the self and the world or through the dissolution of the very concept of self" (10). This is the tension with which psychology struggles.

Conclusion

Though there was a significant shift from "love of wisdom" to a "quest for certainty" within modernity (Toulmin 1990, 55–56), modernity's emphasis upon reason is directly in the lineage of the Greek tradition where the "love of wisdom" steers the path to self-definition and identity.

A Hebrew sensibility begins in a very different place. Levinas began with the "wisdom of love," rather than the "love of wisdom." Truth, in Levinas's thought, is made possible by goodness, not vice-versa: the "wisdom of love" provides the context for truth and beauty to be brought to the height of goodness, justice, and righteousness. That is, *from* love comes wisdom, thought, rationality, knowledge, subjectivity, and consciousness. In Levinas's thought, the very condition for truth and rationality is the ethical relation with the other. Love is when the other's needs become my needs. Levinas often quoted the Jewish proverb: "My spiritual needs are the other's physical needs." Cohen (1986) explains, "Levinas raises anew the question of the limits and nature of knowledge, the question of the status of thought itself. What is unique about Levinas' answer is that it binds thought not in the name of the *true*, but in the name of the *good*" (vii). Reason, at its most reasonable, is open to being disturbed, interrupted, made unreasonable, and made nonsensical. It does not need to reify into shielding and calcified renditions of experience. Love must be the starting place, not the ego, rationality, or any other immanent principles.[10] It is to the immanent source of scientific "truths" that our attention now shifts.

4

The Normal Bell-Shaped Self
From Immanentization of Knowledge to Transcendence of the Other

> *To die for the invisible—this is metaphysics.* (Levinas 1961/1969, 35)
>
> *The domain now supervised by psychiatrists, as well as other specialists in the deeper understanding of man, is the* self. *It is another one of the discoveries made in the state of nature, perhaps the most important because it reveals what we really are. We are selves, and everything we do is to satisfy or fulfill our selves.... We are suffering from a three-hundred-year-old identity crisis.* (Bloom 1987, 173)

Levinas's fundamental criticism of the West centers on its use of the immanent order—nature and history—as a viable source of meaning and definition for the self. According to Levinas (1976/1990b), "If 'know thyself' has become the fundamental precept of all Western philosophy, this is because ultimately the West discovers the universe within itself. As with Ulysses, its journey is merely the accident of a return. The *Odyssey,* in this sense, dominates literature" (10).[1] Levinas (2004) dislodges the primacy of the natural self lived "for-itself," making it clear that the observable order or natural order must be reversed and interrupted by that which is infinite and transcendent. Ethical relationship to the other upsets the definitions of selfhood based within these ontologizing principles, interrupting the visible and measurable and calling the ego beyond itself. According to Levinas (1974/1998c), the face of the other bears the trace of the Divine, a transcendent calling that is the location of the "break up of...synchrony" (85) within time and history. The face is a violation of the sovereignty of our natural proclivities and categorical distinctions.

This chapter engages Levinas's critique of the immanentization process through his concepts of "the ennui of egoism" and "the face." Later, I employ a Levinas-inspired exposition of the psychological discipline's reliance on nature, history, and science through my notion of the "normal bell-shaped self."

THE EGO CALLED FORTH: THE ENNUI OF EGOISM

> *Physical things can be defined in terms of objective properties; man can be understood only in terms of the demands he is called upon to answer. The chief problem of man is not his nature, but what he does with his nature.*
> (Heschel 1963, 10)

Ernest Becker's (1973) book *The Denial of Death* provides helpful insight into the formation of an immanent version of the self. Becker describes how humans pursue "cosmic specialness" (5) as a means of denying the reality of death. He explains that, much like any natural organism, persons seek self-preservation. Yet, with the added capacity of consciousness, this "natural instinct" becomes a pursuit of self-importance, an assertion of the primacy of the self, and a drive toward heroism. Consciousness becomes a tool by which the eventuality of death is denied or deferred; persons develop a variety of processes whereby they can feel a form of pseudoimmortality. They yearn to become the hero in their stories, a demigod that is the center of the stage of life. In the face of the nothingness that lies before them is a wish to sustain meaning. This consciousness, consumed with its own destiny, lives out of a self-configuration aimed at its expanded duration or, as Becker put it, "limitless self-extension" (3).

The drive toward heroism and self-importance emerges from what Becker (1973) describes as an "organismic narcissism" (1–8). In relationship to others, Becker likens the human person to a transplanted organ fighting to maintain its existence and to protect its integrity against the "foreign matter" that surrounds it (2). In the face of mortality, persons view luck as "when the arrow hits the other guy" (an aphorism often attributed to Aristotle). Persons naturally seek preservation, longevity, and self-importance, leading to an intrinsic and inevitable narcissism. The other becomes an adversary, who threatens my primacy in the world. Rather than rupturing the immanence of my natural will, the other further entrenches me within it. My bulwark thickens and I repel the other. Sartre (1944/1948), then, was accurate in saying, "Hell is other people" (61).

Levinas does not contest that the ego's natural orientation is toward itself and "for-itself." He writes, "What is an individual, a solitary individual, if not a tree that grows without regard for everything it suppresses and breaks, grabbing all the nourishment, air and sun, a being that is fully justified in its nature and its being? What is an individual, if not a usurper" (1976/1990b, 100)? The opening pages of *Totality and Infinity* (1961/1969) provide an analysis of the human condition prior to ethical transformation. In this state, self-regard and egoism are fundamental characteristics of enjoyment and our constitutional capacities. A person's very corporeality and perceptual apparatuses orient the ego into an endless cycle of coincidence with itself—sameness. The ego experiences the world around it as its possessions. The ego is self-obsessed, self-absorbed, and fundamentally turned back upon itself. This is what Levinas refers to as the "concreteness of egoism" (38). In this place, the other is not Other. The subject/object distinction is operative, with the other becoming a character in my play, a reader of my script, and a possession caught in the vortex of my needs. This is a violent place where the face of the other is mere physiology. It is an ego unaccosted by the Other.

However, for Levinas, egoism is not the end of the story. The solitary ego is never allowed to rest content. It is plagued by "ennui." The *ennui of egoism* is a boredom with the sameness of self-reference and self-regard, a restlessness and discomfort within one's own skin. It is as though the skin is too tight, constricting (Levinas 1974/1998c).

Levinas (1961/1969), here, rejects the complacency of Euro-American identity and denies the homeostasis of the natural ego. Instead, he (1974/1998c) asserts that the ego is "hunted" and uncomfortable, wrest from its safety and at-homeness by the other: "The identity of the subject is here brought out, not by a rest on itself, but by a restlessness that drives me outside of the nucleus of my substantiality" (142).

The "ennui" of egoism leads to what Levinas (1961/1969) calls "metaphysical desire," a desire for that which is outside of our self-system, our egoist fantasies of a world of our own. In contrast to the self which is a private property, at home with itself, Levinas describes metaphysical desire as that which "does not long to return, for it is desire for a land not of our birth, for a land foreign to every nature, which has not been our fatherland and to which we shall never betake ourselves.... It is a desire that cannot be satisfied" (33–34). The biological drives (needs) of the ego do not constitute the self. Levinas (1989) maintains, "The concept of the incarnate subject is not a biological concept" (99). There is a yearning beyond the ego's functions, a desire for the other.

Here again one witnesses Levinas's translation project. Levinas frequently compares the Greek myth of Ulysses to the Hebrew story of Abraham as a means of describing two modes of understanding the trajectory of selfhood; the former remaining complacently within the self-reflexive trajectory of the ego and the latter driven from its at-homeness. He states, "To the myth of Ulysses returning to Ithaca, we wish to oppose the story of Abraham who leaves his fatherland forever for a yet unknown land, and forbids his servant even to bring back his son to the point of departure" (Levinas 1986b, 348). Instead of the prodigal trajectory of Ulysses who returns home after his journey, from the ego back to the ego, Levinas posits the exilic trajectory wherein Abraham is called forth, never to return home (Levinas 1986a, 1976/1990b, 1974/1998c; Robbins 1991). The demanded self is not settled within itself or on a journey back toward itself. It is forever commanded outside of itself.

Levinas is inspired by a different imperative than natural and historical situatedness; his imperative arises in encounter with the other. The normative discourses of ontological and expressive individualism are guided by and fortified by a history and sociopolitical lineage that dominate the *self out of which we live*—a prodigal and self-returning orientation. Reaching beyond the "horizons of history," Levinas (1976/1990b) finds in his Judaism a sensibility and "extreme consciousness" (6) that promote a countercultural and counternormative source of human identity. The calling to an Abrahamic narrative speaks of leaving the complacency and comfort of one's home in the self.

However, the "concreteness of egoism," according to Levinas, is the inevitable state of the modern self—both complacent and self-protected—whose egology is the beginning and end of the story.

This self is unable to move toward radical exteriority in relationship to the transcendent other. It is a life trapped in the circuitry of its own history, its own habitualities, and constructional abilities, without a means of escape. Its gaze is sameness, overlapping with itself over and over. Moreover, this is all that it knows. As Cushman (1995) puts it, "the eye cannot see *how* it is seeing" (300). This epitomizes Levinas's concept of the temptation of temptation. The self is constructed and lived out in such a way that it cannot get outside of itself anymore. The modern individual, the psychologized self referred to earlier, renounces the marvel of metaphysical desire in its very definitions. This "complacency-in-being" (Levinas 1985) remains the arrested state of modern consciousness. The Western ego denies the Other in its own freedom and self-assertion.

THE POWERFUL POWERLESSNESS OF THE FACE[2]

> *When a man truly approaches the Other he is uprooted from history.* (Levinas 1961/1969, 52)

> *Rather, it is as if the face of the other man, who from the first "asks for me" and orders me, were the crux of the very scheme of this surpassing of God, of the idea of God, and of every idea in which He would still be intended, visible, and known—and in which the Infinite were denied by thematization, or in presence or representation. It is not in the finality of an intentional aiming that I think infinity. My deepest thought, which carries all thought, my thought of the infinite, older than the thought of the finite, is the very diachrony of time. It is noncoincidence, dispossession itself.* (Levinas 1982/1998b, xiv)

Freedom does not come from the ego. Freedom is not in the fulfillment of needs. The ego does not *need* the other. It is threatened by the other (Levinas 1961/1969, 1974/1998c). Its sovereignty is called into question by the other and its identity reconditioned. According to Levinas (1961/1969), "The I loses its hold before the absolutely Other... (it) can no longer be powerful" (17). In proximity to the other, self-assertion fails. Levinas's description of the face of the other and its inversion of intentionality is helpful here.

It has been argued that the ego reduces that which is other than itself to perceptual and experiential categories. The ego's need is safety and assurance of self-preservation. However, the face of the other interrupts this "natural" process. The other is completely other than the ego's categories. This alterity ruptures the immanent order (needs and conceptual apparatuses) out of which the ego functions. The other is analogous to the infinite and the transcendent; rendering the totalizing processes of the ego impotent (Huskinson 2002). The face of the other, in Marion's (2005) words, is a "saturated phenomenon" (23).

The face, in its transcendence, refuses to be reduced (Levinas 1961/1969). Instead, it bears a command: "thou shalt not kill." It halts the reductive nature of the ego and "checks my habitual economy...it interrupts the play of the same" (Robbins 1991, 141; see also Levinas 1991/1998a, 222). Levinas claims that the trace of the divine in the face of the other powerfully decenters egoism and provides the possibility of a self that is given instead of possessed. That is, the other's alterity breaches my lackluster being and bestows upon me an identity born out of infinite responsibility. Levinas writes, "A calling into question of the same—which cannot occur within the egoist spontaneity of the same—is brought about by the other. We name this calling into question of my spontaneity by the presence of the Other ethics" (43). Instead of the ego calling its surroundings into question, the ego is called into question. The face of the other creates this inversion and "breaks the secret of Gyges" (Levinas 1974/1998c, 145).

Upon what basis is this inversion possible? First, pervasive in Levinas's thought is a sensibility that the self is born from ethical relation to the other, not out of essential characteristics (e.g., rationality, relationality, etc.). The self is not a discernable structure with a universal nature. It is without a home within the "is." Cohen (1985) explains,

> Ethics, in Levinas's view, occurs "prior" to essence and being, conditioning them. Not, however, because the good is instilled in a Heaven above or an identity behind identities, for this would just take the ontological move one step back, would again fall back into onto-theology, once more confusing ethics with ontology, as if what "ought to be" somehow "is."...Ethics does not have an essence, its "essence," so to speak, is precisely not to have an essence, to unsettle essences. Its "identity" is precisely not to have an identity, to undo identities. Its "being" is not to be but to be better than being. Ethics is precisely

ethics by disturbing the complacency of being.... "To be or not to be," Levinas insists, is not the question. (10)

The given, the natural being or order of things, is not cognizant of that which transcends it and precedes it. Rather, the face of the other introduces and welcomes the "presynthetic, prelogical" (Levinas 1974/1998c, 107) and "immemorial" past that is older than essence and nature (Levinas 1991/1998a). The other calls the ego outside of itself and its self-reflexive questions onto a journey beyond itself. Levinas is a philosopher seeking exit from this static and ataractic existence (Kunz 2006). For Levinas, exit is not found in choice or agency, not derived from a rational approach or an inherent drive toward freedom. It is not a throwing off of the shackles of the social order and its conditions of worth. The self, in and of itself, cannot achieve exit from its "for-itself." Rather, according to Levinas, the self is commanded outside of itself only by the other.

Second, this "unsettling" of essences transpires in proximity to the face of the other. Levinas (1986a) writes that "essential nature is put into question. It is a reversal starting from the face of the Other, where at the very heart of the phenomenon in its light there is signified a *surplus* of meaningfulness that one could designate as glory. Does not what is called the 'word of God' come to me in the demand that summons me and appeals to me and, before any invitation to dialogue, that rends apart the form under which the individual, who resembles me, appears to me and alone is shown in order to become the face of the other man?" (39). This is what Levinas (1974/1998c) refers to as the "religiosity of the self," a self-emptying in proximity to the face of the other, the infinite to which we are primordially exposed (117). This relationship with the other commands me and creates me before I even have *being*. Levinas emphasizes the created status of humanity, as opposed to the coming to fruition of naturalistic principles (Levinas 1974/1998c). Before we exist, we are called forth. "What Adam hears first is a command" (Heschel 1963, 97). There was a demand upon the self before it had consciousness (Levinas 1974/1998c). And, ultimately, this demand conditioned the nature and formation of consciousness. We are always being addressed.

This command is an ethical injunction for the self to be utterly responsible for the other, all the way to being responsible for the other's responsibilities (Levinas 1974/1998c). It is an avolitional and preconscious calling or demand to substitute one's life, identity, and very existence for the neighbor and the stranger. It is witnessing the commandment of "thou shalt not kill" in the other's face and responding by taking the food out of one's own mouth for the sustenance of the other (1974/1998c). The beginning of subjectivity and identity is an exposed and vulnerable posture before the Other and an ethical responsiveness to the other's needs. Levinas (2004) remarks, "I am defined as a subjectivity, as a singular person, as an 'I,' precisely because I am exposed to the other. It is my inescapable and incontrovertible answerability to the other that makes me an individual 'I.' So that I become a responsible or ethical 'I' to the extent that I agree to depose or dethrone myself—to abdicate my position of centrality—in favor of the vulnerable other. As the Bible says, 'He who loses his soul gains it'" (Levinas 2004, 78).

For Levinas (1988/2007b), identity's starting place is kenotic.[3] The process of self-emptying is central to Levinas's idea of substitution and expiation for the other; the decentering, dethroning, deposing, and divesting of the self's "enchainment to itself where the ego suffocates" (Levinas 1974/1998c, 124). Levinas challenges the Western philosophical enterprise to engage in a "de-reification" and "de-substantiation" (127) of the subject (ego) so that the ethical can inform interhuman relationships instead of the essentialist pictures of human nature that can merely point to solitary existence.

According to Levinas (2004), Western philosophy's understanding of identity in terms of history and "presence" (72) inevitably leads to an egology. Ethics before others is more primary than the mechanisms or shared characteristics in conventional definitions of selfhood. Before ontology, knowledge, and consciousness (all of which are extensions of totality), there must be a conditioning from this preoriginal, dyadic, interpersonal, asymmetrical state that creates an "optics" (Levinas 1961/1969, 29; see also Levinas 1976/1990b, 159) out of which I experience, perceive, and live. The face of the other is the beginning of this conditioning. The question is whether the self out of which we live is an optics that can witness this face or whether it retains its grasping function.

The face of the other, in Levinas's thought, did not denote actual physiognomy. Levinas (1985) even said, "You turn yourself toward the Other as toward an object when you see a nose, eyes, a forehead, a chin, and you can describe them. The best way of encountering the Other is not even to notice the color of his eyes! The relation with the face can surely be dominated by perception, but what is specifically the face is what cannot be reduced to that" (85–86). The face is an *approach* whose proximity appeals, caresses, and ultimately deposes the ego from its throne of being and mastery. In the presence of the face, the self is exposed to persecution, accusation, guilt, and a remorseful "gnawing" at one's self (Levinas 1974/1998c). The process of thematization, locating the other in a totalizing discourse, and cutting the other to the size of my horizon/ego is expressed as forming a "plastic image" of the face that is no longer a signification of the Divine, nor capable of making an ethical claim on my identity (1961/1969). Levinas accuses Western philosophy as functioning within this plastic imagery and idolatrous realm of presence and being. According to Cohen (2002), "To have seen that the core of what it is to be human, the distinctively human, the very psyche, is from the first and at the bottom to be conceived—and not merely conceived but lived—within the imperative vectors of morality and justice, rather than in terms of the motivations, drives, and interactions of instincts or knowledge, creativity or productivity, technology or ontology, or aesthetics—this is the challenge of Levinas's thought" (42).

IMMANENT PSYCHOLOGIES: SCIENCE, HISTORY, AND THE PLASTIC FACE

> *Our failure is due to our regarding the realm of values as a superstructure of existence, deriving the 'ought' from the 'is,' 'norms' from 'facts,' spirit from nature, requirement from measurement.* (Heschel 1963, 96)

> *Ethics is not derived from an ontology of nature; it is its opposite, a meontology which affirms a meaning beyond Being, a primary mode of non-Being (me-on).* (Levinas 2004, 76)

In modernity, nature's order, discerned by reason, became the parameter for understanding human beings. Following Descartes, "The universe was to be understood mechanistically, by the resolute/compositive method pioneered by Galileo. This shift in scientific theory...involved a radical change in anthropology as well" (Taylor

1989, 144). If that which is ordered, discernible, and visible to quantification and measurement becomes the rule by which the self is understood, then the self is increasingly understood strictly in these terms (Danziger 1990). Gergen (2000) facetiously states, "Science teaches that the world is composed of fixed and knowable entities. The same should be no less true of persons" (38). He continues, "It was psychologists who undertook the task of illuminating the nature of the basic self. The systematic application of reason and observation was to make 'man's nature' known to 'himself'—to generate fundamental knowledge of the knowledge-maker's foundations" (39). From this, structuralist, functionalist, behaviorist, cognitive, and psychoanalytic theories have been generated that, in varying degrees, have attempted to distill the human self into particular characteristics and qualities generalizable across the human species. Hydraulic, machine, animal, and computational metaphors for human reasoning and experience have dominated psychological paradigms up to and including the present.

The Normal Bell-Shaped Self

Modern psychology has adopted empirical methodology from the natural sciences.[4] In contemporary contexts, rationality, delimiting data, and observable and replicable patterns have become the basis for "truth," "fact," or "law." The modern psychological self, for example, can be thought of as a normal bell-shaped self, derived from detached measurements of what is normative in a particular historical location (Burston and Frie 2006). For the self to be reformed and defined within the strictures of science (e.g., Locke), it needed to be made measurable, to fit the requirements of empirical observation, and to be reduced to a statistically meaningful form. Danziger (1990) explains, "Statistical constructions represent work done on some raw material that already has a numerical form.... [I]ndividuals who are counted must also be endowed with countable attributes" (136). Hence, persons are transformed into countable entities. This can be seen in the pioneering and influential work of the psychologist Thorndike who developed a "metaphysics of quantification" (146). Thorndike (1918) famously states, "Whatever exists at all exists in some amount" (18). As such, persons become attributes, characteristics, and constellations of features. Persons are reduced to their "plumbing" and placed in "zoomorphic" categories that consist of observable features (Heschel 1963, 23–24).

The psychological sciences' emphasis on empirical methods is evident in their dependency upon statistical constructions of normality (Danziger 1990). Modern psychological methodology and theory, particularly in its use of normality as a definer of human nature, provide a clear illustration of how this works.

> When experimental methods were extended to the investigation of complex, molar behavior patterns—for which they had not originally been considered suitable—the use of average data seemed to provide an acceptable way of coping with the utter lack of consistency that was characteristic of complex individual behavior forced into the quantitative mold. Individual behavior might show little or no consistency from one occasion to another or from one experimental situation to another, but if data from many individuals were pooled, certain statistical regularities sometimes emerged. These regularities were to form the basis of psychological generalizations, even though the average pattern might not correspond to the actual behavior of a single individual member of the statistical group.... Henceforth, the use of average or group data was to become the norm for this prestigious area of basic research. (153)

Normality, a mere snapshot in history, is often the foundational base of modern psychological definitions of selfhood. That is, psychological studies measure a cross section of history and this, then, becomes the prescriptive frame for defining the self. This process frequently takes place through the following steps: first, normative results are shown to be replicable and even predictable. They represent what "is." Second, and subsequently, these results are understood to be representations of laws, natural processes, or objective reality. Third, these natural processes are reified into an ontological status. Modeled after the natural sciences, the existing order or normative arrangement is defined as "human nature." These definitions are believed to be based upon a universal and transhistorical human nature that scientific methodology is able to access. R. Bernstein (1976) states this clearly: "There has been an overwhelming tendency in mainstream social science toward reification, toward mistaking historically conditioned social and political patterns for an unchangeable brute reality which is simply 'out there' to be confronted" (106; see also Bernstein 1983).

In short order, theories that proclaim themselves to be ahistorical and universal are generated based upon normative measures, providing naturalistic explanations for the given order that appear to justify (if not even prescribe) the given normality.[5] The *status quo* is thus maintained. The normal bell-shaped curve is transformed from a description of the *is* into a universalizing system and metalinguistic framework that drives the justifying paradigms of a particular configuration of the Western self. Ultimately, it is a picture of sameness, a totality in which every person is located. A present moment in history is morphed into an exhaustive descriptor of the human self. The measured norm of the status quo is not questioned or challenged, but rather becomes the litmus test of the self's essential nature.

The normal bell-shaped self is thus derived from an empirical measurement in time. In much of contemporary psychology, humanity's current historical location becomes the source of meanings and definitions for human identity. History, with its sociopolitical movements and patterns of being, becomes the progenitor of meaning, the normalizer of persons, and ultimately the determinant of health and pathology. It is a conversion of the given order into a construct of the self that is ultimately adopted and disseminated as an empirically validated norm. It becomes an overextended and reductive basis for understanding selfhood. As a socially sanctioned definer of the self, modern psychologies become the source of relaying the given into the prescriptive. They make normative what is already popular, giving it a language and, through therapy, provide for their consumers a more sophisticated means of maneuvering within the norm.

Levinas's Critique of Scientific Theory

Within Levinas's thought, the natural order is not the origin of theory, nor are systems of meaning and calculated measurements the sources of reason. Rather, "the one-for-the-other is the foundation of theory" (Levinas 1974/1998c, 136). Science esteems the immanent order and its discernable laws, principles, and repeatable themes. Levinas refers to this thematization as a blanket under which the infinite—that which exceeds and calls—is lost. Fearing that science, with all of its "marvels of technology," traps the person within a discourse that excludes the other, Levinas (1989) exclaims, "[T]here is no outside here! What immanence!" (239). He continues, "The contemporary world, scientific, technical, and sensual, is seen to be without issue, that is to say, without God, not because everything is permitted and is possible by means of technology, but because everything is the same" (245). Modern psychologies work within the realm of totalizing descriptions and the immanent order; Levinas believed that this totality must be conditioned by the infinite.

In its natural form, the ego is concerned for itself and consumed with its own death. Modern psychologies have codified this into an ontological account of human existence, the observable, normative, and hence natural state of the human self. In this form, the ego's appearance is very much like the "organismic narcissism" aptly described by Becker (1973). Modern psychologies, many of which are committed to a natural scientific model, assume the natural, self-important state of the human person: by the very nature of its physio-chemical makeup and instinctual response, the ego *is* interested in establishing its freedom, preserving itself, and assuring its safety. Hence, the "natural state" of egoism becomes the definitive gauge of human identity and selfhood. Kunz (1998) articulates this well: "Psychology has nearly deified the self, paradoxically by reifying it as a natural force. The implicit natural law of self-interest acts as the core principle upon which much of the social sciences are founded" (xvii). We start as egos and amass a system of meaning around this ego. Self-interest is natural and the search for "cosmic specialness" is normative (Becker 1973, 4–5).

In Euro-American cultures and psychological practices, then, the "concreteness of egoism"—measured in history, in nature, and in relation to explanatory systems without ethical reference—is the foundation of the self. Modern psychologies take the *is* (the egoism of the organism and natural state of consciousness as self-preserving and self-asserting), reify it as definitively normative, and this normativity becomes the self out of which we live. Nowhere on our horizon is the possibility of the next step. We are halted in our egoism by contemporary constructs of the self. We are deafened.

Levinas's placement of "ethics as first philosophy," on the other hand, makes that only the beginning of the story. For Levinas, egoism is how we begin *and then* move beyond in the presence of the other. The "arbitrary and unjustified" quality of egoist freedom is "detestable" (1961/1969, 88). For Levinas (1991/1998a), if we remain in this place of ego-primacy and sameness, we are caught in the temptation of temptation with no susceptibility to being "wounded by the infinite" (222). There must be, as Levinas (1982/1998b) states, a "rupture of immanence" (1), that takes us beyond being, death, and organismic response. There is a calling from outside of nature and norms.

Levinas did not understand ethics to be an extension of nature. Speaking directly to Darwinian biology and psychoanalysis, Levinas (2004) states, "Ethics is...*against nature* because it forbids the murderousness of my natural will to put my own existence first" (75–76).[6] Levinas (1976/1990b) asks, "What is signified by the advent of conscience, and even the first spark of spirit, if not the discovery of corpses beside me and my horror of exiting by assassination?" (100). That is, beyond one's egoism and concern for his or her own death is the recognition of the other and the primacy of the other's death over my own. Using Levinas's thought, we quickly detect that modern psychologies' leap from a description of organismic self-protection to prescriptive ethics is faulty. The natural will or essential nature does not have the final word."The celebrated 'right to existence,' which Spinoza calls the *conatus essendi* and defines as the basic principle of all intelligibility, is challenged by the relation to the face. Accordingly, my duty to respond to the other suspends my natural right to self-survival, *le droit vital*. My ethical relation of love for the other stems from the fact that the self cannot survive by itself alone, cannot find meaning within its own being-in-the-world, within the ontology of sameness" (Levinas 2004, 75). The face of the other ruptures the complacency of a self lived "for-itself," and calls it to what is beyond, an ethical responsibility that violates the natural laws and principles out of which the ego lives. The face is a reminder of what is beyond physiology, drive, fulfillment, and need. There is something supremely more original and higher than self-propagation that calls me outside of its banality (Cohen 1994).

At issue here is whether the ego can become what Levinas describes as a "self" without passage through an ethical relationship to the other. This question is rarely (if ever) asked in contemporary society and psychological paradigms. The temptation of temptation derives from trusting the "natural order" and what *is* without reference to what lies behind and beyond it.

Modern psychologies emphasize sameness rather than otherness. In front of the other, the Euro-American self is still not in proximity to him or her. In the physiognomy before the self, the face of the other is not seen, the trace of the Divine undetected. And without an openness or exposure—an orientation toward the other—we remain oriented toward ourselves, trapped in the modern prison of individual consciousness, a solipsistic consciousness deaf to what is outside of itself. We live within our own world, a Gygean world with a "richly furnished interior" (using Foucault's words), and modern psychologies assist us in being "geniuses" about this world (Rieff 1987, 32). Becker (1973) argues that these psychologies offer the false salvation wherein "the myth is paradise through self-knowledge" (271). Nothing outside of ourselves truly calls us out of ourselves.

The "organismic narcissism" described above comes in many variations within psychological theories and is a contemporary, Euro-American example of the temptation of temptation that anesthetizes the consciousness of persons to others, and perpetually orients the self "for-itself." Levinas (1961/1969) states: "The ideal of Socratic truth thus rests on the essential self-sufficiency of the same, its identification in ipseity, its egoism. Philosophy is an egology" (44). This, then, becomes another form of philosophical egology and the "sufficiency of the same," though it comes to us in the form of a Darwinian "survival of the fittest" and a normativity that appears to justify it.

Furthermore, inasmuch as the language used in therapy remains ontological language, therapists are teaching patients to understand their reality within the given and natural order. The prophetic calling of the other's face is drowned out. Clinicians, then, further bolster the natural state of the person, providing minimal assistance in exposing themselves to the face of the other (Sayre 2005). Heschel (1963) argues that "openness to transcendence is a constitutive element of being human" (66), but this transcendence is often lost in the immanent skew of psychological constructs. Rosenzweig uses tragic heroes in Greek dramas "to illustrate the basic nature of the human untouched by the divine. This is a tale of fundamental alienation from the other. The hero of tragedy lives a life of isolation and self-containment, which culminates in his or her self-destruction" (Oppenheim 2006, 32). The ego dominant in most psychological frameworks and propagated in our culture is similarly ethically unaware, untouched by the other, untouched by the Divine. This self is a perceiving, cognitive, being-in-the-world without moral qualifications or implications. It is a subject that is subjected to nothing beyond itself.

Reforming Science

Levinas (2004) reminds us of Heidegger's statement that science "calculates but does not think" (73). This is an essential starting point for uncovering some of the methodological fallacies behind applying empirical methods and historical norms to discourses on human identity. Science is a method for observation and description, not a meaning-making or value-creating enterprise.[7] It is descriptive and cannot (appropriately) function prescriptively.

One of science's great strengths is its incisive methodology that forces it to set parameters around itself that allow controlled claims to be made (Faulconer 2005; Heidegger 1977). Its empirical methodology only considers the *is* or the given order of things. Scientific inquiries, by building a particular horizon with artificial limitations, necessarily ignore other facets and levels of the object (or subject) in question. This is not inherently problematic; there is no question that the objectifying picture produced by science is useful for particular inquiries.[8]

However, science (in its chronically parentified state) becomes dangerous when its narrow scope is forgotten and its findings become totalizations transformed into prescriptions. It violates its own parameters and its "hegemonic inflation" becomes dangerously constricting (Cohen 2002, 37). This forgetfulness and totalizing tendency has been a feature of many modern psychologies. Particularly in empirical and positivist versions of modern psychologies, scientific methods are applied in such a way that essentially denies their inherent limits. Their minute snapshots of a particular section of "what-is" are interpreted as definitive for the human person. Science's inherently narrow methods are used to form totalities; and in this way modern psychologies are guilty of methodolatry.[9]

Science, the parentified child-turned-dictator, must be allowed to develop without the impossible and violating pressures of a dysfunctional family system. Heidegger, Levinas, and a variety of postmodern thinkers contend that science functions best when it is not overextended and forced into violations of its own parameters. A science restored to a healthy dialogue with philosophy and theology—used as an adjunctive means as opposed to a foundational arbitrator—will develop and flourish into a beneficial maturity, assuming its healthy place in the family again (as a sibling according to Gibbs 2000).

Science's application of the discoverable *is* to constructs of human identity is an overextension of its own ideology/methodology. The *is* cannot appropriately define the self without entering (however implicitly) into the realm of the *ought;* a realm wholly off limits to a descriptive enterprise. Modern psychologies' definitions of the human self, emerging from their normative and naturalistic paradigms, are a breach of self-definition; they become a system of religious thought with implicit values and morality (Browning 1987; Clouser 2005). By inadequately responding to postmodern critiques that work to wrest from them the power given over to science within modernity, psychologies remain in their parentified form, continuing to be the informers of meaning and functioning out of a "physics envy" that furthers the illusion of legitimization (Leahey 2004).

Modern psychologies have often been critiqued for adopting methods from other sciences, particularly the naturalistic sciences, and assuming the appropriateness and fit of this methodology on the object of its study, the human person (Faulconer 2005; Richardson et al. 1999; Williams 2005). Richardson et al. use Gadamer's thought to critique the pervasive "methodologism" in the social sciences and show the fallacy in applying natural scientific methods in the study of persons (222–44). One would not transfer methodology in physics to biology without making significant changes and alterations to account for the new dimensions of the object being studied. To borrow the methodology of the naturalistic sciences, whose objects of study are inanimate or nonconscious, and apply it to conscious, social, volitional, and ethical beings is to fail to consider how the object being studied demands a different form of method to study it (Faulconer 2005, 6).

The strength of the scientific method—detached measurement and unconfounded deductions born from numerics—avoids the illusory correlations and overconfident judgments of individual subjectivity. However, a human being introduces new dynamics—intentionality, meaning-making, will, relationship, ethics—that confound the accuracy of overt observation. Science can only take a snapshot in history, or a series of snapshots (using complicated analyses) that create a sophisticated image, like the detailed images furnished by an MRI. This discerns bone mass exceptionally well, but methodological snapshots of persons cannot capture the dynamic creativity and dynamism of human relationality and experience. One can delicately capture a picture of someone's patterned tendency toward particular behaviors and place it in a matrix of other people with similar demographics and family of origin characteristics. However, to use science's methodology to discern human experience, meaning, and identity is to adopt a narrow narrative that does not even begin to allow for more substantive meaning to appear on its horizon.[10] Instead, it leads to a ready application of medical language to selfhood, demonstrated by the current explosion of "medical model" psychologies.

In short, the scientific gaze is so precise that it cannot attend to the excess or surplus of human identity, which exceeds even itself (Levinas 1974/1998c). Psychology can speak to patterns, correlations, and causations but without regard for what is more "original" to the human being—ethics, relationship, dynamism, choice, and experience. Empirical descriptions of the self are truncations and "objectifications" (Richardson, et al. 1999, 33), a boxing up into concepts that cannot contain their contents (Critchley 2007). The self out of which we live is often lived out of these truncations. Experience itself—limited by the modern psychological gaze—has thus become "flatter and less nuanced" (Cushman and Gilford 2000, 989), and, with it, human identity. Science is a process of homogenization, its gaze functioning as a procrustean bed.[11]

Modern psychologies continue to mine history for ontological truths and naturalistic explanations through their dependence upon the normative order. These psychologies' measurements of the given order in history become totalizing systems of discourse, exhaustive conceptualizations that are marketed as universal, acontextual, and ahistorical understandings of the human person. The "normal" person, to use Heschel's words, is merely a "homunculus of statistics" (38). Modern psychologies' measurements—taken from the observable, given order of things—yield normative data that is merely a dipstick measure of a given historical context. Human identity becomes supremely tied to a reified moment in history. Burston and Frie (2006) describe how this reification "fosters a *profoundly ahistorical mode of consciousness* that mistakes the existing state of affairs for a merely 'natural' one" (56). The conflation of the given or natural order with human nature is an ironic result of modern psychologies' methodological avoidance of historical and tradition-based epistemologies, which, in turn, creates a more insidious and blind dependency upon history and tradition (see Danziger 1990).

The result is a normal bell-shaped self that becomes the currency of psychological theories and practice. It is marketed in psychotherapeutic interventions and permeates the surrounding culture's discourse. It is the assumed point of origin for modern psychologies' operational definitions, technologies for healing, conceptualizations, questions, and diagnostic systems. Ultimately, this version of the self filters into the culture at large and psychotherapy patients in particular. It becomes, unreflectively, the functional core of the hermeneutic with which persons understand themselves and others. The normal bell-shaped curve becomes an exhaustive tool for understanding the self. In a sense, history becomes the source of meaning when it has none to give. The self is flattened to quantifiable elements, generalized/universal characteristics, and the given order. Furthermore, the use of the given order (i.e., the natural and sociocultural present) to form a universal depiction of the self reduces and traps the self in its current historical configuration. Freud suggested that an aim of therapy is to help the patient behave normally.[12] The given order becomes our "normative unconscious" (Layton 2009). Working only within the normative order, modern psychologies cannot extend beyond themselves to question the "goodness" of their constructs. They measure (allegedly) without value, implicitly giving value to the status quo. And, particularly in the West, the normative cultural milieu is one of fundamental narcissism, a monadic conception of the human being with rights attached (to be argued more fully in the next chapter).

CONCLUSION

Working from within Levinas's criticisms, humans cannot be understood merely by taxonomic categories or an "ontology of sameness" (Levinas 2004, 75). That is, a democratically agreed upon self that is flattened for the sake of universal discourse is not an acceptable source of meaning and identity. The "category of human is not simply derived from the category of being" (Heschel 1963, 29), the "natural" and "describable" not the first order from which constructs of self should be established. Rather, the moral event and ethical responsibility out of which the self is borne create a "reversal of the normal order of things" (Levinas and Robbins 2001, 47). This is not to deny the biological, descriptive, and normative, but rather to locate them more appropriately subsequent to ethical relationship. This is Levinas's fundamental critique: being and presence (history and nature) must be infused with meaning from beyond themselves, from the anarchic nature of the primordial, ethical relationship with the other. Levinas (1993/2000) writes: "In this initial passivity, in this accusative preceding every nominative, the self (soi) abrogates the imperialism of the Same and introduces *meaning* into being" (183). Ethical relation and goodness are a "better" source from which identity, constructs, and meaning can arise (Levinas 1985). Levinas (1976/1990b) refers to Judaism in the following way: "It has a painful experience of living on; its performance accustomed it to judging history and refusing to accept the verdict of a History that proclaimed itself judge" (166).

Modern psychologies can be prophetic or collusive in their theories and practice. Their application of scientific epistemologies has contributed to a commitment to collusion. Instead of assisting persons beyond the present order, calling into question their moral anethesization, these psychologies have often helped persons adapt to or function more effectively within this order. Psychology, in conversation with Levinas, can instead take a prophetic practice that asks the difficult and ethical questions of its surrounding context. As a "moral discourse" (Cushman 1995; Doherty 1995), psychology can question the goodness of the accepted knowledge of the day and the versions of the self that it promotes. There must be a means of living beyond the default, of challenging rather than bolstering the status quo. The current configuration of the self must always be conditioned and pulled forward by something beyond mere measures of historical norms and naturalistic principles. As Levinas (1961/1969) writes, there must be something beyond history to judge history. If psychology does not have this self-honesty and questioning, it is not serving

Western societies beyond providing its population with a "frictionless" adaptability to the present order (Burston and Frie 2006, 4; see also Fox and Prilleltensky 1997; Fromm 1955; Laing 1969).[13]

The fact that human beings tend to put themselves first does not justify this disposition. Murphy (2005) states, "Psychologists can measure human qualities and determine the norm. But is it a good thing for humans to fall within the capacious middle of a normal distribution, or is there some *ideal* state, out at the right tip of the distribution, that is the true goal of the human race?" (53). "Normality" is not "goodness." To assume that what *is* is what *ought* to be is to assume and embrace the primacy of the given historical order. Upon what basis is the present order determined to be prescriptive?

A reorientation of science is needed, one that helps science heed its own self-defined limitations and prevent an "empire of the empirical" (Cohen 1994, xiii) wherein the measurable given order, or what "is," discernible through rational inquiry, is afforded the status of what *ought* to be. This need not be a denigration of science, but rather a removal of an inappropriate burden, a reorientation, a recognition of science as a narrative, tradition, methodology, and not the grand arbiter. According to Critchley (2001), the impetus behind much postmodern thought is to argue that "the natural sciences do not provide human beings with their primary and most significant access to the world" (v). Science cannot provide the model for the human self without condoning an organismic narcissism and the normative discourses that reinforce it.

5

The Buffered Self
From the Individual Subject to a Subjected Individual

> *The subject—the famous subject resting upon itself—is unseated by the other [autrui]... The position of the subject is already his deposition. To be me (and not I [Moi]) is not perseverance in one's being, but the substitution of the hostage expiating to the limit for the persecution it suffered.... For it is only then that we witness... a dereification of the subject, and the desubstantialization of the condition, or noncondition, which qualifies the subjection of the subject.* (Levinas 1993/2000, 181)

A BBC series was produced in 2002 under the title *The Century of the Self*. Referring to the twentieth century, Adam Curtis (the series creator) explores the radical alterations that took place in how the human self was perceived amidst tectonic shifts in modernization, technology, consumerism, and the social sciences. As the title of this documentary further denotes, the twentieth century witnessed a valorization of the self wherein the self emerged as a centralizing and dominant new figure on the world stage. Changing sociopolitical, economic, and ideological arrangements ushered in an epistemological shift, giving birth to the psychological sciences that made this self its "subject" (Danzinger 1990, 1997). This chapter explores some facets of this story and explores how defining the self[1] in such a way creates obstacles for ethical encounter.

IDOLATRY: THE NARCISSISTIC SELF OF THE PRESENT ORDER

One of the most radical contributions of the modern period was its reification of the "masterfully bounded," "self-reflexive," "autonomous," "rights-based" self. As nation-states became sovereign entities and began to turn inward and focus on their own inner workings, so also did the persons living in those contexts (Toulmin 1990). Taylor (2007) characterizes this as a move from a "porous self" to a "buffered self" (38), self-reflexivity becoming its increasingly central feature. Cushman (1995) chronicles some of the growing self-reflection and expanding sophistication of internal language during this phase of the modern era in literature. The Cartesian "cogito" and the Lockean "punctual self" were versions of the self that could disengage and observe their own processes (Taylor 1989, 2007). Kant explains this new reflexivity as Enlightenment, "man's release from his self-incurred tutelage. Tutelage is man's inability to make use of his understanding without direction from another.... Sapere aude! Have courage to use your own reason—that is the motto of enlightenment" (ctd. in Leahey 2004, 153). The modern self is a self turned increasingly toward itself.

One significant part of the modern era's "change in the fundamental arrangements of knowledge" (Foucault 1970, 386–87) was the individual's internalization of authority and power that, beforehand, had been held by ecclesial and political overlords. The rational person became the source of sociopolitical, economic, and epistemological meaning and the constituter of reality. "Ironically, just as science was 'proving' that the earth was not the center of the physical universe, the Enlightenment philosophers were arguing that the center of the moral universe was located within each individual" (Cushman 1995, 377).

Over time, the modern emphasis upon the individual subject morphed into an individual*ism* that is well documented throughout contemporary sociological literature. The loss of social capital and communal practices (Putnam 2000), privatization of life and morality (Bellah et al. 1985; Bloom 1987), and rising narcissism (Lasch 1979) within Western cultures have become staple features of Euro-American economics, politics, and identity.[2] Rieff (1987) observes that De Tocqueville, John Stuart Mill, and others worried about what would happen to public life once individualism had sapped its virtues. For the individual would no longer feel committed to the "chain of all the members of the community." "Democracy," De Tocqueville concluded, "breaks that chain and severs every link of it." The individual is thus, in De Tocqueville's grand diagnosis, the defaulted citizen; he has cut off his feelings from communal affections. Individuals learn to feel that "they owe nothing to any man, they expect nothing from any man; they acquire the habit of always considering themselves as standing alone, and they are apt to imagine that their whole destiny is in their own hands." In a highly differentiated democratic culture, truly and for the first time, there arose the possibility of every man standing for himself, each at last leading a truly private life, trained to understand rather than love (or hate) his neighbor. (70)

The focus of society became fixed upon the individual subject and the human subject became fixed upon him or herself.

The liberal democratic emphasis upon individual rights, romantic notions of individual freedom, and depictions of human nature as "essentially self-interested" (Long 2006, 79) have bankrupted current configurations of the self, leaving persons living with anemic versions of sociality and interhuman relations. Laing (1969) and Fromm (1955) point out that a schizoid self-alienation became preponderant and normative in American culture. Laing (1967, 1969) refers to the "normal" person as living within a "pseudosanity" in the context of "collective alienation" where a "schizoid existence" was normative. Laing further argues that this configuration of the self stultifies "the yearning for transcendence and the ability to love and to connect with others authentically" (Burston and Frie 2006, 226). Cohen (2002) writes that the self-aggrandizement of the modern self has ultimately created the opposite of its intended effect upon human identity: "paradoxically, this grandiose enlargement of the self has never seemed so small. Alienation, estrangement, isolation, 'the lonely crowd,' anomie, loss of meaning, and now, the question of otherness, haunt the modern psyche and its brave new world" (35).

Speaking to the loss of communal cohesion and identity formation within Western civilization, Rieff (1987), an American sociologist, was highly critical of the therapeutic culture Freud ushered in. With caustic style, he describes how we have become "psychological men" and our language of self-understanding has become oriented around the individual subject (instincts) and his or her "manipulable sense of well-being" (13). Though mourning this shift in society, Rieff expresses a degree of sympathy for Freud's reorientation toward the inner and monadic world of the individual. He suggests that Freud's emphasis upon the inward realm of the individual was, in part, due to the lack of a meaningful support system in wider society: "Freud saw no alternative to a strengthening of the individual ego, for he...saw no therapeutically effective communities to which he could refer the patient in the post-analytic situation" (75). Freud's thought was the product of a culture that could no longer integrate the individual "under the sway of its communal purposes" (73). Thus, therapeutic culture became a set of doctrines "intended to manage the strains of living as a communally detached individual" (74). Psychology became a means of managing the effects of a society whose sociality had been lost.[3]

Certainly, before modernity there was differentiation between persons, and the inner self was part of the pre-Cartesian subject. Murphy (2003) reminds us, "Augustine is credited with the invention of the concept of inner space" (41). However, this achieves a whole new level within modernity. Taylor (1989) argues, "The modern epistemological tradition from Descartes, and all that has flowed from it in modern culture, has made this standpoint fundamental—to the point of aberration.... It has gone as far as generating the view that there is a special domain of 'inner' objects available only from this standpoint; or the notion that the vantage point of the 'I think' is somehow outside of the world of things we experience" (131). Murphy describes the two changes that took place with the modern version of this inner space. First, during and after modernity, the "real I" could be found nowhere other than in this inner region and the choice of entering and exiting it was no longer there (2003, 43). This notion fixes us into our inner world; it is from within that we assess what is without. Heidegger describes this modern notion of knowing as being within a box, experiencing only what comes into it (Williams and Gantt 1998). The self, in modern discourse, is trapped within itself, relating to others through the constituting capacities of its rational ego (see chapter 3).

Second, Murphy (2003) suggests that the "outside" is now closed off from direct access, and truth is only known through the filtration of sensory organs or through the unadulterated access of one's mind to universal principles. In modernity, the self is first and foremost a consciousness whose principle purpose is the construction of knowledge. Rationality is an individual process and the defining characteristic of human experience and identity. Locke's understanding of personal responsibility involves taking charge "of constructing our own representations of the world" (Taylor 1989, 174). This is, in part, the beginning of our "reflexive expressions" such as "the 'self', the 'I', and the 'ego'" (175). The indirect effects of this sentiment have altered the very constitution of the Western self. As MacIntyre (1998) states, at present, humanity is working with a "meager stock of description" and "an impoverished view" of itself, particularly in its descriptions of the self apart from another person (100).

This leads into another core critique that Levinas developed concerning the Western self. He rejected depictions of the self founded on being (existence) and as a bearer of rights. Highly critical of the disengaged, autonomous, and egoist individual subject, Levinas stood fundamentally opposed to the Cartesian subject, its Lockean derivative, and the psychological permutations that have followed in their wake. The individual subject—as epitomized in Husserl and Heidegger—were "imperialistic" (Levinas 1974/1998c, 112), falsely sovereign, and violently egoistic. "The Cartesian subject," Huskinson (2002) writes,

> sees itself as subject by reference to the non-self. Levinas adapts the Cartesian argument to show that the ego is not primary but is dependent on the Other (the Self) for its constitution. Levinas thus wants to undermine the ontological authority of Western thought which is essentially an egology that asserts the primacy of the ego, the Same, the subject or Being. In Western philosophy the infinite Other is acknowledged only in order to be suppressed or possessed by the ego, it thus claims that the totality of the ego is without flaw and is all-encompassing, and that the subject receives nothing and learns nothing that it does not know or cannot possess. (444)

Along with other Jewish thinkers such as Buber, Rosenzweig, and Heschel, Levinas interrogates the Cartesian version of the ego that sees autonomy, self-sufficiency, self-reflection, and individual needs as central to selfhood. Indeed, Levinas's critique followed a line of numerous negative appraisals of the Cartesian "disengaged" *cogito* over the last two centuries. From Hegel's master-slave dialectic to

MacIntyre's (1999) *Dependent Rational Animals,* many camps have been critical of the monadic person seemingly central to the Enlightenment project. However, Levinas critiques the Cartesian *cogito* in a unique way, putting the question of holiness, goodness, and ethics first. He works to lift the individual beyond (or *otherwise than*) the essentialist categories of being. Yet, this is not for the sake of further freeing the individual from constraints or romanticizing the notion of selfhood.[4] Rather, it is for the sake of restoring an ethical transcendence. As Heschel (1963) argues, "Here is a basic difference between the Greek and the biblical conception of man. To the Greek mind, man is above all a rational being; rationality makes him compatible with the cosmos. To the biblical mind, man is above all a commanded being, a being of whom demands may be made. The central problem is not: What is being? but rather: What is required of me?" (107).

The self and psyche within Levinas's work is understood as "moral attention" (Cohen 2002, 50). Aronowicz (1994) writes that "for [Levinas] the primary sense of subjectivity is not a private universe, a sealed interiority, but an unparalleled attention, a response to what is outside, the most outside of which is the other human being" (xxi). Humanity does not consist of uniquely constituted selves with complex constellations of characteristics. That would be, for Levinas, merely a reified version that totalized persons into forms of being. The self is a moral exchange, an ethical interchange, a substitution for another, and a "moral event" (Gantt and Williams 2002, 6).

"Conatus Amandi" Rather than "Conatus Essendi"

> *As gift and call, love is both the description of life and the prescription for life.* (Olthuis 1996, 143)

Throughout his writings, Levinas made reference to *conatus essendi* as a foil for his understanding of an ethically constituted self. *Conatus essendi* was a phrase coined by Spinoza, making reference to the value of existence. According to Spinoza's perspective, existence begs for, defends, and has a right to its own perseverance. Existence, itself an inert and abstract subject, somehow confers rights upon its subject. The ontological existence of a being, then, becomes a centralizing component of and value for selfhood: every human has the right to exist, and thus that right should be protected. The political, social, economic, and epistemological rights attributed to the atomic, human subject are a derivation of this understanding of existence and its shaping influence on the self's organization in modernity.

Levinas views the Western ego as functioning fundamentally from an ontological position that values existence for the sake of existence, and he argues for an alternate metaphysics. Though Levinas does not deny the crushing power of mortality and death upon human consciousness, he calls for an ethically constituted consciousness wherein the other's death takes precedence over one's own, creating a "forgetting of death" (1974/1998c, 141). This is a "fundamental difference" between Levinas and Heidegger (ethical vs. ontological, respectively). Levinas (2004) states, "Whereas for Heidegger, death is *my* death, for me it is the *other's* death.... Heidegger defines *Dasein* in almost Darwinian fashion as 'a being which is concerned for its own being'... as that of *mineness*" (77). For Levinas, this "mineness" needs to be abdicated in the presence of the vulnerable other. The trace of the Divine is a transcendent reminder that reframes and decenters our immanent engrossments. "Subjectivity... obligated with regard to the neighbor, is the breaking point where essence is exceeded by the infinite" (1974/1998c, 12).

The other is a threat to my existence inasmuch as my existence is prized as primary. And, the other is a threat inasmuch as I conceive of the other as a competitor for existence and a powerful contender that brushes up against my rights. These are basic assumptions behind social contract theories that undergird Western society and that filter into constructs of the self.

However, Levinas asserts a different picture of the human person. Putnam (2002) writes that "in contrast to what Levinas sees as the Enlightenment radiant image of the human essence," he stresses the "*vulnerability* of the other" (45). Instead of questioning how the other is usurping my rights, Levinas imposes the question of how I am usurping the rights of the other. How is my space in this world taking away from the space of another? More concretely, how do the clothes that I wear or the coffee that I drink (i.e., my enjoyment) fall on the shoulders of others (e.g., sweatshops, coercive trade agreements)?[5] How does my "place under the sun" rob someone else of his or her place? This is the origin of what Levinas refers to as "guilt"

(Levinas 1974/1998c, 1985; Levinas and Robbins 2001). Existence does not offer rights; it requires persons to perpetually recognize and account for their potential violence toward others. The self must be forever apologetic.

Levinas's concept of "asymmetry" is helpful here. Whereas the ego works to take precedence over the other, thinkers such as Buber (1958) argue that there must be mutuality between persons. Levinas critiques Buber for not being radical enough.[6] The other's needs as *more important than* my own is an asymmetrical requirement made upon the self. Levinas (1985) writes, "It is the exigency of holiness. At no time can one say: I have done all my duty" (105). This is what leads Levinas (1961/1969) to argue that there is a "surplus of my duties over my rights" (159). That is, the other is weak and vulnerable, which requires me to forego and relinquish my rights in his or her presence. Cohen (2002) states that in Levinas's thought, "Responsibility for the other cuts deeper than egoism's for-itself" (42). This, for Levinas, is the source of "human rights," not some ontologically derived or essence-based quality of being (Burggraeve 2007). The individual is subjected to the other.

Here is yet another example of Levinas's translation project. The face of the other is not to be understood in terms of comprehendible or generalizable qualities, but rather as the widow, orphan, and stranger described in Hebrew Scriptures.[7] The face of the other is first a command and request from a vulnerable stranger, whose hunger, fear, nakedness, and death are of greater importance than my own. Malka (2002/2006) expresses this as follows: "Levinas reclaims an old Jewish optics that sees the fragile face of the Other and, simply by seeing it, stands infinitely in its debt. Vulnerability as such is reclaimed as the source of all prescription" (xxii). This vulnerability inverts the egoist fantasies and realities of the self. Levinas (1988/2007b) writes,

> There is the possibility of a responsibility for the alterity of the other person, for the stranger without domicile or words with which to converse, for the material conditions of one who is hungry or thirsty, for the nakedness of the defenseless mortal. Where is the person who would not come toward me in that essential misery, whatever countenance they may put on? The other, the one separated from me, outside the community: the face of the person who asks, a face that is already a

request.... In that weakness there is the commandment of a God or an authority, and, despite all they say, there is a renouncing of the force of constraint. And from that moment forth, in this self persevering in being, there emerges mercy and the overturning of beings' tautology of pure "being *qua* being." (119)

The beginning of wisdom and holiness is to be found in *conatus amandi;* an evocation of love wherein the other is loved through a recognition of and attention to his or her needs. For Levinas (1988/2007b), "being's fundamental *obstinacy* in *being*, the priority of the *conatus essendi*, is put into question in the love of one's neighbor and the stranger" (xx). Levinas recognizes the radicality of this claim within Western thought when he states, "This is an odd recommendation for an existence summoned to live at all costs" (119). Nonetheless, Levinas (1991/1998a) explains that love breaks "the equilibrium of the equanimous soul" (168). Love allows the other to interrupt the narcissistic processes inherent in ego function, and mourn the loss of sovereignty. "It brings into question the 'self-care' that is natural to beings, essential to the *esse* of beings" (Levinas 1982/2007a). It involves carrying the weight of the other's existence, not a preoccupation with one's own. Levinas (1993/2000) writes, "Suffering the weight of the other man, the 'me' [*moi*] is called to *uniqueness* by responsibility" (176).

INDIVIDUAL UNIQUENESS AS NONINTERCHANGEABLE RESPONSIBILITY

> *This constitutes the foundation of the inestimable or absolute value of every self and all receptivity, in this revelation which is non-transferable, like a responsibility, and is incumbent afresh upon every person and every epoch.* (Levinas 1982/2007a)

Definitions of selfhood derived from the immanent order are distillations of generalized principles. In Euro-American thought, a person's uniqueness is derived from the distinctive conglomerate of attributes and the unique history of experiences that he or she has accumulated. In this sense, the individual subject "possesses" and lives his or her own identity.

This definition of the subject has come under massive attack from postmodern thinkers such as Foucault and Derrida. The validity of the "individual subject" and "ontological individualism" has been increasingly called into question[8] (Bellah et al. 1985; Burston and Frie 2006; Gantt and Williams 2002; Gergen 2000, 2001; Stern 2003). George (2007) wrote that two tragic deaths took place in the postmodern era, the death of God and the death of the subject.

Levinas offers an alternative to postmodern skepticism, where the individual subject is dismembered and left for dead. Levinas's critique against the modern self is just as trenchant as that of Derrida and Foucault but does not leave the reader in the abyss of nonmeaning. Levinas proscribes the modern self as it currently stands, a radically self-reflexive self that functions idolatrously in its relationship to others: "The grandeur of modern antihumanism—which is truly beyond its own rationale—consists in making a clear space for the hostage-subjectivity by sweeping away the notion of the person. Antihumanism[9] is right insofar as humanism is not human enough. In fact, only the humanism of the *other man* is human" (Levinas 1993/2000, 182).

Levinas (1961/1969) does affirm the individuality of each person and their separateness from one another, but with a twist. The unique constellation of features that each person holds is not, in and of itself, the basis of value, worth, and humanity. Rationality, meaning-making, will, and choice are not the determinants of the self. Neither these things, nor the very fact of existence, provide the value that entitles us to "rights." Rather, it is the distinct qualities of my history and response-abilities to the other whom I encounter that bestow uniqueness upon me. "My uniqueness lies in the responsibility I display for the Other" (Levinas 1976/1990b, 26). The uniquely constellated self is singularly able to respond to the needs of another in a particular way. The self is "ethical singularity" (Bloechl 2000)—a "non-interchangeable identity" (Levinas 1982/2007a), each self able to hear and respond to the needs of another in a way that another cannot because each self bears a unique revelation. Levinas (1989) writes that "this desire for the non-desirable, this responsibility for the neighbour, this substitution as a hostage, is the subjectivity and uniqueness of a subject" (112; see also 190–210). For Levinas (1974/1998c), uniqueness is equated with being "chosen" and "elected" to responsibility for the other. He states, "This summons to responsibility destroys the formulas of generality by which my knowledge (*savoir*) or acquaintance (*connaissance*) of the other man re-presents him to me as my fellow man. In the face of the other man I am inescapably responsible and consequently the unique and chosen one" (Levinas 1989, 84).

The contrast between a uniquely responsible self (demanded self) and the modern self is stark. The modern self begins with the self and ends with itself. The journey along the way is through the universalizing, normative, organismic, and ultimately abasing generalities through which one comes to understand him or herself. It is an idolatrous circuitry in that the self begins with itself and ends with a truncated ego, "for-itself." The subjected individual or demanded self, on the other hand, begins with the ego—need, self-preservation, etc.—and is broken free in proximity to the face of the other. The demanded self cannot return to itself; it is in perpetual exile—away from complacency and identity—and entering into moral covenant. "The human I," states Levinas, "is not a unity closed upon itself, like the uniqueness of the atom, but rather an opening, that of responsibility, which is the true beginning of the human and of spirituality. In the call which the face of the other man addresses to me, I grasp in an immediate fashion the graces of love: spirituality, the lived experience of authentic humanity" (Levinas and Robbins 2001, 182).

While he never denies the faculties of perception and intentionality as "*consciousness of*," for Levinas, cognitive faculties and adaptive function do not define selfhood. When one looks at a rock or the ocean, perceptual categories dictate what is being seen, how it is being fit into prior experience, and how to assimilate or accommodate this information in terms of categories of being and presence. However, Levinas argues that this does not extend into the interhuman. That is, in proximity to the face of the other, these faculties are shown to be fundamentally lacking. There is an interruption of objectivity and horizonality in the other's excess. One's history no longer adequately accounts for one's "experience" of the other, which is no longer even an experience; it is an epiphany. Subjectivity is the reversing of the tide, a being *subject to* instead of merely a subject. The other—bearing the trace of the divine—denucleates my facilities and ultimately and primordially calls me forth. It is no longer subject relating to object, nor even a subject relating to a subject. The ego fissures in the presence of the other, and the psyche is born into a demanded and ethically constituted self. According to Levinas,

> The psyche involved in intentionality does not lie in *consciousness of...*, its power to thematize, or in the "truth of Being," which is discovered in it through different significations of the said. The psyche is the form of a peculiar dephasing, a loosening up or unclamping of identity: the same prevented from coinciding with itself, at odds, torn up from its rest, between sleep and insomnia, panting, shivering. It is not an abdication of the same, now alienated and slave to the other, but an abnegation of oneself fully responsible for the other.... In the form of responsibility, the psyche in the soul is the other in me, a malady of identity, both accused and self, the same for the other, the same by the other. (1974/1998c, 68–69)

The demanded self is defined by its moral shape—a life lived toward the outside, sacrificing one's identity for the sake of the other. This "moral shape" enables the self to hear the call of the other and does not deny it through detachment, indifference, and self-aggrandizement. It is a self that is given as a gift to others, living in hospitality and welcome to the other. Hence the subtitle to Levinas's (1961/1969) *Totality and Infinity* is *An Essay on Exteriority*. This exteriority is, in a sense, a return to the Platonic idea of the Good in that morality is not an internal practice of will, consciousness, or contract, but rather the very aiming of identity to that which exceeds itself. Goodness is not detached rationality; it is the lived and dialogical condition by which rationality is made just. Relationship is the very condition wherein goodness can take place. Without the other, holiness is not possible.

Levinas affirmed the individuality of each person, but displaced the individual from its status as primary within Western thought. The individual is no longer the constituting, authoring source of reality. It is not that which relates to others through detached reason, "windows closed and doors shut" (Levinas 1961/1969, 173). Rather, the self is "for the Other," an identity lived outward that is then given back as a gift from the other (Marion 2003/2006; see also Horner 2001). Levinas (1989) writes, "Its exceptional uniqueness in the passivity or the passion of the self is the incessant event of subjection to everything, of substitution" (96). The self is a lived love, a sacrifice.

Levinas sought to define the self anew, within the freedom of responsibilities and the wisdom of love. He hoped to show that "the nonidentity of the self has higher priority, is more important, is better, than the complacency of identity" (Cohen 2002, 48). Levinas (1974/1998c) suggests that there is a "plot larger than the apperception of the self" (76). He states, "I am trying to show that man's ethical relation to the other is ultimately prior to his ontological relation to himself (egology) or to the totality of things which we call the world" (Levinas 2004, 72).

EGOLOGICAL PSYCHOLOGIES: SAMENESS WITHOUT EXIT

> *I do my thing, and you do your thing. I am not in this world to live up to your expectations, and you are not in this world to live up to mine. You are you and I am I, and if by chance we find each other, it's beautiful. If not, it can't be helped.* (Perls 1969, 4)

> *We are all responsible for everyone else—but I am more responsible than all the others.* (Dostoyevsky 1880/2004)

Alienation of the "Masterfully Bounded" Self

Referring to psychological discourse, Laing (1969) states, "The words of the current technical vocabulary either refer to man in isolation from the other and the world, that is, as an entity not *essentially* 'in relation to' the other and in a world, or they refer to falsely substantialized aspects of this isolated entity" (19). Laing and many others ask what is concealed by this language, which precludes a glance beyond the immanent, beyond the flattened sameness of secular, Enlightenment discourse. Its language favors evolution over revelation, measurability over incarnation, and individual rights over ethical responsibility. Vulnerability and exposure to the call of the other is absent (Layton 2009; see also Butler 2004), and with it the possibility of hearing an ethical imperative in relation to the other.

The other, our neighbor, is no longer a constitutive part of our definition of the self. Each individual is a "masterfully bounded" self that happens to relate to other "masterfully bounded" selves (Cushman 1995). Firm, "non-porous" boundaries demarcating the self from the other lead to versions of the self that are self-reflexive and seemingly free of ethical injunctions. Fromm (1947) describes his position as being in "contrast to the trend prevailing in modern psychology which emphasizes 'adjustment' rather than 'goodness'....

[P]roblems of ethics cannot be omitted from the study of personality" (viii).[10] Psychological discourses for selfhood—derived from natural processes, normative practices, and the historical status quo—are without the resources for rich ethical relationships between selves, their questions about the self wholly separated from questions of goodness.

Levinas accuses Western philosophy of being an "egology" (1961/1969, 44), and modern psychology contains the same obsession with being, idolizing of the immanent order, and illusory safety of self-mastery and meaning-making. The psychological self is self-constituting and at home in itself, a well-boundaried, "buffered self" whose rights and needs are perpetually active (Levinas 1974/1998c). Dueck and Parsons (2007) write, "Levinas recognizes this self pejoratively as the Cartesian ego that functions in a mode of unrestricted freedom. The Other is there for the ego: the Other gives the sensory experience of pleasure and pain. When the ego reduces the Other to sameness, the Other becomes an extension of the self. The ego is the 'melting pot' of otherness" (275). Levinas charges this "masterfully bounded" self, the child of Western philosophy, as being a bulwark of imperialistic practices, definitively without ethical cognizance, and without a Desire for what is beyond, behind, and instead of itself.[11]

This egoism is the preponderant state of the modern self, unable to move from interiority to the outside, toward the other. It is a life stuck in the circuitry of its own history, without a means of escape. This ego, severely detached, hears the sameness of itself in the other's voice instead of hearing the other's voice in its own. The other has little constitutional capacity. Intimacy is alien even in the presence of eros (Williams and Gantt 1998). Without an openness or exposure—an orientation toward the other—the self remains oriented toward itself.

This Euro-American subject, propagated in a variety of forms in psychological theory, provides no means of escape from itself, no transcendence. Rather, its language of fulfillment, adaptation, and ego function/boundaries, in their common use, further reifies and facilitates this way of being. This language feeds into constructs of the self that are definitively egoist, leaving the needs of the other outside of the purview of human identity.

Levinas (1961/1969, 1974/1998c) contends that this egoism and its alienating function is pandemic in Western thought. Alford (2007) writes, "People are always complaining, says Levinas, that they can't get close to other people.... Forget about trying to get close, Levinas responds. Try to get more distant! Get far enough away to feel the awe as the sheer otherness of another person. Then maybe you will feel the wonder of a world filled with others" (547). If we locate the other in the themes of our systems, we "hear" the other through our own knowledge and not through the true exposure that is laced with an inexhaustible responsibility. In such a place, the other cannot demand anything of us beyond the dictates of social contract.

As a principally normative science, contemporary psychological constructs of the self have both reflected and propagated a monadic, individualistic trajectory, as evidenced by current theories and practices in modern psychologies that revolve around the individual subject (Cushman 1995; Kirschner 2005; Kunz 1998; Richardson et al. 1999). Richardson (2006) states, "Psychology, in representing normative culture, maintains and constructs a self that privileges freedom and autonomy, rejects authority/power other than from self, and is a puppet of individual liberalism." Following the modern project out of which modern psychologies were spawned, theories generated about the self are oriented around the observations of the present order. They make sense, thrive, and are propagated not because they tap into some form of universal truth or essential element of human nature. Rather, they are congruent with and are in the flow of the current horizons of experience, within a particular time and place. Therapy may be experienced as "effective" and "meaningful," but these terms are always referential to the overarching framework of what one values. The "value neutrality" dominant in clinical practices might be better understood as subscription to the default cultural and philosophical practices. It is the uncritical valuation of the immanent order. It is a passive submission that ends up being an active collusion.

Long (2006) argues that many psychological theories about the self are arranged "according to the dominant vision of physical reality" (78), leading to a portrayal of the human person as "essentially self-interested" (79). As a result, the ego's function and needs of the organism become primary focal points (see Heschel 1963). As such, health and pathology have become about an individual's mental hygiene, adaptability, rationality, vulnerabilities, and resiliencies. Kunz (1998) expresses a similar point: "Psychology has a difficult time describing human experience and behavior other than as events of an ego-centered being solely concerned with itself: either an ego forced by biological and instinctual causes, similar to plants and animals, or a willing ego empowering itself for personal self-esteem" (9). This has led to what Bloom (1987) referred to as an "enlightened selfishness" (175), a configuration of the self that is justified rationally by the observation of nature and lived out normatively in Western society. Bloom wrote, "Hobbes blazed the trail to the self, which has grown into the highway of a ubiquitous psychology without the psyche (soul).... Hobbes and Locke assumed that most men would immediately agree that their self-preservative desires are real, that they come from within and take primacy over any other desire. The true self is not only good for individuals but provides a basis for consensus not provided by religions or philosophies. Locke's substitute for the virtuous man, the rational and industrious one, is the perfect expression of this solution" (175).

Many sociological critiques have been levied against modern psychologies and their psychotherapeutic practices, particularly their role in the reflection and propagation of this insidious individualism (Cushman 1990, 1995; Fox and Prilleltensky 1997; Prilleltensky 1994; Rieff 1987, 2006; Vitz 1994). Richardson et al. (1999) articulated one such critique: "To what degree does twentieth century psychotherapy represent a significant contribution to human welfare and the struggle for a good society? Is it possible that the modern therapy enterprise to some extent subtly reinforces a shallow, one-sided individualism in our kind of society? Does it help perpetuate such modern social ills as the loss of community, the decay of any sense of individual purpose beyond shallow and self-serving ends in living, emotional isolation, alienation, and emptiness?" (4).

If, as argued in chapter 1, the self is a story that both includes some facets of experience and excludes others, then the normative and preponderant individualism espoused by most psychologies may be an example of psychology's role in the narrowing of our understanding of the human person (Hillman and Ventura 1992). Cohen (2002) observes, "We find ourselves in a world whose meaningfulness is increasingly explained by psychology.... Psychology, not metaphysics, supports and explains our new monadic lives" (33).[12] Though it is unfair to unidirectionally blame modern psychologies for the rise of individualism and its societal consequences, many of these psychologies have reflected and propagated the status quo and have further developed and entrenched individualism's status as the given order (Cushman 1995). The interplay of countless forces and variables gives rise to a particular self out of which we live. These psychologies pick up and reflect this emergent self and give it a language, integrate it into convention, and normalize it. And, in doing so, they blindly disseminate the given state as definitive.

Individual fulfillment, autonomy, individuation, rationality, agency, adaptation, and functionality are the promoted *lingua franca* of contemporary psychological constructs of the self. Totalizing descriptions of human health and pathology are produced and marketed, both in the context of therapy and in our "therapeutic" society, appealing to a general sense of "well-being" and shedding any system that incorporates "moral demand" (Rieff 1987, 13, 30). The "masterfully bounded" self and the "sovereign I" (Levinas 1985, 101) are preeminent.

Due to its invisible, assumed, and insidious nature, the normative self is not challenged, but rather is valued as the foundation of psychological concepts and practice. However, remaining passively committed to the given order or normative pictures of the self is to blindly trust a myriad of natural and historical forces to appropriately define the self out of which we live. It is to unreflectively function as a puppet in the puppet show of history. And, the culpability of clinical psychologists—whose work revolves around assumptions about the self and their transmission to patients through "technologies of healing"—in perpetuating a particular version of the self is obvious.[13]

The question arises whether the monadic and individualistic definitions or constructs out of which we unreflectively live and experience are a product of deadening political, economic, and social practices.[14] Gergen (2000) warns, "If there is one message writ large within the annals of anthropology, it is to beware the solid truths of one's own culture.... we find that what we take to be 'reliable knowledge' is more properly considered a form of folklore. Consider the very definition we hold of a single, autonomous individual. We more or less take it for granted that each of us is a separate individual possessing the capacity for self-direction" (8).

Countercultural Therapy and a Demanded Self

Many psychologists who use Levinas's work challenge the "masterfully bounded" version of the individual subject (and the derivative models of psychotherapy and psychopathology that emerge from it) by attempting to show how morally laden human suffering is (Gantt and Williams 2002; Marcus 2008). Psychotherapy, in this emerging conversation, is less interested in therapeutic "interventions" from within models that emphasize empirical validation and symptom reduction (Clegg and Slife 2005) and is more concerned with persons trapped within themselves, seeking escape and responsibility for the other (Alford 2007; Atterton 2007; Cohen 2002, 2005; Kunz 1998; Marcus, 2007; Williams 2007; Williams and Gantt 1998). Williams (2007) writes, "For those who seek therapy because of the heavy burden of self-creation and a poignant sense of nothingness, or for those who are lonely even in the midst of unbridled autonomy, a Levinasian account of life, relationships, and infinity whispers of hope and wholeness. These are to be found not by concentrating ourselves inward, but outward" (695). Cohen's (2005) description of suicidality from within a Levinasian frame illustrates this point:

> Instead of conceiving suicidal inclinations as the desire of a desperate soul to escape from life, one rather should think of these inclinations as the ultimate expression of the failure to find an escape from self-absorption. That is to say, the potential suicide is he or she who has not found a "way out," has not found an escape, lacks the humane and humanizing experience of transcendence, despairs, and gives up all hope of ever finding one.... The therapeutic response to such feelings of entrapment, and to all the conscious psychic distortions that come with these feelings, would be to re-connect the individual to a genuine inter-subjective life, life with others. (111)

For Levinas, "The subject exists, but not in isolation, only in relationship to others" and furthermore "Levinas.... is not looking for comfort. He is looking for an exit. My infinite responsibility to the infinitely other allows me to participate, in as much as humans are able to participate, in transcendence, understood as leaving the burden of my being behind as I devote myself to others" (Alford 2007, 540). An alternative paradigm to conventional discourse about pathology might consider the ways that persons are impeded in living a life of love, justice, sacrifice, and attunement to the needs of the other (Marcus 2007). This means that psychologists might orient their work around treating the wounds that continue to orient their patients toward themselves, and assist their patients to act justly toward others.

Might therapy help individuals, and society as a whole, to witness how they have been tempted by temptation, how they have used knowledge and the current disposition of the human self and their own needs as a means of protecting themselves from exposure and proximity to the other? Might therapy provide a context wherein persons can dismantle their "defenses against the ethical encounter with [their] neighbor" (Santner 2001, 128)? Therapy could be a location where one learns to hear not just one's own voice, but the revelation gifted from the trace of the Divine: seeing the face of the other again and hearing, "thou shalt not kill." How do we, as psychotherapists, introduce to our patients the countercultural approach of emptying themselves of their natural impulses toward self-preservation, self-regard, self-interest, and self-assertion? If it is the face of the other that ruptures the sameness of our patients' egos, then how can we restore a nontotalizing vision of this face? How do we overcome a cultural narrative with its normative and consumerist discourse that deafens us to others and that is a blind coextension of the natural proclivities of our self-interested egos?

Possibly, in relationship to a therapist, patients can learn a way of letting go of themselves and laying their lives down for their neighbors, of seeing in the face of the other that which trumps, overwhelms, and calls toward a freedom that only can come from responsibilities. This is a freedom alien to a culture tempted by temptation and to our derivative communities that revolve around the heroism of each individual.

Psychotherapy coming from the concept of the demanded self might be a process that "calls me into question" (Levinas 1989, 83). It decenters individuals' sense of self (Sayre 2005), and moves them increasingly toward openness to the mystery and surprise of the other. It is a process of self-emptying or kenosis in which a person increasingly releases his or her sedimentary layers of identity, control, and consciousness for the sake of exposure to the other. Being exposed to the needs of the other and being utterly accused lays the groundwork from which subjectivity and consciousness emerge. However, this is a subjectivity and consciousness born out of an ethical encounter, not a "true self" buried within or a reintegration of the ego free from "conditions of worth." It is a subjectivity and consciousness that recognizes obedience as more fundamental than autonomy and individuation, passivity as more primary than rationality and agency, and ethical responsibility as a greater concern than functionality.

The demanded self does not shore up its walls, ensure its rights, and function unto itself. For Levinas, "The road from mental illness to mental health is not to create from a shattered ego a fortress ego, but to regain one's obligations, one's responsibilities to and for the other" (Cohen 2002, 48). The demanded self is susceptible to the madness and insomnia of being ruptured, taken hostage, by the face of the other (Levinas 1974/1998c)."The subject—the famous subject resting upon itself—is unseated by the other (autrui), by a wordless exigency or accusation, and one to which I cannot respond with words, but for which I cannot deny my responsibility" (Levinas 1993/2000, 181). It is a self decentered in its being that can experience the trace of God in the face of the other. The demanded self sacrifices personal illusions of sovereignty and comforts of identity for the goodness of the other's needs. Brueggemann (1999) captures this when he states, "Thus the 'othering' process admits of no settled self, because the self is always reengaging self in an ongoing covenanting exercise" (15) and further writes, "'[S]pirituality' is the enterprise of coming to terms with this other in a way that is neither excessively submissive nor excessively resistant.... This Thou always undermines whom we have chosen to be. The presence of the other always reminds us that we are addressed, unsettled, unfinished, underway, not fully whom we intend or pretend to be. For that reason, so much of life consists in fending off this life-threatening, life-giving otherness, for the other evokes in us terrible fears—phobias, we call them" (2).

Levinas (2004) hopes to take advantage of a "golden opportunity for Western philosophy to open itself to the dimension of otherness and transcendence beyond Being" (79). Likewise, the work of a therapist is an incredible opportunity to help patients open themselves to a dimension of otherness and transcendence beyond the sameness of their own being. Therapy, instead of restoring persons to the cultural status quo, might be better understood as a process wherein persons redefine their personal freedom (Dueck and Parsons 2007), becoming less concerned about autonomy and rationality and more concerned with being ethically subject to others.[15]

Freedom is redefined and reconditioned by Levinas's thought (Alford 2002). It does not come from unencumbered sovereignty of the ego, self-creation, or autonomous rationality. It is not in living congruently with nature and one's needs. Rather, it is a life of perpetual sacrifice, of laying down oneself to the needs of the other (Levinas 1991/1998a, 1974/1998c, 2004). It emerges in the trauma of exposure to the other and is a freedom born from responsibility to this other. Freedom, in its self-referential form—needing to be protected and conserved—must instead be given away and relinquished (Levinas 1968/1994; Robbins 1991). In giving away a lesser freedom (i.e., unencumbered being)—a greater freedom is given by the other to the self. Levinas (1947/2001) states, "This is the most profound paradox in the concept of freedom: its synthetic bond with its own negation. A free being alone is responsible, that is, already not free" (78–79).

Conclusion

While the philosophical presupposition that the self is the center of the self has been the firm foundation of psychology, it has encouraged an egocentrism that sabotages itself. (Kunz 1998, xix)

According to Levinas, the self is always affected, involved, called, and demanded. The self is irreducible to generalizable rationality (genus), the immanent order, or the monadic and disengaged, self-interested organism (ego). The normal bell-shaped self with its preeminence of autonomous reason, constriction to the given historical and natural order, and its preoccupation with the individual subject must be called into question.

Defining the self without ethical reference to the other is a common trend in Enlightenment-derived thought (the Greek self), epitomizing the creation of a form of knowledge that allows for detached representation. Identity is constituted by an abstraction, a generalization of the themes of a particular historical situation. This is another means of distancing myself and others from an identity forged within the moral imperative of relationship. Definitions of self that emerge from the normal bell-shaped curve, to use Levinas's words, "express the most flat banalties, taking their meaning from a system" (1974/1998c, 70). Levinas (1982/1998b) refers to this as the "normative allure" (4). It is another means of possession, control, and safety.

The current self out of which we live is an idol, pointing persons back to themselves and to the surrounding culture and history. It cannot point beyond itself. Born in modernity, it is a picture of the self whose reason and identity are divorced from ethics and responsibility. The West lives out of a version of the self that is not truly exposed to the calling of the other, but rather only the closed circuitry of its own calling for fulfillment, adaptation, and resolution (Harrington 2002; Heschel 1963). The dominant configurations of the Euro-American self reflect this alienation, self-absorption, and schizoid orientation and, some argue, psychotherapy often merely functions as "modernism's therapeutic arm" (Olthuis 2001, 30).

I pose this as a metalinguistic challenge to the dominant epistemologies, methods, and constructs within many modern psychologies and their healing technologies and norms propagated in general culture. When applied to clinical psychology, I suggest that mental health is not merely realigning misaligned cognitions, shoring up ego strength/boundaries, or reconditioning a patient toward greater adaptability for the sake of reduced symptoms or increased normality. These models of psychotherapeutic treatment are the logical conclusion of naturalistic, immanent, and reason-based constructs of the self: health and pathology are located in the mechanisms and universal functions within each individual. Sameness of being allows the therapist to conceptualize the patient from recognizable characteristics, symptom clusters, and a preassessed understanding of what a healthy person looks like. These dominant models of psychotherapy reflect and encourage egological models of human health in which autonomy, rationality, freedom, and functionality are espoused as the litmus test of psychological health.

The self out of which we live, reflected in psychological practices, is a self that is defined and lived in such a way as to blind us to that which is behind and beyond mere constructions, the ethical call of the other. In Western history, there has been a metaretreat from ethics through our constructs. Our very constitution, our lived self, has lost its capacity to hear the primordial call to be responsible for the other, our brother or sister.

Part Two

The Demanded Self:
Clinical Applications

6

Hineni and Transference
The Remembering and Forgetting of the Other

> *Meaning is found in responding to the demand, meaning is found in sensing the demand.* (Heschel 1963, 108)

Tucked away in the hills of France, there is a small town named Le Chambon. During World War II, Jews, fleeing from other regions of Vichy-controlled France and the advancing forces of Germany, were sheltered in its homes. At great risk and peril to themselves, the Chambonnaise opened their lives up to these refugees, provided them with ration cards, food, and clothing. Raids were frequent; some villagers were arrested, interned, and killed, and threats were ever present. Thousands of Jews were saved in this town, many of them children (Hallie 1979/1994).

After the war ended and word of Le Chambon spread, its anomalous status in the ethos of wartime Europe attracted reporters. The responses of some of the citizens interviewed were enigmatic in light of conventional ethical theories. One interviewer wrote: "When I asked [one of the Chambonnaise] why she found it necessary to let those refugees into her house, dragging after them all those dangers and problems...she could never fully understand what I was getting at. Her big, round eyes stopped sparkling in that happy face, and she said, 'Look. Look. Who else would have taken care of them if we didn't? They needed our help, and they needed it then...there are no deeper issues than the issue of people needing help then" (Hallie 1979/1994, 127). Many of this reporter's interviewees "scoffed at words that express moral praise" (20). One interviewee even exclaimed, "How can you call us 'good'? We were doing what had to be done.... And what has all this to do with goodness? Things had to be done, that's all, and we happened to be there to do them" (20–21). Many Chambonnaise did not know how to answer the questions concerning why they cared for the Jews when it meant much sacrifice and danger to themselves and their families.

For them, it was not a matter of consciously performing the categorical imperative or calculating right and wrong through the heuristic of some abstract moral judgment. The moral cognitions of the Chambonnaise people were not of an accelerated caliber: they would likely respond to Kohlberg's Heinz dilemma as an average person would, and their scores probably rank unremarkably on Kohlbergian scales of moral consciousness. Their ability to formulate and articulate what is "good" and "right" was relatively unsophisticated in the terms of ethical theory. Nonetheless, their moral or ethical response was clear.

The moral actions of the Chambonnaise people were not, first, rational decisions. Their actions emerged out of a psyche oriented toward the other, the very configuration and shape of their selves lived out as *hineni,* a perpetual "Here I am" (*me voici*). Levinas (1989) wrote, "The for-the-other characteristic of the subject can be interpreted neither as a guilt complex (which presupposes an *initial* freedom), nor as a natural benevolence or divine 'instinct,' not as some love or some tendency to sacrifice" (114). It was, for Levinas, responsibility; lived action. It was an ethical response before deliberation, not the emergent property of intellectual faculties. In *Difficult Freedom,* Levinas (1976/1990b) states, "Moral consciousness is thus not a modality of psychological consciousness, but its condition" (293). Recent literature within "moral psychology" has concurred with the assertion that moral judgment and moral consciousness are not the best predictors for moral behavior (Blasi 1983).[1] It is not rational deliberation and sophistication that determines whether one hears "You shall not kill" when in proximity to the other. According to Levinas (1993/2000), "Responsibility... has no cognitive character. Responsibility is not a knowledge" (186). Instead, responsibility is an embodied memory or remembering of the other.

Levinas (1976/1990b) asserts, "To see a face is already to hear 'You shall not kill,' and to hear 'You shall not kill' is to hear 'Social justice'" (8–9). Justice was an outgrowth of the Chambonnaise people. They lived out a responsiveness to an imperative that could only be heard through a shape of the self radically exposed to and oriented toward the other—a demanded self.[2] Cohen (2002) writes, "Contrary to Socrates, for Levinas, one does not first know the good in order to be able to do the good. To do the good one must first be responsive to the order of the good" (62).

The following chapter further considers what a demanded and morally shaped self looks like within Levinas's thought. It is obvious from the start that describing the self as having a specific "structure" with certain definite characteristics already stands in fundamental opposition to Levinas's work (1993/2000; see also Cohen 2002). On the other hand, Levinas provides the space for the formation of a self conditioned by ethical relation and points to some of the ingredients needed to shape such a self.

My Brother's Keeper?

> *To recognize the Other is to recognize a hunger. To recognize the Other is to give.* (Levinas 1961/1969, 75)

For Levinas, the question "Am I my brother's keeper?" inherently assumes that the other is not my business (Levinas 1976/1990b) and is "already too late," already an "evil" (Cohen 2002, 62). The question only has meaning "if one has already supposed that the ego is concerned only with itself, is only a concern for itself" (Levinas 1989, 107; Levinas 1974/1998c, 117).

The prodigal orientation of the self that lives without substantive ethical recognition of the other is readily propagated by modern psychologies. It asks the question "Am I my brother's keeper?" and asserts a definitive "No." It has been argued in the preceding chapters that the self found throughout the egological tomes of psychological literature is a self shaped in a prodigal arch (Robbins 1991); an instinctual, physiochemical, and existential being "for-itself." It is a justification of the *conatus essendi*. Speaking about substitution and exposure, Levinas (1974/1998c) argues, "These are not events that happen to an empirical ego, that is, to an ego already posited and fully identified, as a trial that would lead it to being more conscious to itself, and make it more apt to put itself in the place of others" (116).

For Levinas (1995/1999), the other is "my business" (32). However, Levinas is careful to evade an essentialist or ontological definition of the I. The other is my business not because of the topography of my ego—its attributes, traits, and abilities (1993/2000, 179). The calling, command, demand, and election comes from the other. Furthermore, and more radically, this beckoning from outside of myself is actually the source of the self. Levinas (1989) writes, "I exist through the other and for the other, but without this being alienation: I am inspired. This inspiration is the psyche" (104). That is, the activity of my consciousness and attributes is not the source of identity and goodness; rather it comes from the other and names me as an "I." Cohen (2002) represents this sensibility when he suggests, "'I am my brother's keeper' is for Levinas literally true: the I is I as, and insofar as, it is its brother's keeper" (57).

However, even though ethical response to the other is not born from my attributes and qualities, it is the shape of the self—its lived configuration—that allows for a hearing of the other. Levinas (1974/1998c) clarifies, "Substitution is not the psychological event of compassion or intropathy in general, but makes possible the paradoxical psychological possibilities of putting oneself in the place of another. The subjectivity of the subject, as being subject to everything, is a pre-originary susceptibility, before all freedom and outside of every present" (146). The command comes from outside of ourselves, but the receptiveness to it is, in part, a product of how the self is shaped and oriented.[3] "The ethical relationship is not a disclosure of something given but the exposure of the 'me' [*moi*] to another" (Levinas 1993/2000, 186). Whether the other can be heard as other, and with it the moral injunction inherent to relationality, is influenced considerably by the self's orientation toward the other. Does the self respond with a "Here I am" or out of a preservation of rights and assertion of a being lived "for-itself"? Is it a self that hears the other behind history or is the volume of its own history so loud as to mute the command?

"Self," in Levinas's thought, is conditioned by ethical relation. It is "through and through a hostage, older than the ego, prior to principles" (Levinas 1974/1998c, 117). Throughout his work, the shape of the self oriented toward the other is referred to as *hineni*, which, for Levinas is interchangeable with the word "I": "Under assignation, the pronoun 'I' [*je*] is in the accusative: it signifies *here I am*" (1993/2000, 188; see also 1989, 104).

SELF LIVED AS *HINENI*

> *The Torah is given in the Light of a face. The epiphany of the other person is ipso facto my responsibility toward him: seeing the other is already an obligation toward him. A direct optics—without the mediation of any idea—can only be accomplished as ethics. Integral knowledge or Revelation (the receiving of the Torah) is ethical behavior.* (Levinas 1968/1994, 47)

Hineni represents one of Levinas's many allusions to Scripture throughout his philosophical writings.[4] Abraham, Jacob, Moses, and Samuel all respond to God's voice with this word (see Gen. 22:1; 46:2; Exod. 3:4; 1 Sam. 3:4). It is an immediate acknowledgment of a calling from on High and a mobilization of responsibility. Rather than an assertion of one's rights or a statement of individuation, it asks, "What would you have of me?" It is a responsiveness before God, a receptivity. Critchley (2002) writes, "As Levinas puts it...my first word is not Descartes' 'ego cogito' ('I am, I think'), it is rather 'me voici!' ('here I am!' or 'see me here!'), the word with which the prophet testifies to the presence of God" (22).[5] Before God one does not assert one's rights. One does not author God, but rather is authored by God. In relationship to God, one offers oneself, recognizing an inexhaustible responsibility.

Likewise, the other comes to me from such a height (Levinas 1996; see also Cohen 1994). He or she bears a trace of the Divine and in proximity to him or her, I am not a subject (an agent), but rather am *subject to*—I am a response (Levinas 1974/1998c). Instead of possessing myself as a subject, I greet the other with an openness as though it were "towards-God...*à-Dieu*" (Levinas 1989, 7).[6] In a self lived as *hineni*, my identity is not monadic and mine, but rather is an ethical response.[7] I hear my name always in the accusative, an apology required for my existence.

In the following section, the self lived as *hineni* is described through five interrelated qualities. This self is attuned to the immemorial; open and receptive; divested of itself; radically passive, exposed, elected and chosen; and oriented toward the outside.

First, the self lived as *hineni* is attuned to a history more original than its own. In the progression of history, there is a temptation for the ego to find rest in its self-possession. It is a temptation for the ego to calcify a secure means of being in the world, finding safety in predictability, the familiar, and control. Trapped within one's history, the accumulation of one's past becomes the means of maneuvering and negotiating within the world. One identifies primarily with the emergent character of one's amassed experience, which inevitably leads to automatically living out or embodying this accrual. From such a place, "The unknown immediately becomes familiar, the new, habitual. Nothing is new under the sun" (Levinas 1989, 245). One's self becomes equivalent to one's history. The circuit of life is sameness—a déjà vu.

In contrast, the self lived as *hineni* is attuned to an immemorial past where its identity is born from its responsibility to the other. Levinas (1961/1969) argues that the other addresses me from beyond history (23). Behind our consciousness and freedom is a "pre-original, anarchic" identity, "older than every beginning" that comes from "the extreme exposure to the assignation of the other" (Levinas 1974/1998c, 145). Our consciousness is not privy to this past, though it lies behind its very constitution. This attunement is a remembering that is not cognitive or rational; it is an embodied remembering. Levinas (1995/1999) describes it as

> a past irreducible to the present that seems to signify in the ethical anteriority of responsibility-for-the-other, without reference to my identity assured of its right. Here I am, in the responsibility cast back toward something that... *does not come back to me from memory*. Ethical significance of a past that concerns me, that "regards me," that is "my business" *outside all reminiscence, all retention, all representation, all reference to a remembered present*. Significance in the ethics of a pure past, irreducible to my present, and thus, of an *originary past*. Originary significance of an immemorial past, based on responsibility for the other man. (32)

A self lived as *hineni* is a remembering of this "pre-history of the ego" (Levinas 1974/1998c, 117), an immemorial past that perpetually breaks into the present with a calling to responsibility. It is a recognition (not merely cognitive) that "before being dedicated to myself" I was "exposed and dedicated" to the other as a "vow or a votive offering" (1991/1998a, 170). Time, for Levinas (1961/1969), is a curvature where this immemorial past and the present are folded together in sociality, in the intersubjective context of the interhuman. Before consciousness, volition, action, and being—"'before' eternity, before the accomplishment of history"—there is an identity where individuals are called "forth to their full responsibility" (23). And, this immemorial past is a "past that is on the hither side of every present" (Levinas 1974/1998c, 12), a diachronic and anarchic haunting of the present. It never allows the present to become settled.

Instead of consciousness merely coagulating into the "complacency of being," this attunedness to the prehistory of the ego keeps the I from maintaining a placeholder in being. In everyday life, this means that I lose my place as primary and live my life as a gift unto the other (Marion 2003/2006). My "shelter in being" (Levinas 1974/1998c, 185) becomes less true than the needs of the other. Levinas (1968/1994) writes, "Reason, once it comes into being, includes its pre-history" (38). Knowledge, then, is not a means of possession and comprehension, but rather is a tool for the calculation and implementation of justice and a loving response: caress rather than grasp (Faulconer 2005). I realize that freedom is in sacrifice to the other, not self-authorship.

Second, the self lived as *hineni* is open and receptive to that which is not itself, does not fit within its experience, even threatens itself. Levinas's thought was a response to a deeply entrenched trajectory within Western philosophy that esteemed the I as an intending, constituting, detached, and conscious observer. Ultimately, this I cuts its experiences to the size of its cognitive apparatuses and knowledge base, dictating the realities that it experiences, all the while remaining safe within its invisibility. It is a disengaged subject interacting with nondemanding objects, a self-reflexive orientation that rewards the self with the status of "heroic I," the center of its own story. It is a self that remains within the sameness of Being, the constricted circuitry of his or her own history and nature.

The self lived as *hineni* is a self, first and foremost, forever responsive to the other. It is a subjectivity susceptible to the other. It has no immunity, not even in its perception. The self is not primarily identified with its attributes or the perseverance of particular traits over time. It is not an atomic entity, constituting its surroundings. Rather, it is an opening to the other, a vulnerability to what is not itself; something wholly other. It represents an inversion of intentionality, a being *constituted by* (Levinas 1961/1969; see also Malka 2002/2006, 276). The calling of the other, the voice/face/trace, does not first move through the constituting and deciphering apparatus of consciousness.

Rather, the opening of the I to the other means that the I is first accused, guilty, hostage, and obedient to the other and from this place, consciousness is born. I. F. Stone (1998) explains, "Our relationship to the other precedes thought, precedes our thought of ourselves, precedes our very idea of self. In fact, our sense of self arises from our relationship to another.... We are created by another's love and create ourselves by accepting the burden of this love and its obligations.... Before philosophy, there is responsibility" (8).

Egoism often functions out of an accumulation of experience with which one overidentifies. It forms a bastion out of the mortar of one's own history. One's history, a testament to self-consciousness and self-reflexivity, does not accommodate what is completely other than itself. It must be breached to remind me of what is other than my constricted "economy of being," the sameness within which I live. Levinas (1993/2000) writes, "The psyche is that animation and inspiration of the Same by the Other; it is translated into a fission of the core of the subject's interiority by way of its assignation to respond... It is like a *despite myself* that is more me [*moi*] than myself: it is an election" (187). This stance prevents others from merely becoming players in *my* story. I cannot come back to myself to "understand," but rather must be maddened and humbled before what I cannot grasp. Levinas (1989) observes, "Responsibility for the others has not been a return to oneself, but an exasperated contracting, which the limits of identity cannot retain" (104). The other is anarchy to my history.

Furthermore, living in a receptive and responsive "Here I am" "brings me out of invisibility" (Levinas 1974/1998c, 150). I cannot remain immune, but rather live fully before my brother or sister. The widow, orphan, stranger, or alien in my land is my responsibility. I cannot observe without welcoming. From such a place, "The Other is not only known, he is greeted" (Levinas 1976/1990b, 7).

Third, the self lived as *hineni* divests itself of its need to "be" and self-assert. The modern era bred a considerable sociopolitical shift when it located "rights" within the individual person. The self became private property (Taylor 1989) and a right to exist (*conatus essendi*) became commonsensical. This has generated a somnabulatory stance wherein persons live within a drunken rationality, intoxicated by a version of reason that justifies this "sovereign I" (Levinas 1982/1998b, 16).

The self lived as *hineni* recognizes the "surplus of my duties over my rights" (Levinas 1974/1998c, 159). I, as first person singular, am particularly "called" to "exceptional duties" not "exceptional rights" (Levinas 1976/1990b, 176). The self is not a possession—an earned right to itself based on its ontological status. Levinas recognized that the "natural" state of the ego is one of self-preservation and self-extension. However, the "religiosity of the self" (1974/1998c, 117) is a movement beyond this constricted narrative. It links up with a living past more fundamental than the sequence of history or natural processes. This immemorial past invokes a "metaphysical desire" that drives the I beyond its own satisfaction and "place under the sun." In loving the other before the self, the I must kenotically loosen its grip upon itself. This is how Levinas describes the "structure of ethical subjectivity" (Critchley 2002, 20). The self is disequilibrium and a non-identity following denucleation by the other (Levinas 1974/1998c). It is a relinquishing of being.

Levinas (2004) refers to this "psyche" as a "perpetual leave-taking" (74). Responding with "here I am" is a giving up of oneself, a responding beyond the limits of who I currently am. I am not a bearer of attributes or a "node of interactions" (Cohen 2002, 41). Instead, Levinas (1989) states, "Its exceptional uniqueness in the passivity or the passion of the self is the incessant event of subjection to everything, of substitution. It is a being divesting itself, emptying itself of its being, turning itself inside out, and if it can be put thus, the fact of 'otherwise than being'" (106). The game of being is rendered obsolete in this relation. It is a place where the face of the other "suspends the efficacy of all my horizons" (Westphal 2004, 194).

Fourth, the self lived as *hineni* is radically passive, exposed, elected, and chosen. In modern psychology, the self is loaded with active drives and constituting faculties. The self is agentic, powerful, and self-creating. The self is responsible for its own representational capacities and self-actualizing processes. As "masterfully-bounded" beings, nothing outside of the Euro-American subject is its responsibility. It might be expected that close kin will fall under the purview of the self's responsibility, but even that is decreasingly emphasized in contemporary society (Bloom 1987; Clapp 1993). The self is responsible only to itself except for on the occasions where being responsible for others conveniently parallels the more primary responsibility to oneself.

The self lived as *hineni* does not conflate his or her drives and nature with identity and goodness. The passivity of this self leaves it always exposed to the needs of its neighbor;[8] responding with "here I am" means being open to what one is being called to. One is "exposed to the other's needs as if they were one's own" (Cohen 2002, 57).

Levinas repeatedly refers to the self as radically passive. Levinas (1993/2000) states this "passivity prior to all receptivity... transcends the limits of my time" (177) and is an "exposure to that obligation for which no one else can replace me, and which strips the subject right down to his passivity as hostage" (161). This self is guilty before the other. And, it is elected by the other in its calling to responsibility.

The self is a sentient vulnerability (Critchley 2002, 21). Our very skin makes us vulnerable and affected. Levinas (1993/2000) writes, "It is as if, declined prior to any declension, prior to any position within a nominative, the 'me' were awakened as one possessed by the other" (188). Levinas's ideas of substitution and expiation for the other require a decentering, dethroning, deposing, and divesting the self of its "enchainment to itself where the ego suffocates" (1974/1998c, 124) and also a taking of the food from my own mouth and giving it to the hungry other. It is both hearing "thou shalt not kill" and also giving shelter to those at risk. Levinas (1993/2000) referred to this as "giving with hands full, a being bound to corporeity; the body is the very condition of giving, with all that giving costs" (188).

Fifth, the self lived as *hineni* is oriented "toward the outside," recognizing the other as "first come" (Levinas 1968/1994, 35). Western thought, on the other hand, has a "great tradition of interiority" (Robbins 1991, 71). For Levinas, the enjoyment of sensation and its interiority are but the beginning of human experience, a state that is dephased in sociality. Hence, the reification of interiority and the naturalistic justifications that codify it as an exhaustive system of explanation were the main aims of Levinas's critique. The inevitable egoism that derives from this overextended interiority keeps the windows closed and the doors shut (Levinas 1961/1969).Exteriority, most poignantly known in the command issued at the face of the other, comes from a height—it is a revelation—from which an ethically constituted consciousness is issued. The immanence of "consciousness of" does not allow for the appointment that comes from above and conditions the totality of being.

The self lived as *hineni* functions within an exteriority that constantly calls the self beyond itself, outside of itself, and toward the other. Even in one's own voice the other speaks; the self's "soul is the other in me" (Levinas 1974/1998c, 191). Critchley (2007) describes this "ethical subject" in the following way: "the inside of my inside is somehow outside, the core of my subjectivity is exposed to otherness" (61). Levinas (1985) writes,

> Interiority is consequently not a secret place somewhere in me. It is that reverting in which the eminently exterior, precisely in virtue of this eminent exteriority, this impossibility of being contained and consequently entering into a theme, infinite exception to essence, concerns me and circumscribes me and orders me by my own voice. The commandment is stated through the mouth of him it commands, the infinitely exterior becomes an interior voice, but a voice testifying to the fission of the interior secrecy, signaling to the Other. (110; see also 1974/1998c, 147)

This self oriented toward the outside, recognizing both the height and the destitution from which the other speaks, does not seek symmetry, mutuality, and reciprocity: "If you recognize my worth then I will recognize yours." Rather, it experiences the command of the other as a demand made upon the self as if from God. And, God, in Levinas's thought is wholly and completely outside of and other than the self (radical separateness). He went to the extreme of referring to the self as being atheistic to establish this point (Levinas 1961/1969). To be oriented toward God and the other is to be oriented toward a "point of exteriority," outside of oneself (Critchley 2002, 17). This is less about increased openness to relationship—an intersubjective field and matrix—and more a recognition of and exposure to the height from which the other calls me. It is a hearing of the command for love, sacrifice, and generosity in this relation.

FORGETTING *HINENI*

> *This is the obligation to compare unique and incomparable others; this is the moment of knowledge and, henceforth, of an objectivity beyond or on the hither side of the nakedness of the face; this is the moment of consciousness and intentionality. An objectivity born of justice and founded on justice, and thus required by the for-the-other, which, in the alterity of the face, commands the I.* (Levinas 1991/1998a, 166–67)

If we are unlimited in our responsibility for the other and are hostage to his or her ethical injunctions, then why does egoism reign supreme in how we relate? If we are utterly responsible to the other, then why *do* we *still* ask, "Am I my brother's keeper?" If the fundamental quality of subjectivity is its stance in the accusative and "initial passivity" (Levinas 1993/2000, 183) where we respond with "here I am," offering ourselves, then where and how is this lost? How did the Shoah take place? How can multinational corporations build their capital on the backs of sweat shop workers? How can one spouse beat another?

Levinas (1968/1994) gives clues to the answers in his descriptions of how consciousness and knowledge are formed.[9] In the primordial dyad (myself and the other), the question of my own being has no bearing. The other's call forges my subjectivity. However, it is inevitable that this shifts in the presence of a third person—"another neighbor" (50). Levinas describes how the "third party," that is, the presence of the other's other, requires a "weighing of matters" (50), calculation, and thought. Consciousness and knowledge are born in this process. Their purpose is to convert the ethical injunctions of the dyad into justice in relationship to a third party. Institutions, politics, and economics are put in place to attend justly to a populace of neighbors, strangers, widows, and orphans.[10]

For Levinas, consciousness and subjectivity are secondary steps following the prior, primordial encounter. However, one cannot remain in full proximity to the other in a world where there are many others. In the presence of the "third party," the ethical basis of relationship to the other must transform into a system of justice wherein the third is also accounted for. This is where community takes form. This is where I become an other to others (Levinas 1974/1998c). Consciousness is the formation of a systematized ethics or justice wherein the primordial ethical responsibility is transmitted into a lived world of language, economics, and constructs.

However, according to Levinas, we risk forgetting the primordial in the process of transmission, and, "In this forgetfulness egoism is born" (1968/1994, 50). The constituting (intentional) ego forgets its nonoriginal and nonultimate place and is tempted by a Gygean self-interest and distance. In the process of moving from the ethical into the relationship to the third, which is that of society beyond the dyad, the ethical is forgotten. The primacy of reason and knowledge becomes unhinged from the memory of the primordial dyad, and results in the temptation of temptation. It is a shift in constitution and lived experience. The self becomes conflated with detached reason and disinterestedly relates by knowing. The calling and demand that was prior to knowing are now lost in the centralizing and seductive power of knowledge, thought, and rationality. We become our own gods when our autonomous and rational identities become the idols through which we live. When we forget the ethical relation, we create meaning through our individual cognitive apparatuses, personal histories, and preferences. The pursuit of justice can be forgotten in the formation of consciousness. The ego becomes enamored with "a pure possession of self by self" (Levinas 1993/2000, 183). Levinas (1982/1998b) writes, "The prereflective I, the I without a concept, the I anxious about its right to be before the face of the other...has shielded itself, but has also forgotten, under the generality of the concept, the first person who is subject to others and incomparable to others, and who is precisely not an individual of a genus. In the first person it is an Ego [*un Moi*] and, in the equity of the concept, it is a pure individual of the genus in perfect symmetry and reciprocity with the other Egos. It is the equal, but it is no longer the brother of all the others" (169).

In the accumulation of experience and the forward movement of history, there piles up a sedimentary version of the self, a self whose memories coalesce into attributes and whose history becomes the greatest determinant of experience in the present. The optics of this self have the cataracts of Being and presence, and the other cannot be seen through the opaqueness of one's history. One is blind to the excess found in the newness of the other.

Conceptual Case Study: Transference

> *You claim you love me but you keep suffering. You say you love me in the present but you're still living in the past. You tell me you love me but you refuse to forget....The truth is that I am nothing to you. I don't count. What counts is the past. Not ours: yours. I try to make you happy: an image strikes your memory and it is all over. You are no longer there. The image is stronger than I. You think I don't know? You think your silence is capable of hiding the hell you carry within you?* (Wiesel 1960/1990, 302)

A self lived as *hineni* is attuned to a history more fundamental than accumulated experience. This history is precognitive and is "remembered" not through cognitive apparatuses, but rather through a lived responsibility and embodied exposure to the other. *Hineni* is embodied remembrance. Transference, on the other hand, is an example of a precognitive forgetting of the other, a learned and lived defense. Instead of "remembering" the primordial dyad, it is an unconscious[11] forgetting of anything beyond the calcification of one's own history.

For Levinas (1995/1999), ethical relation is "a past irreducible to the present" (32); transference, on the other hand, is a present reducible to the past. My past folds on the present as my historical particularities are imposed and concretized upon the present other, reducing and totalizing the other into the accumulation of my lived experience. This puts the other in my mold, robbing them of their otherness and of an authentic encounter. Transference is thus an embodied forgetting of that which is before and other than one's self.

Within the psychoanalytic tradition, transference is a central therapeutic concept and has a substantial history of research and literature. The term attempts to capture a phenomenon that frequently takes place within the relationship between the patient and therapist. Freud, its innovator, refers to transference as a "reviving" of the past and its application to the person with whom one is relating in the present moment (Caper 2000, 35). Joseph (2001) described transference as when "our patients bring into the relationship with the analyst their internal world, their archaic ways of relating" (186). Typically, these unconscious organizing principles from the past guide present interactions: "Patient's experiences of the analyst and his or her activities is unconsciously and recurrently patterned by the patient according to developmentally preformed meanings and invariant themes" (Stolorow, Atwood, and Brandchaft 1994, 81). This "preformed meaning" and these "invariant themes" are carried into present relationships and experience is then organized around these thematized categories. These definitions, in no way comprehensive, should be sufficient for our purposes here.

Though my intent is to stay true to much of the psychoanalytic literature regarding the meaning of transference, it is necessary to broaden its parameters in order to apply it within the confines of this work. Transferential consciousness is a vibrant illustration of what Levinas describes more generally to be the Western ego and consciousness. As such, some of the usual frame, which locates transference only within the therapeutic relationship will be violated in order to draw on the richness of this analogy to further illuminate the contrast between a self lived as *hineni* and a self lived transferentially.

First, the self lived transferentially is blockaded in its own history, unattuned to a history more original than its own. Freud understood the origins of transference as having to do with living out characteristic ways of being loved—learned repeatedly in life—and then reapplying them to the person at hand. As such, when a patient encounters the therapist, he or she is encountering the repeated patterns of a forgotten history.[12] From a psychoanalytic perspective, discarded and unattended to facets of a person's psyche and history end up recycling and repeating within one's present. Freud (1914/1958b) considered how repetition is a form of lived remembering when conscious remembering is disallowed. In this way, history is perpetually oppressing the present. It is an unconscious and noncognitive reliving, reexperiencing, and redoing of an event or relationship in one's past. It is an entrapment and entanglement in history. Mitchell (1988) referred to this as "living subjectively in the past" (297).

From a Levinasian perspective, this historical oppression and subsequent repeating is party to the forgetting of a history more original and fundamental than one's own. Gibbs (2000) described how Levinas represents the past and present as relating in a "rhythm" "without becoming identified." Transference is an overidentification of the present with the past. Gibbs further emphasized the importance that this bears for Levinas's thought by stating that if the "past throws its light on what is present," it "would only show in the present what the past had already contained, and so the present moment would be subsumed" (364). The present has no chance of being haunted by a more "originary susceptibility" because it is oppressed, prepackaged, and wired to a compulsory and binding past.

Paradoxically, then, forgetting one's history leads to forgetting that one's history is not the totality in the present. Remaining unconnected to one's own history can lead to an imprisonment in one's history. The past is destined to repeat and the present can never reach beyond or behind itself.

Second, the self lived transferentially is closed off to what is not itself, closed off to what cannot be assimilated into its experience, and defended against the threat of mystery. Transference reduces the present into the known. It takes experience of the other and converts it into experience of the Same. Levinas (1974/1998c) beautifully expresses this point: "Without the proximity of the other in his face everything is absorbed, sunken into, walled in being, goes to the same side, forms a whole, absorbing the very subject to which it is disclosed. Essence, the beings of entities, weaves between the incomparables, between me and the others, a unity, a community (if only the unity of analogy), and drags us off and assembles us on the same side, chaining us to one another like galley slaves, emptying proximity of its meaning" (182). Experience remains a possession, a form of control and safety. When what is known is used to translate what is transpiring, experience homogenizes into my categories of being. It is a form of slavery. Present relationship, then, is experienced as an extension of one's internal world and relational repertoire and not as a proximity to what is other than oneself. In speaking about certain types of consciousness, Levinas (1989) refers to them as reducing "every experience to an element of reminiscence. Reason is alone. And in this sense knowledge never encounters anything truly other in the world" (39).

Transference is a deafening and muting of otherness. Instead of seeing the face of the other before him or her, historical voices, images, and representations mediate and subsume the experience. Parental voices in the past thicken and block the experience of the other's voice that is different than my own. Instead of "Thou shalt not kill" spoken through the other's face, I hear him or her say, "You are worthless" as historical voices impede the primordial.

Levinas (1989) refers to the relationship with the other as "a relationship with a Mystery" (43), and this is precisely what transferential consciousness eschews. Mystery is to be defended against; it is intolerable. It is experienced as a rupturing of the known and a dangling over the chasm of oblivion. No surprises are permitted (Levinas 1974/1998c, 99). Proximity, then, is impossible and only an impoverished relation is allowed.

Third, the self lived transferentially is a perpetual self-assertion. If no space is allowed for what is other than me and my history, then life remains a constant autobiographical reminder. In this transferential consciousness, every interaction remains about me. We hear our own history about ourselves. There is a "mineness" by which life is experienced.

Separation is an essential facet of Levinas's thought, because it ultimately allows for proximity and caress, instead of fusion or generalization. *Hineni* is a remembering of what is other than myself; that I am separate and the other is not my alter ego. Instead of the self being divested, transference involves the constant investing of the ego, the entanglement of the other in the morass of my lived autobiography. Instead of being "denucleated," transference draws one invariably into the nucleus of every experience and relationship. With nothing outside of myself to remind me that I am not sovereign, I remain within the "concreteness of egoism" (Levinas 1961/1969, 38) and its myths of self-importance and self-exaltation.

Fourth, the self lived transferentially is actively constituting and unexposed. The transferring of one's past onto the present is a habitual activity. Transference is a perpetual "consciousness of," with one's range of vision formed by the habitual horizons or history of the observing subject: the "light" of one's consciousness illuminates the meaning of experience.[13] Levinas (1961/1969; 1989) was highly critical of Husserl's "consciousness of" as being definitive for all experience (see also Husserl 1901/2001), viewing it as another manifestation of the active and sovereign ego (cogito) to which all experience bends.

Transference is not a passive receptiveness to newness or otherness, but rather an active coopting of experience. Instead of being infused by the demand of the other, this self infuses the encounter with meaning that robs the encounter of its authenticity and the other of his or her alterity. The question that the other poses upon the self cannot be heard. My own questions hijack the relationship. The other whispers, "I am hungry. Will you feed me?" My transferential response is, "Is she mad at me for not feeding her? Does she blame me for her hunger?" *or* "What if I am not adequate to the task of feeding her? Will I still be worth anything?" *or* "Why am I always having to feed everyone? Doesn't anyone think enough of me to feed me for once?!" The other's voice cannot be heard because I am already speaking. My activity prevents my exposure. I hear my own voices and questions without true exposure to the questions of the other; it is a preoccupation within myself.

Relationship, within transference, takes on a Gygean, detached form that places upon the present the activity of its constantly effervescing past. It imbues every present with the colors of its own perception. It elects and chooses experiences, protecting itself from the demands made upon it. The passivity of the ethical encounter is lost, and intimacy is made impossible (Williams and Gantt 1998). The gift of identity, given by the other, is rejected in this counterfeit consciousness that falsely promises safety and the possibility of resolution.

Fifth, the self lived transferentially is oriented self-reflexively, as a prodigal returned to itself. The transferential orientation is an arrangement that forever curbs the subject from exiting the confines of his or her own consciousness. The subject remains undisturbed by what is outside of itself because the outside merely remains a reminder of what is inside. Triggers come from the outside, but they are experienced through the confines of the interior.

Transference is a defensive posture born out of fear and learned in the pain of trauma, sadness, or neglect (Stone 1984). It guards against further encroachment and trauma by constricting one's posture, hunkering down, or closing up (see chapter 8). The outside is an unknown and symbolizes terror, oblivion, and annihilation. The inside, though steeped in pain, remains familiar and manipulable. The inside is preferred. A world of binaries, blacks and whites, and knowable truths remains far more tolerable than the blurring lines and paradoxical tensions of what lies outside of one's experience. Klein's concept of the "paranoid-schizoid position" is a helpful illustration of this tendency. The other and his or her otherness signifies the terrors of the cosmos. If love, as Levinas (1976/1990b) suggests, is a "perfidious arrow" (7), then transference is the fortified breastplate that prevents its penetration.

A self lived as *hineni,* as suggested earlier, hears the other's voice in one's own. Subjectivity is oriented toward the outside, bringing that which is outside and other into the same. In a transferential consciousness, one is only able to hear one's own voice. Though this voice is likely the emergent conglomeration of introjects and the accumulated voices of significant others, these voices can stagnate into a repetitious cycle of sameness, keeping us from responsiveness to the present other. Such a consciousness lives the present out of coagulated voices from the past. The other's voice is not heard in my own voice. The psyche is a return to its own past, with no access to the outside or the present. This is a prime example of what Levinas refers to "in-itself," a closed egoism that takes an unsurprised stance and an identity that is merely in coincidence with itself. It ventures only within the constricted playpen of its own history, a horizon that attenuates out what is in excess of its own self-sameness. It is living within the circuitousness of interiority without the dynamic interplay of an exteriority that sends one into exile from the patterned history of being. Levinas (1976/1990b) writes, "The violent man does not move out of himself. He takes, he possesses. Possession denies independent existence. To have is to refuse to be. Violence is a sovereignty, but also a solitude.... To know is to perceive, to seize an object—be it a man or a group of men—to seize a thing. Every experience of the world is at the same time an experience of self, possession and enjoyment of self [*jouissance de soi*]: it forms and nourishes me" (9). Further, he (1961/1969) reminds us, "The essence of reason consists not in securing for man a foundation and powers, but in calling him in question and in inviting him to justice" (88). Psychotherapy should provide such a questioning and invitation.

Psychotherapy as Remembering

Remembrance is not about recalling the past or about preserving it, but is needed to disrupt the present. (Gibbs 2000, 354)

Freud (1905/1958a) refers to transference as an "inevitable necessity" that is analysis's "most powerful ally" (116) and "greatest obstacle" (117). Transference can be the forgetting and totalizing of the original dyadic relation, but it can also be helpful in recovering that relation.[14] For Freud, mining transferential meaning provides the most significant material for therapeutic progress. In language more congruent with recent *relational psychoanalytic* thought, working within transference can allow something new to emerge for the patient as he or she moves from a more obstructing transference to a remembering of the other.

More recent relational psychoanalytic and intersubjectivity literature speaks of the "third" that is created in the psychotherapeutic context (Aron 1996; Benjamin 1998; Ogden 1994). A unique constellation emerges in the context of relationship, as though the interhuman forms something other than both sets of subjectivities.[15] And, in relating to this "third," a space is opened up wherein the efficacy of our patient's horizons (and our own) might be suspended (Westphal 2004, 194), and the "closed circle of totality" might be broken into by the infinite (Levinas 1961/1969, 171). During this process,

> The analyst discovers himself a coactor in a passionate drama involving love and hate, sexuality and murder, intrusion and abandonment, victims and executioners. Whichever path he chooses, he falls into one of the patient's predesigned categories and is experienced by the patient in that way. The struggle is toward a new way of experiencing both himself and the patient, a different way of being with the analysand, in which one is neither fused nor detached, seductive nor rejecting, victim nor executioner. The struggle is to find an authentic voice in which to speak to the analysand, a voice more fully one's own, less shaped by the configurations and limited options of the analysand's relational matrix, and, in so doing, offering the analysand a chance to broaden and expand that matrix. (Mitchell 1988, 295)

Levinas (1974/1998c) suggests that "newness comes from the other" and with it, a transcendence and signification that is "otherwise than being" (182). Psychotherapy provides a context wherein the history of two persons can, in the moments of meeting, create a fissure in history. It is the formation of something new in the present relationship with the other (the therapist). History is typically an individual experience, but when the interhuman takes place, history is arrested, and something anarchic occurs. Psychotherapy can be a place where the power of one's history is slowly disarmed and a memory of what is beyond and more fundamental than history is given space. The freedom to live and love—found in an embodied remembering where the currents of the past are given caring attention and contained—allows the present to run its unhindered course. Therapy is a journey into this embodied remembering, session after session, day after day, week after week.

Conversation, as simple as that might seem, can loosen the hold that history has upon the patient's being. Levinas (1976/1990b) writes, "The banal fact of conversation, in one sense, quits the order of violence. This banal fact is the marvel of marvels" (7). In the therapeutic relationship, this conversation allows something more original and distant than history to call the patient's history and his or her accumulated identity into question. The face-to-face allows for the conditioning of time (Levinas 1989). The intersubjective relationship stalls history's perfunctory movement. The patient's story and its layers of identification in the world are no longer the dominant means of being in the world. The arrow of intentionality is inverted, removing from the patient a perpetual self-authorship. Instead, the therapeutic dyad, a relation with the other (the therapist), begins to author the patient's psyche. The author is outside, calling, writing and rewriting.

Remembering involves an inbreaking of the original dyad,[16] and psychotherapy provides a place for this relational rewiring and reexperiencing, a freeing from the shackles of historical oppression. By attending to the transference, inviting openness, and exposing the violence handed down and relived in the present (Butler 2005), the therapeutic relationship becomes a place of love and caress where grasping and defense become increasingly less necessary, where one has the possibility of orienting anew, hearing a past more distant than one's own. It is a place where the therapist is allowed growing intimacy, becoming increasingly other. In this process, in this unshackling of ubiquitous reduction, the patient becomes free to experience that other.

In relationship to the therapist (an other), history has the possibility of ceasing to be merely synchronous and linear. We are, as Gadamer suggests, historically situated beings, but, for Levinas, it is a history that is curved and inclusive of the more originary memory of the ethical dyad.[17] The ethical relationship to the therapist is anarchic and diachronic. Anarchically, it is a disruption of the lineage of time in history, something new. Diachronically, it is something more present than any present, more ancient than any past, and more promising than any future hope (messianic eschatology). In the present, there is experience that is not experience within its usual strictures (Levinas 1976/1990b). Gibbs (2000) writes, "For Levinas there must be a moment that is not available to me in memory, a moment I cannot knit up in a narrative, and in that moment, to which I have no access in consciousness, I am chosen, elected, obliged. My narration is broken into by something that I cannot make part of the story.... Levinas calls this a past more distant than any past, and eventually a past that was never present" (30). The intersubjective in the therapeutic relationship is a conversation that wounds the banality of historical progression, a new history in the making (Levinas 1976/1990).

Therapy is a process of opening to something other than being within history, of forming a self whose shape points to what transcends the restrictions of synchronous time, accumulated experience, and natural instincts. Animals are defined by stimulus-response histories. Humans are defined by a "religious shape"—an ethical responsiveness in sociality—that is called through "illuminated living faces" (Levinas 1976/1990b, 25) that bear the trace of the Divine. The other is a promise from beyond history, though it is a promise known in the lived responsibility of concrete history and life. Transferring our past upon the present is suspended and a new history, an intersubjective creation within the dyad, gives a new definition to the situation, and to myself.

Exploring what facets of the self prevent exposure to and maintain structures of perceptual and emotional sameness are essential facets of a "Levinasian animated psychoanalysis" (Marcus 2008, 13) and/or therapy. Instead of merely hearing one's voice and those internalized voices that lay the landscape to which one's horizon points, therapy might begin the process of hearing the other's voice in my own (not the other way around). The compulsive drive for possessive interpretation must be slowly and gently dismantled throughout the therapeutic journey. Therapy holds out the promise of a more lively and dynamic relation where the present lives within itself, disrupting itself, without the crushing sameness of a transferred and malignant past. It is a movement toward exteriority, a passivity where experience shapes and calls instead of being constituted and ego-determined. It is where "identity is inverted" (Levinas 1974/1998c, 115).

Ultimately, then, one of the goals of a Levinasian psychotherapist is assisting a patient to a lived remembrance, so that a patient begins seeing in the other's face a command that exceeds him or her rather than a reminder of an experiential category. Mitchell (1988) asserts, "The aim is to broaden the analytic relationship, and by extension the analysand's other relationships as well, into richer, more dialectical exchanges" (300). It is an expansion out of the smallness of interiority, a dispossessing of an active and protective consciousness, and an exposing of the patient to the other's needs, calling, election, and welcome. In Levinas's (1976/1990b) words, "the moral relation... reunites both self-consciousness and consciousness of God" (17). Remembering means one's consciousness is conditioned by and oriented toward the other and, more radically, to God (*à Dieu*), toward a love that draws him or her beyond the constricting, historical ego. Levinas (1989) opines, "The human is the return to the interiority of non-intentional consciousness, to mauvaise conscience, to its capacity to fear injustice more than death, to prefer to suffer than to commit injustice, and to prefer that which justifies being over that which assures it" (86).

Systematizing Levinas? The Clinical Conundrum and "Idea of Possibility"

There is an important tension in this work. Levinas did not want his thought to be used to form ontological or totalizing principles, even a depiction of the self as "ethically constituted." As Williams (2007) writes, "Were Levinas himself to comment on the application of his work to psychology, he might well resist such a project and warn us against any system of constructs, principles, or pronouncements that could constitute a psychology" (683). To even begin speaking about forming a configuration of the self that is constitutionally ethical or oriented toward the ethical risks losing sight of Levinas's project. As such, throughout this work, it is unclear to me whether these pages have creatively applied Levinas's work to constructs of the self within modern psychologies or whether it has fallen prey to systematizing Levinas's thought in such a way as to remain untrue to it. Levinas, however, left little in the way of application, implementation, and operationalization of his thought. In short, the dilemma is that Levinas's thought cannot maintain its integrity while being systematically applied. This leaves two options: First, Levinas can remain an inspirational coach on the fringes, who forever whispers into our ears the necessity of humility and the limitations of our perspectives (something done by many others as well). He will have merely spoken of a distant idealism, a utopian primordial state that informs our attitude, but does little to assault our constructs. Or, second, we can enter dangerously into the world of totality, funded by Levinas's ethical injunction. We can, in applying Levinas to a science of which he was unfamiliar, struggle to reconstitute our theories, reshaping an enterprise that is a blind derivative of the modern philosophical enterprise toward which Levinas levied his strongest critiques. As Levinas (1995/1999) states, "I do not know how to draw the solution to insoluble problems. It is still sleeping in the bottom of a box; but a box over which persons who have drawn close to each other keep watch. I have no idea other than the idea of the idea one should have. The abstract drawing of a parallelogram—cradle of our hopes. I have the idea of a possibility in which the impossible may be sleeping" (89).

Working from within his "idea of a possibility," this work builds upon Levinas's sensibilities. To justify this move, Levinas's own concept of the "third party" is invoked which allows for the formation of calculation, consciousness, systems, institutions, and justice. In speaking of a "therapist" or a "patient," we have already allowed the "third" to enter the discussion. We are no longer speaking from the dyadic *saying*, but rather have entered into the ontological and the *said*. When addressing the field of psychology, case conceptualization, health, pathology, identity, and treatment, we are inevitably addressing a system. Systems and knowledge are not inherently problematic, but both must be conditioned by the infinite, called into question, held accountable by justice, "subjugate[d]...to the ethical" (Clegg and Slife 2005, 71), and "must always be held in check by the initial interpersonal relation" (Levinas 1985, 90). The formation of a type of self (i.e., the demanded self) is an attempt to apply Levinas's thought to the third party that is psychology. This is a tightrope walk.

An element of the strain in applying Levinas's work to the clinical setting is its inherent resistance to generalization and its contention that ethics comes from a first person singularity. It is how I am to come to you. I am exposed, persecuted, and responsible in proximity to the other, but there is no reciprocity in Levinas's account. The other is not demanded by me. If a code of ethics operates in dyadic relationship, then a rationalistic, naturalistic, ontological, and/or disengaged quotient mediates the relationship between myself and the other. This is intolerable to Levinas and sits at the core of much of his contention with Western philosophical systems.

As such, instead of orienting the clinical illustration in the following chapter around how the therapist might assist the patient toward becoming more of a demanded self, it is more conducive to Levinas's project to consider first how the therapist might live out of a self oriented in the fashion described thus far in this work. As such, chapter 7 provides a clinical example of a demanded subjectivity from the place of the therapist and explores its importance in my work with Samuel. The last chapter will then move into the riskier territory of pushing back on some of Levinas's thought by considering its shape and meaning in reference to my work with Jill, a trauma survivor.

Conclusion

Only a free person knows that the true meaning of existence is experienced in giving, in endowing, in meeting a person face to face, in fulfilling higher needs. (Heschel 1963, 61)

The modern self defends from being infringed upon. Individuation, differentiation, and ownership are its mottos. Freedom comes from being unencumbered. This chapter has argued for a self that is radically different, a self lived as *hineni*, whose freedom is borne from its responsibilities to the other. Freedom is *being encumbered* by goodness. Freedom is found in love, and love can be nothing less than responsibility and holiness.

For the Jew, the Torah is not merely a set of commandments. It is an obligation and duty, but, ultimately, it is a delight and a freedom, a gift from God that promises a fullness of life. Justice is full of life. Responsibility is freeing and allows for love. Brueggemann (1999) captures this Jewish sentiment well: "In the end, the obedience of Torah piety is not 'must' or 'ought' or 'should.' It is rather the kind of delight whereby friendship ripens into love, and obligation is the chance to please and delight the other, the Thou who hopes and delights in us, as well as commands us. It is this strange process, whereby duty becomes delight without ceasing to be duty, that is expressed in Simhat Torah, the festival of the 'joy of the Torah'" (31).

Levinas (1988/2007b) states, "To shelter the other in one's own land or home, to tolerate the presence of the landless and homeless on the 'ancestral soil,' so jealously, so meanly loved—is that the criterion of humanness? Unquestionably so" (86). The citizens of Le Chambon lived out of the joy of the Torah. May the psychological profession and the patients we serve be called to a self lived as *hineni*.

7

Hearing "Thou Shalt Not Kill"

Psychoanalysis, Enactment, and Levinasian Ethics

> *Psychotherapy is a religious event. Levinas says, "We propose to call 'religion' the bond between the same (self) and the Other."... The primitive meaning of the word religion is to bind oneself in obligation, to transcend the self to serve others. Psychotherapy is "attending to another to heal." The therapeutic relationship is religious. The goal of therapy is to seek this primitive religion, commitment to others.* (Kunz 2006, 10)

Looking over my patient's chart, I read the same disturbing comments found in many of the files: "Sexually molested by grandfather." "Ritually beaten by his alcoholic father before the abandonment." "Mother in and out of jail—can't keep the needle out of her arm." "Major behavioral and emotional disturbance and difficult to manage." "Several psychotropic medications already administered by the age of seven, with minimal benefit."

After 14 foster home placements, Samuel (not his real name) had finally been plopped into a residential treatment facility (at the age of seven). It was here that I met him in the special education classroom. He was bright, creative, moody, and energetic. About three months into his time in my classroom, we had several consecutive weeks of exciting progress. His math lessons were coming along with lightning speed. Also, his warmth and ability to connect were becoming more evident—after a very rough start, he was starting to attach. He was beginning to tell the residential staff that I was his favorite.

One afternoon, I was kneeling next to Samuel's desk working on a complicated math problem with him. As usual, elated at his ability to master the equation, he grinned wildly at my encouragement. The moment came quickly with no premeditation, no preparation, and no warning. As I looked down at his page to scribble a note, I felt a fist come across my face and heard the loud crack of his knuckle bones against my cheek bone. I felt a sharp pain, my eyes teared up immediately, and my self-protective systems came fully online. Shock and anger exploded into my consciousness, and my body flooded with powerful instinctual reactions. Protect self. Fight back.

What took place next remains seared into my mind. I looked up at Samuel, his face a foot and a half away from mine. His chest was heaving; his eyes were filled with tears. But besides this, there was a look of desperate expectation. His eyes exclaimed, "Hit me! Push me! Shove me away! Hate me! I am truly intolerable, unlovable, and disgusting.... I just proved it!"

This story is emblematic of particular types of encounters with patients in psychotherapy. Unlike young children, adults often cloak their fear, angst, and brokenness in more hidden and "sophisticated" forms. Years of socialization give adults less obvious ways to express their fears, repeat their pain, and relive their pasts. However, in these moments, the message to the therapist is the same: "Thou *shalt* kill."

Levinas argues that the face of the other exclaims the opposite command, "Thou shalt *not* kill." But what if this command is so contrary to one's lived experience that it is no longer recognizable? What if, instead, the face of the other pulls, tugs, and screams to be murdered, strangled, debased, and reduced? What if one's "way of being" in the world has been nothing but the renunciation of life, worth, and love?

From the frame of Levinasian ethics, the psychological violence by which a patient is victimized becomes the responsibility of the therapist. Levinas clearly articulates this ethical framework but is less clear about the developmental and psychological processes involved in enactment—the psychoanalytic notion that past and present violence endured by the patient can become calcified into current relational patterns that lure others (including the therapist) into participating in this reductive violence. On the other hand, psychoanalysts delineate the processes involved in enactment and merely assume an ethical response by the therapist. Conversation between the two might be fruitful. Building on the concept of *transference* and *psychotherapy as remembering* put forth in the previous chapter, this chapter provides an example of the translation project inherent in Levinas's work through a conversation between Levinas's Jewish ethical phenomenology and one of psychoanalysis's current conceptual/clinical emphases.

ENACTMENT IN PSYCHOLOGICAL PERSPECTIVE: RELATIONSHIP AND REPETITION

Ultimately, Freud and Levinas agree that within the interhuman and intersubjective space—in the presence of an-other—time is curved upon itself. The present moment is not merely *now* nor the accumulation of the past, but the past alive in the present, the ancient in the new. While the effect of the intersubjective upon time and what is meant by the "past" mean very different things for Freud and Levinas, a conversation between Levinasian thought and the psychoanalytic concept of enactment can enrich the ethics of psychoanalytic language.

For Freud, and the psychoanalytic tradition that followed in his wake, persons relate to others out of reminiscence of their past relationships. Described in greater depth in the previous chapter, transference involves encountering the present other as a repeated experience of a past attachment figure, or an amalgam of figures and experiences. It is not a *memory* based on past experience, but rather a present interrupted and shaped by a *lived remembering without memory*—that is, the process is unconscious (Freud 1914/1958b; Ginot 2007). Freud (1914/1958b) writes that "we may say that the patient does not *remember* anything of what he has forgotten and repressed, but *acts* it out. He reproduces it not as a memory but as an action; he *repeats* it, without, of course, knowing that he is repeating it" (150).

As the patient acts out the past in the present relationship, the therapist finds him or herself activated and unconsciously responds out of his or her own relational past; this is called counter transference. Ultimately, the combined effect of the transference and counter transference is the "interplay" (Maroda 1998, 517) referred to in psychoanalytic literature as *enactment*. Enactment describes the *folding over* of the past upon the present within the intersubjective space between the therapist and patient. It is the unconscious dance of two psyches, a tug and pull of affective histories and unresolved traumas.

Enactment is not a monolithic term with a clear meaning in psychoanalysis. It has evolved and taken many shapes and forms. Furthermore, there have been and are differing opinions in the psychoanalytic literature about the dangers and benefits of enactment (Aron 2003; Chused 1991; Gabbard 1995). For some analysts, enactment is the very grist for the mill wherein transformation takes place. It provides access to lived patterns in a way that bears significant substance and meaning. At worst—when the therapist is not functioning out of intention or volition, but rather is "acting out" of his or her own elicited psychic material—enactment retraumatizes the patient.

Thus described, it is hard to imagine enactments as therapeutic or good. However, without this risk, therapy remains too buoyant and consciousness-oriented. In a recent panel discussion, Nancy McWilliams (2008) explained that contemporary psychoanalysis *assumes* that therapists will wound their patients and that this is integral in the process of healing. Her point is that entering into the mire of lived relationship and the covert patterns repeated there inevitably leads to recreating wounding experiences, to enactments. To encounter the patient—the other before us—requires a level of exposure and proximity that precedes and violates intelligibility, active consciousness, and intentionality. Our controls, in this space, escape us (at least in part). Mitchell (1988) elaborates this point: "Unless the analyst affectively enters the patient's relational matrix or, rather, discovers himself within—unless the analyst is in some sense charmed by the patient's entreaties, shaped by the patient's projections, antagonized and frustrated by the patient's defenses—the treatment is never fully engaged, and a certain depth within the analytic experience is lost" (293). In lived relationship, we engage one another a few steps apart from conscious reflection. Levinas mirrors this assertion when he writes, "Consciousness is always late for its meeting with the close other" (qtd. in Smith 2005, 229).

That both therapist and patient live out of alluring patterns from their pasts is part of the process of therapeutic engagement. Maroda (1998) provides helpful nuance when she reminds about the danger of "counter transference dominance" in enactments (522). She states that for enactments to be therapeutically useful, "In general, one can safely say that the goal should be that more of the patient's past be recreated than the analyst's, and even more important, that the patient have every opportunity to safely work through these events within the boundaries of the analytic relationship" (530). Nonetheless, the therapist *is* a partner in enactment; he or she is an "enactor" (Hirsch 1994). There has been a growing recognition that the analyst cannot remain a "blank screen" or uninvolved member of the dyad. Over the past couple of decades, conversations in relational schools of psychoanalysis have called for a "two person psychology" rather than the "one person psychology" that had preceded it (Aron 1996). The intersubjective space is jointly constructed.

Other than the sheer inevitability of enactment in lived relationship, what are its therapeutic benefits or possibilities? One answer to this question is that enactments provide an opportunity for communication beyond words and outside of signification. Enactments are moments of profound vulnerability for patients. Patients engage in an expression without exact words or clear symbolization, a sacred whisper of need. Without awareness, patients welcome the therapist into a space outside of the safety of the known. In these contexts, the patient has little means of communicating except through "acting out" or eliciting an alteration in the relationship itself. By pulling for some patterned way of being/feeling. Anna Ornstein (in press) describes this as a simultaneous "dread to repeat" and a "need to repeat."

In this way, enactments are a kind of preverbal communication of a patient's wounds (Bromberg 2003). In therapy, the patient "cannot escape from this compulsion to repeat; and in the end we understand that this is his way of remembering" (Freud 1914/1958b, 150). Patients "act out" (in the sense that Freud understood it) to communicate that which has not been formulated, processed, or placed into other modes of expression (Stern 2003). Reductive transferential pulls are communications (Boesky 1982, 46) that may be "impossible to communicate through verbal description" (Chused 1991, 637). However, the unconscious and preverbal quality of an enactment does not minimize its felt reality for either patient or analyst. "During an enactment, the patient has a conviction about the accuracy of his perceptions *and* behaves so as to induce behavior in the analyst which supports his conviction" (Chused 1991, 617). This can be done with words, gestures, a certain form of presence, or an absence (Gabbard 1995; Ginot 2007). It is an embodied expression that attends to both "word and deed" without dichotomizing them (Aron 2003, 624).

Samuel's story illustrates this first point concerning the vulnerability in enactment. Upon being struck, without thinking, I wanted to kill, hurt, and yell. My automatic response was natural, based out of my own physiological reactivity and threat response. Immediately, I no longer wanted to work with Samuel. He had violated the most basic building block in our relationship: respect. My immediate desire was to push away and punish him for this violation. If he could not respect me, then I would abandon him. However, why my emphasis upon "respect"? Was that merely a causal derivative of a natural self-protective process, or was there more behind this than appeared at the surface? In my own history, after my mother passed away from cancer when I was 16, my father abandoned me; the word "respect"—or, more clearly, his need to feel respected—was his confusing rationale for leaving a well-behaved teenage son. My dad's rigid, warped, and self-aggrandizing need for respect from his adolescent son as the basic condition of love remained a wound that I carried into a variety of future relationships. Now, here it was again with Samuel. However, this time I was the perpetrator. Just as I was abandoned for "respect," I was about to do the same to Samuel. Without respect, my love for him was threatened. He had violated the conditions of my love for him, successfully eliciting one of my ongoing unconscious struggles and a complex vein in my convoluted history. Chronology and lived relationship at that present moment were pregnant with both of our pasts.

Complexly and simultaneously, my internal experience mirrored and paralleled Samuel's emotional needs at that moment. He communicated, exposing his wounds, offering me a chance to become his abusive father, his absent mother, his invasive grandfather, and his inconsistent foster home caretakers. In order to remain within a world that was slightly predictable and tolerable, he needed to live out a repetition of what he had known (Boesky 1982). Sameness is safe and works smoothly within the implicit grooves that we all readily live out. It is not that Samuel wanted me to reject him and abuse him. In this case, it was Samuel's unconscious means of protecting himself from the terror of something unknown: trust, connection, and love. We had become close, and this was intolerable. Also, the enactment was his means of bringing me into his experience, his internal conflicts, and his relational history. It was the only way he knew how to share his past. It was, simultaneously, a means of expressing, remembering, and protecting. And, in this instance, his way of bringing me into his experience was by inciting my places of pain and pushing me beyond the functions of my consciousness.

In many ways, the therapist's psyche is borrowed by the patient so that he or she can communicate and express broken processes, unconscious stuck points, and unformulated wounds (Bromberg 1998; 2006; Stern 2003). For wounded patients, suffering is lived in the raw, not subject to conscious or rational engagement alone. Persons play out and repeat painful interactions in current relationships, their enactments arrowing toward a previous place of murder: "Injustice took place, here!" But the "here," is confused, something lived both then and now and many times in between. In this way, enactments also express deep relational pain and locate profound vulnerability.

Levinas and Enactment: Violence and Expiation

> *In order for any good to come from what we do, it is necessary that we try to subordinate the primacy of our own needs, that we never presume to know the ground on which we tread or claim right of access to posted fields.*
> (McLaughlin 1995, 435)

Lewis Aron, a leading psychoanalyst at NYU, recalls, "In his Clinical Diary, Ferenczi (1932) asserted that, as the analysis of a traumatized patient progressed, the analyst would unavoidably 'have to repeat with his own hands the act of murder previously perpetrated against the patient' (2003, 52). Ferenczi claimed that it is the intensity of the interpersonal experience that is transformative and that what differentiates analysts from others is their commitment to face honestly and acknowledge their role and participation in these enactments without hiding their complicity from their patients" (624).

This statement bears a profound Levinasian ethic, recognizing the sacredness of the other's vulnerability and the therapist's responsibility for these wounds.[1] Indeed, in describing the process of enactment, psychoanalysts assume that therapists recognize their role to care for the patient and seek a nonhostile way of being with the patient. However, the grounding for this ethical injunction is less clear in the literature of the field than the articulation of the nuts and bolts of the enactment process. For that reason, I turn to Levinas for his ethical perspective grounded in the face of the other and the injunction of sacred texts.

Understanding how enactments allow something new to develop that interrupts the violence of the patient's lived experience requires a deeper examination of Levinas's ethical concepts of radical responsibility, expiation, substitution, and guilt. Levinas claims that we are responsible for the wrongs done to the other. We are responsible for the murders performed upon him or her. As Alvin Dueck and I pointed out in an earlier work (2007), even if we are not party to the initial moment of terror—even if our hand was not the tool of abuse—this guilt still rests upon the therapist/analyst: "In an encounter with a client, we have before us an individual exposed, nude, vulnerable, and with a history of being psychologically murdered. In seeing the face before us, we lay down our lives before the patient. We expiate for the murders performed.... We now sit with the broken, persecuted state of the other and experience with them in the pangs of exposure. We are responsible for this drama of self-mutilation, and we are not finished with our 'duty' until the other has been emptied of the terror" (612).

Enactment is a specific and concrete illustration of how therapists enter into and are responsible for the continued violence against their patients. Engaged in true relationship with my patients—within the morass of the intersubjective space—my past and the patient's past are folded into an inscrutable "entanglement" (Ginot 2007, 317). Consciousness is eclipsed in the cloud of enactment. Without clear intent, the patient invites me to perpetrate violence, and I find myself enticed toward particular feelings and forms of action. Ultimately, as I live in this allurement and act out of this place, I become complicit in continued violence against my patient. As my psyche carries some of the expression of the other—the other alive in my flesh (Levinas 1974/1998c)—I become identified with the negligent, hateful, lustful, and violent figures who torment my patient. My identity *is*, in part, drawn to reduction, totalization, egoism, defensiveness, protection, complacency, and even murder. In being radically exposed to a patient's needs, desires, and history my psyche is truly persecuted and pulled to its extremes. Rage. Hate. Eros. Love. Affection. Madness. Facing Samuel, for example, I immediately wanted to strike back or yell. At the very least, I wanted to withdraw from the relationship and abandon him without looking back. These thoughts and reactions were my own, but they were also extensions of his past (and perpetually present) psychic trauma. I became responsible for his trauma and guilty of its continuation.

However, this is not the end of the story. The therapist's psyche can be a gift (Marion 2003/2006) if it receives the patient's message and responds, ultimately, without violence. Substitution takes place as the therapist's psychic protection is "denucleated" and he or she becomes hostage to the patient's terror. The therapist's passivity means offering the flesh of one's body and the content of one's psyche to the needs of the other. With Samuel, my instinctual responses to either push away/withdraw (i.e., flight) or strike back/punish (i.e., fight) had to become secondary to my love for him. The "murderousness of my natural will" (Levinas 2004, 75–76) must be called into question by a history more fundamental than the patient's accumulation of violent experiences and my patterned reactions. This requires a passivity and kenotic stance that makes recognizing this claim and responsibility possible. It means that I, as therapist, must hollow out and witness the other *in* my own sameness. I must call into question my tendencies and activities and sacrifice their primacy for the patient. As Levinas (1974/1998c) beautifully writes, it is moving "from the outrage undergone to the responsibility for the persecutor and in this sense from suffering to expiation for the other" (111). This sometimes means uncomfortable self-disclosure (Ginot 2007; Sorenson 2004) and entering into the "cloud of unknowing" where one's footholds are not as clear.

Expiation takes place when, instead of, or in spite of, "acting out" upon this highly affected state, the therapist remains attuned to an immemorial history. When the therapist remains committed to history not remembered through experience, violence is closed down. It is here, in this primordial level of relation, that the therapist can hear the command "thou shall not kill," despite all evidence to the contrary.

Behind the repeated pattern that is comfortable and begged for, we witness the request that this mundane story might have a different ending. Behind Samuel's desire for me to hit him back is the desire for caress (Levinas 1961/1969). His yearning for a dad who did not beat him is resident in his provocation. It is a perverted and distorted means of requesting love—it contraindicates love. But, this is the potential gift of therapy. I must watch for the contraindications that might lead me into harm, hatred, and violence. From these calls to murder I must witness the prior claim that the other has upon me, a claim behind my patient's history and my own proclivities, a sacred claim that is witnessed most poignantly in the patient's vulnerability.

The therapist's psyche is a gift when the therapist takes responsibility for his or her murderousness. The violence resident in the acting and reacting cycle is interrupted and subordinated in this substitution and radical responsibility. The therapist lives out of an alternate ethic, one of nonpossessive and primordial love. Hospitality and welcome replace murder and violation. Gentleness stands in the place of violence. Expiation takes place, a new ending to the narrative formed from a different ethic.

CONCLUSION

> *As we thread our way through the patients' brambles, we trip over the big feet of our self-interest, then stumble to those same feet to resume the quest for the other.* (McLaughlin 1995, 435)

Patients often live out of choreographed histories from which they cannot find escape. Hopefully, the therapist maintains a deeper sensibility, a remembering of the more primordial calling of the face. Despite the *said*, found within the words and behaviors that pull for enactment, the *saying* demands a reversal of history, a reversal of this natural course toward reactive violence (Levinas 1974/1998c). We raise the knife, but, hopefully, recognize this posture before the blade falls. Behind the patient's blatant "Murder me," we hear him or her whisper, "Please do not kill me." We witness in the face a more original calling.

As Samuel's eyes watered and my face reddened, I was stunned by the look of expectation and terror upon his face. My rage went from boil to simmer. My mind raced to understand what had just befallen me *and* us. We had become close, too close, intolerably close. We had passed the thresholds that he had come to know. He needed to push me back, keep me from moving into the tender areas where I could hurt him. He would hurt me first, giving himself some degree of control over and comprehension of how and why I would hurt him back. If he brought it about, then my violence toward him would be predictable and known. Sensing this, I found myself growing in compassion and empathy for this protected place that he had just shown me. It was the most primal of communications. He had expressed what he could find no other way to express. He lived it and forced me to live it with him. We sat, looking one another in the eyes, for about 30 seconds before words came to me.

"Samuel, why did you do that? It really hurt. I don't understand."

His breathing remained shallow and rapid. A droplet rolled down his right cheek.

"I thought we were working well together and enjoying the work. Was I wrong?"

His shoulders shrugged and then returned to their tense posture.

I rubbed my cheek bone. "I don't understand what's going on. Are you as confused as I am?"

He remained quiet but seemed to loosen up a bit as my tone became even softer.

"I'm going to take some space and take some deep breaths so that I can get myself back together a bit. But, I will be back in five minutes so that we can take another pass at the math problem we were working on. If you want to talk with me about this, I am happy to talk about it anytime. I'm here, okay?"

Samuel slowly nodded, looking a bit bewildered. I stood up and worked to center myself at my desk, still within Samuel's eye sight. Five minutes later, I returned to his desk, and we carried on as though nothing had happened. Since he was seven, I respected his inability to really address and consider what happened. Much of it could not be symbolized or verbalized. But our relationship from that point on had a different quality: it somehow felt more real. He had communicated with me, and I had listened. He had asked to be killed, and I had heard his deeper request. I had not struck back or abandoned him. No perfect ending, but we both witnessed something new and good.

This story ends without a true enactment coming to pass. Though Samuel's transference and "acting out" elicited a profound intrapsychic response in myself that linked up to my unconscious processes around abandonment and respect, my impulse to react ended up being short-circuited before it was enacted. Chused (1991) states,

> In the best of all possible worlds, an analyst is sensitive to his patient's transference, as expressed in either words or actions, but does not act. Sympathetic with a patient's pitiful state, he does not nurture; temporarily aroused by a patient's seductive attacks, he does not counterattack. An analyst contains his impulses, examines them, and uses the information gained to enrich his interpretive work. This best of all possible worlds is the ideal, something we strive for, but often fail to achieve. In the second best possible world, where most of us dwell, an analyst reacts to his patient—but catches himself in the act, so to speak, regains his analytic stance, and in observing himself and the patient, increases his understanding of the unconscious fantasies and conflicts in the patient and himself which have prompted him to action. (616)

This story ended "in the best of all possible worlds" because of Samuel's age. The look on his seven-year-old face, the tears in his eyes, the history in his chart, and the linkage between his lost childhood and my own gave me a sensitivity that I otherwise might not have had in other situations and with other patients. Seeing a small child expressing his wounded past through violent action felt far more obvious (and less layered and hidden) than my work with so many adults. The complexity of enactments with adults frequently muffles the "thou shalt not kill" far more effectively. It may not be until one is in the center of an enactment or even fully on the other side of an enactment that it begins to make some sense or emerge as a meaningful expression or relational possibility. Samuel's story is a particularly poignant illustration mainly because of the palpable tension between the commands of "thou shalt kill" and "thou shalt *not* kill" resident in his actions.

Enactments are a reliving of past experience that produce possibilities of deeper entrenchment (eliciting murder yet again) or reparative relation (violence interrupted). In relationally and ethically oriented psychotherapy, what "patient and analyst do to and with each other" (Aron 2003, 625) remains the emphasis. Healing and transformation come from ongoing collaborative witnessing of relational patterns and implicit processes, in the heat of their manifestation. This provides both an "opportunity for meaning and symbolization" (Ginot 2007, 325) and reparative ethical experience. A different ending is forged to an otherwise infinitely repeated narrative of violence. Substitution and expiation allow for these possibilities.

Enactment allows for dialogical and midrashic transformation. It is a lived, breathed, and embodied experience of something new, of something ethical, and of nonpossessive love. From a Levinasian frame, it is the meeting of sacred vulnerability and sacred responsiveness. Into this space, the Divine is invited.

8

The Psyche Awakened
The Other as a "Trauma Which Heals"

C. S. Lewis's (1946) compelling allegory of heaven and hell, *The Great Divorce*, begins with its nameless main character standing in line at a bus stop in the civic center of a "grey town" that is "always in the rain and always in evening twilight" (1). Surrounding the bus stop are residences spread out in concentric circles, littering the dull landscape as far as the eye can see.[1] Without a clear understanding of why he is doing so, the main character boards the bus that takes flight above the seemingly enormous expanses of Hell and takes the passengers on a day trip to the outer recesses of heaven. Upon arriving, the passengers are met by figures who they had known in their earthly lives. In his conversation with his "Teacher," the main character describes where he has just come from. The conversation plays out as follows:

> 'The big gulf, beyond the edge of the cliff. Over there. You can't see it from here, but you must know the place I mean.'
>
> My Teacher gave a curious smile. 'Look,' he said, and with the word he went down on his hands and knees. I did the same...and presently saw that he had plucked a blade of grass. Using its thin end as a pointer, he made me see, after I looked very closely, a crack in the soil so small that I could not have identified it without this aid.
>
> 'I cannot be certain,' he said, 'that this *is* the crack ye came up through. But through a crack no bigger than that ye certainly came.'
>
> 'But—but,' I gasped with a feeling of bewilderment not unlike terror. 'I saw an infinite abyss. And cliffs towering up and up. And then *this* country on top of the cliffs.'

'Aye. But the voyage was not mere locomotion. That bus, and all you inside it, were increasing *in size*.'

'Do you mean then that Hell—all that infinite empty town—is down in some little crack like this?'

'Yes. All Hell is smaller than one pebble of your earthly world: but it is smaller than one atom of this world, the Real World. Look at yon butterfly. If it swallowed all Hell, Hell would not be big enough to do it any harm or to have any taste.'

'It seems big enough when you're in it, Sir.'

'And yet all loneliness, angers, hatreds, envies and itchings that it contains, if rolled into one single experience and put into the scale against the least moment of the joy that is felt by the least in Heaven, would have no weight that could be registered at all' (137–38).

The enormity of Hell is an illusion. Hell fits into a crack in the soil of heaven, so small that a butterfly could swallow it. However, one's state of consciousness when in this Hell does not *feel* constricting. Rather, as the main character states, "It seems big enough when you're in it." Perceptually, it appears to expand for eternity. Experientially, Hell is all consuming.

Oddly enough, many of the passengers on the bus—the visitors to heaven—choose to get back onto the bus and shrink into the prison of a miniscule narrative. For a variety of reasons, they are not able to tolerate, recognize, or desire the transcendence of heaven. The Teacher explains, "Their fists are clenched, their teeth are clenched, their eyes fast shut. First they will not, in the end they cannot, open their hands for gifts, or their mouth for food, or their eyes to see" (139). They prefer the sameness of a somnabultory existence and defend against waking to surprise, variety, and otherness.

Levinas wrote extensively about a consciousness caught up in hellacious clenching, grasping, constricting, and egoist slumber. He recognized a human tendency to remain intoxicated by the security of sleep and the safety of totalizing narratives.[2] For Levinas (1985), the complacency of being is the homeostasis point for the ego. Arrested in a protected state of equilibrium and suspended animation, we prefer our stories to maintain a particular course, a predictable frame of reference. Consumable, bite-sized experience is sought in the place of saturated encounter with otherness. We live out of constricted narratives and remain asleep to alterity, in a state of "tranquilized undisturbance" (Kunz 2006, 7).

Levinas's ethical philosophy calls the self to awaken through an inexhaustible responsibility to the other. Haidt (2003) argues, "Morality dignifies and elevates" (852). Levinas would likely agree, but he would eschew any glorification of morality as utilitarian or even pleasant. Rather, morality, from a Levinasian frame, involves violence and trauma to one's ego. Encountering the other brings about a violent awakening to the self, denucleating and dethroning the self's sovereignty and dismembering its sense of security and comfort. The self is wakened from the slumber of being and becomes awake to the point of insomnia. The clinical implications of this slumber-to-insomnia movement are profound.

THE ASSAULT OF THE OTHER

Mitchell (2003) writes about the dysregulating quality of love and the human preference for contrivances rather than the vulnerability inherent in desire for the other. This orientation toward life ensures that we live out of stories for which we already know the end. We may seek the excitement of new experience or the unfamiliar, but typically we modulate this with defensive fall-backs and "hide outs" (Marcus 2008, 59). Mitchell (2003) describes our willingness to take controlled risks as pornographic in nature. That is, we experience the thrill of desire (pseudo-risk) without compromising our safety. We engage in "risk free desire" (137) and never place ourselves in the "risky business" of love.[3]

Current debates involved in the formation of the DSM5 have revolved around the question of whether there are overarching etiological dynamics taking place in most psychological disorders (Siegel 2009). Among the contenders for such overarching causes is emotion and experience avoidance.

Avoidance of the other or otherness might be another way of understanding this. The inherent trauma present in face-to-face relation to the other is defended against and papered over by alternative perceptual, experiential, and egoistic sources (Fryer 2007). As Fryer suggests, "Everyday life is, from a Levinasian perspective, a constant covering over of our original responsibility for the other person, a continual and deliberate forgetting of our fundamental guilt" (584). Bromberg (2006), in his book *Awakening the Dreamer*, observes, "The need to preserve affective safety organizes the mind's responsiveness to novelty.... When self-continuity seems threatened, the mind adaptationally extends its reach beyond the moment by turning the future into a version of past danger" (4–5). The other is reduced to the sameness of one's past that mutes the terror and trauma of alterity. The Divine is intolerable (Levinas and Robbins 2001, 48). In Hebrew Scripture, the consequences of seeing God were fatal. We find means of hiding behind more palatable idols. We lull ourselves to sleep with counterfeit versions or totalizations until the other wakes us.

This waking process and transformation of the ego from self-protective to ethically responsive is described by Levinas in violent, fierce, and tempestuous terms.[4] Visker (2000) explains that the other "divides me, 'denucleates' and beleaguers me, does not leave me alone but instead obsesses me and persecutes me, takes me hostage and traumatizes me, brings me to hate myself, to abdicate my place at the center of my own concerns, to give everything up, to give nothing more to myself, and thus to hemorrhage ceaselessly; the Other burns him- or herself into my skin, and penetrates me—in short: the Other does virtually everything to me, except 'let me be'" (248). The demand from the other is wounding, disrupting, decentering, and jolts the self from its complacent slumber. It is in encountering the transcendence—the irreducibility and infinity—resident in the *visage* of the other that the ego's primacy is called into question (Levinas 1976/1990b). "Hunted" and called beyond its inherent smallness and overdetermined narratives, the ego's protections are neutralized, and the self awakens to an exposed *otherwise than being* that is less buffered, less defended, and less contained.

Levinas recognized that the ego's current configurations and its corollary definitions of freedom in Western thought lead to a possessiveness of identity and a self-protecting egoism that leaves persons alienated, relationally impoverished, and morally anemic. For Levinas (2004), the violence rendered in proximity to the other is necessary in order that our nature be turned "inside out" and to put "our ontological will-to-be into question" (76). The violence emergent from face-to-face relation allows us to be welcomed outside of ourselves, beyond nature, and into a freedom born from responsibility (Levinas 1968/1994). Critchley (1999) reminds us that, for Levinas, "ethics is a traumatology.... The Levinasian subject is a traumatized self" and, for Levinas, "this is a good thing" (185, 195).

The denucleating violence of the other provides a calling to goodness, an elevation of the person and an exit from the false expanses of a constricting Hell. When describing Levinas's concept of substitution, Alford (2002) states, "The other is my saving grace, an alien presence that allows me to open myself to the world, a foreign body that wedges itself between me and my ego, and so allows me to escape my narcissistic soul by devoting myself to the other in me" (29; see Levinas 1974/1998c). Visker (2000) portrays this lucidly:

> The Other does not enslave but liberates, awakens, disillusions, purifies, and elevates. One cannot but conclude: the Other brings me a trauma which heals. Even if the Other 'paralyzes' me...he or she gives the precise movement that I needed—paralyzing my paralysis and so pulling down the walls which had hindered my movement.... The Other's face taps a source in me henceforth not to be closed; it inflicts a wound in me which purifies with its continual flow of blood: the Other does not permit me to be alone, but leaves me no choice than to come out of my shell (for he or she smokes me out of every hiding place, every *refugium*), to step outside, to bare myself and stand in a nakedness which, as Levinas likes to say, is still more naked than that of my bare skin, for it inverts my skin, turns it inside out, so that I become an outside without an inside (*envers sans endroit*) that no longer has any secrets, no longer any interiority, leaving me completely open, empty, without possibility of holding anything within myself and thus without possibility of holding anything *for* myself. One must not forget that it is precisely these extraordinarily violent expressions that Levinas will take up in order to explain what he means by 'proximity,' the nearness of the neighbor. (248)

Seldom in the literature can one find a more poignant and evocative, a more disturbing and inspiring, description of the violent and freeing effect that the other has upon the self.

I use Visker's depiction as a springboard to enter into conversation with Levinas's account of trauma in order to gain a clearer and more nuanced understanding of how Levinas and psychological literature on trauma might condition one another to greater nuance. Levinas is referring to an "original traumatism" (1996, 90), representing a different level of analysis than I am addressing when I speak about a "trauma" victim, but working to engage these meanings with particular patients is necessary in the process of translating Levinas's work into clinical relevance. It is messy and there are incommensurables that I am pretending to be commensurate. In terms of clinical work, much work still needs to be done to understand, nuance, challenge, and deepen the meaning of Levinas's account of trauma.

TRAUMATIZING THE TRAUMATIZED: A NUCLEUS FORTIFIED

Visker's statement and Levinas's deeper point *assume* a narcissism that is upheld by an egoism that wants the world for itself. It notes the phenomenology behind the ego's fantasy and preference for the equilibrium and knowable rhythms of sleep. In other words, Levinas assumes a grandiose ego.[5]

However, there are also ways trauma has *contributed* to our being-trapped in slumber.[6] When Visker (2000) writes that the trauma created in proximity to the other "paralyz[es] my paralysis and so pull[s] down the walls which had hindered my movement" (248) and "the Other brings me a trauma which heals" (248), I cannot help but think about some of my therapy patients who are adult survivors of severe childhood abuse. The clamping down of the psyche into self-protecting and limbic-oriented states is a salient feature of nearly any trauma-related literature in psychology. Sleep—in the form of being closed off to alterity, difference, threat, otherness—is the only means of preserving basic function and preventing the "dread of re-traumatization" (Ornstein, in press), a dismantling of the ego into fragmented shards of insanity and torment. Dissociative states protect the ego (Bromberg 1998; 2003; 2006; Davies and Frawley 1991). Sleep is the alternative to terror, not the terror of Levinas's *il y a* ("there is"), but terror of the other as hell (Sartre 1948).

For many trauma survivors, the other *was* Hell and *remains* Hell. The other is utterly defended against and suffering becomes a suffering by oneself—a "useless suffering" (Levinas 1991/1998a). Experience is closed down into solipsistic trauma responses. Exteriority becomes, too frequently, a source of retraumatization or reactivation, rather than conversation, exposure, or a calling outside of oneself. Disequilibrium certainly takes place, but it is a being off balance that does not denucleate. Rather, it sends persons more fully into the inner chambers of their nucleus. It is a clamoring for nucleation in the experience of fragmentation. And, when this nucleus is constructed, the windows and doors are shut *and* deadbolted. Traumatized persons are not smoked out of their places of refuge, but the smoke—reminiscent of their burns and scars—entrenches them more deeply in their hiding places (Bromberg 2003). The other, transmuted into sameness, typically takes the shape of the underlying emotional scar tissue. As opposed to a "trauma which heals," trauma victims often find that their trauma continues to wound with a pain that separates, isolates, and exhausts their resources to remain awake to the other. Such persons remain within an "enclosure" that Marcus (2008) defines as tomblike (87).

Contrary to Visker's description (and Levinas's thought), this is not a "trauma which heals" but rather a trauma that clots the blood and lodges in dangerous arteries. It is a trauma that creates an automaticity that paralyzes and reparalyzes, constricting the victim further and further into a repetitive and rote series of functions. Movement becomes increasingly rigid. Walls become fortified and shells thickened. Already feeling as though one's skin is inside out, the trauma victim experiences the other as a reversing of this disposition. He or she desperately, and often effectively, becomes an inside without an outside.

In other words, the traumatizing call of the other can synchronize with the lived traumas of one's past in such a way as to bolster and magnify immanence rather than rupture it. Levinas teaches us that otherness is traumatic, intolerable, unmanageable, and dysregulating. However, what he is really saying is that it is these things to our narcissism. He does not address an allergy to the other that is born from being mutilated and crushed by an other. This brings up a series of new questions, ones that any clinician working with trauma cases from a Levinasian frame will undoubtedly encounter.

How can I, as the therapist, *be* a trauma that heals rather than one that triggers/activates/dysregulates? How do I help a patient move from a trauma that anesthetizes to a trauma that awakens? How do I help a patient from a trauma that causes a burrowing into oneself to a trauma that invites one toward the outside?

CASE EXAMPLE: JILL

Jill was a force of nature. When she walked into the room, whether it was the waiting space or my office, a hurricane of energy and intensity came with her. At 34 years old, she lived in a perpetual frenzy, bouncing from job to job, apartment to apartment, and doctor to doctor.

It was not uncommon for Jill to spend large portions of our sessions talking rapidly, tangentially, and aggressively. "Life has no purpose," "Everyone is stupid," "God conspires against me in all that I do," and "Nothing will ever change." There was such momentum in her narration that it almost seemed out of her control. She appeared to have little agency as words poured out of her mouth. At times, evidently embarrassed, she would apologize for "being like this." She could not calm herself down and was disturbed about her snowballing self-presentation.

Jill was tormented by severe anxiety that translated into perpetual worry, intrusive thoughts, constant tension, and panic attacks. She never slept throughout the night, jolting awake multiple times and flinging her body out of bed into a ready state, chest heaving and heart pounding. She would then spend considerable time rifling through her drawers trying to organize or find something. There was never a clear goal, but rather some sense that she was working at something. In sessions as well, she would be pilfering through her purse, tying and untying her shoes, or working at "something."

In addition to this anxiety, Jill was plagued by dissociative experiences that were particularly disturbing to her. She was sent to physical therapy to have her knee worked on. When touched by the physical therapist, she would immediately experience significant chronological confusion. Touch was dysregulating: she wasn't sure if she was about to be touched, was still being touched, or was touched long ago. Furthermore, she would experience cognitive slippage as she began having tactile hallucinations concerning the knee in question. Sometimes when Jill returned home, she felt as though the knee had disappeared, left behind at the physical therapy office. Or, the knee was rotting in the joint and infecting the surrounding area. These were horrifying experiences for her. She lost herself, or parts of herself, in these episodes. Her daily life over the previous 20 years had consisted of these dissociative experiences and a chronic terror/anxiety.

She frequently spoke about a desire for all of it to end, though when asked, she stated that suicide wasn't even a temptation. Walking through a list of gruesome methods, Jill enumerated with great detail the ways that God would ensure its failure and use her suicide attempt as a means to create greater hardship and exact further cruelty upon her pathetic life.

Jill had grown up in a chaotic home where siblings, cousins, grandparents, aunts, and uncles marched through as though it was a train station. Most family members severely abused alcohol and drugs. Sexual, verbal, and physical abuse was basic to the fabric of her everyday existence. She recalls no warmth or responsiveness from her parents, only volatility, violence, confusion, and debasement. Her body was used for others' gratifications, her emotions used as others' sadistic playgrounds, and her mind was used to contain the insanity of her context. By age 11, she was an alcoholic. She kept Jack Daniels in her locker and took swigs between classes. She spent the next decade "walking wounded" (her words). She frequently found herself in bad situations. By the time she came to me, she had been sober for nearly ten years. She had yet to find an alternative means of calming her limbic flames.

Particularly in the first months of therapy, many of my words, my questions, and even my presence were experienced as an assault or what she described as a "penetration" that did not call her out, but rather drove her into greater frenzy and anxious countermeasures. She paced faster on the well-worn path, more aggravated, and less attuned to anything outside. Jill's Hell was a small region of persecution, helplessness, and the expectation of being psychically dismembered.

One day, as I was walking down the front steps of my office building about an hour after a session with Jill, I looked up and saw her seated in her car at the curb. Looking embarrassed, she waved, and I waved back. During our next session, I inquired about her still being there. She admitted that she frequently sat in the car for a half hour to nearly two hours after sessions. In a rare moment of lucidity, she explained that she often vomited after sessions, was highly disoriented, and would get terribly lost, even when driving through neighborhoods that she grew up in. Without me knowing, throughout the entire first year of treatment, this was a normal chain of events.

I inquired further about why she would come back each week considering the long-term pairing of nausea and therapy with me! Sheepishly, she expressed that over the course of the year, she had begun feeling some pockets of "calm." There were moments wherein she felt that things "might be okay." These moments were rare and brand new for her.

She sat with me, horrified and transformed, over the course of the year, generating whirlwinds of information and affective stimuli in the therapy room, simultaneously creating a protective smokescreen and communicating the deep chaos she experienced within. However, each time she came, she sat with an other who worked toward attunement without impingement, care without need for gratification, and safety and consistency rather than violence and mayhem. Slight movement in her perception of the other, her tolerance of otherness, and her way of relating to herself in the presence of the other was apparent. Her ability to unclamp without disintegration in the presence of the other was growing.

Is it possible that one step toward ethical traumatism of the other might be an experience of the other as safe and calming? Might the ability to open and close the doors of one's psyche be a basic prerequisite for a traumatism that heals? Exposed and perpetually raw, her life was oriented toward trying to put her doors and windows—splintered by violent family members—back on their hinges and install a security system to protect herself from the invading other. Therapy was a movement toward helping Jill experience less limbic noise so that she did not feel as though she had to be in a perpetual state of protection against the other.

Insomnia: Self Lived with Windows and Doors Open

Ultimately, I agree with Alford's (2002) assertion: "From the perspective of Levinas, the therapeutic goal is not to refound or reground or integrate the self. The goal is to find productive—that is, involved with other humans—ways to give oneself away" (73–74). However, too much is assumed here about the self's preparedness for such an orientation in relationship to the other. This discussion of trauma needs to be nuanced with a recognition of the developmental process that may require that the self find a foundation, grounding, and integration capable of hearing the brutalizing and welcoming call of the other. This founding, grounding, and integration often needs to look different than present, conventional definitions. This is where

Levinas's thought can profoundly condition and enrich contemporary clinical theories and practices. His recalibration of Western notions of freedom, as described earlier, lays the groundwork for a redefining of the self and its development.

I posit that psychotherapy has at its goal an awakening of the self to the other. In the vicissitudes of the intersubjective journey between the patient and therapist, the patient is invited to a fuller encounter with the otherness of the therapist. A slow and steady dismantling of the broken symbols (to use Paul Tillich's words) and idols that mediate and protect takes place. The movement in therapy is from solipsistic slumber to an unending vigil to the needs of the other. It is the stirring from sleep to wakefulness and further to an insomnia of inexhaustible responsibility. The therapist offers such a welcome to the patient by not reducing the otherness of the suffering in which that he or she is living (Poland 2000; see also Margulies 2000).

Levinas captures something of the violence experienced in exposure to the other. Being called into question, being affected, held hostage, and persecuted by alterity and the fragility of the other is excruciating. Becoming aware and attuned to the gravity of the other necessarily disrupts and unsettles. Waking up is painful. In the original *Matrix* (1999) movie, Neo, after choosing the red pill and being exhumed from the mucous chamber of the machines, states, "My eyes hurt." Awakening to experience unmediated by the protective sheaths of consciousness, there is pain, confusion, disorientation, and terror; so also, when the psyche shifts from its normative discourses to the phenomenological trauma of the face of the other. The return to this preoriginal and anarchic dyad is radical and catastrophic to one's referential system and anchor points for meaning.

For example, my gentle and reassuring presence accosted Jill. It could not be adequately thematized in the neat categories of her history. In psychoanalytic terms, it remained unformulated and inaccessible to her psyche—a threat to the equilibrium of knowable experience. However, her patterns of overdetermined relationality—creating sandstorms of energy and verbage in the therapy room to keep encounter at a distance—became stale for her as time progressed. She could not maintain them; they began breaking down, and she found herself venturing into the nether territories of something different: small amounts of trust, a sense of comfort, hope, and connection. This created horror, vomiting, disorientation, and a psyche awake to something otherwise than her previous being. Her experience of the other (me) was a violent experience.

On the other hand, the rhythms involved in awakening are sometimes peaceful and not violent. Caress to the side of one's cheek, a kiss on the forehead, or a gentle nudge are also ways of being wakened. The assumption of "entrenched" egoism that requires a "shattering of the individual's nature attitude" leads to the violent denucleation in Levinas's thought (Oppenheim 2006, 39). There may be other parts of the self that are awakened in playfulness, safety, and familiarity. The need to sleep as a means of dissociation and emotional avoidance may become less necessary in the context of laughter and comfort. In this way, Levinas's (1961/1969, 1976/1990b) understanding of the other as providing a welcome, an invitation, and a conversation may be preferred.

Jill and I learned to become playful with one another. I frequently made fun of her purses (they were enormous!), and she made fun of the front office staff (making fun of me would come along further into therapy when it was safer). We were doing serious work but were working hard to take things less seriously. Over time, Jill described the therapy room as the place where she felt safest in the world. She could be herself, without (as much) fear of reprisal. Defenses, hideouts, and idols diminished in power as their protective purpose became increasingly unnecessary. Over time, subtly, the knob on her limbic volume was turned to a decibel that allowed for other sounds besides the inner noise that plagued her perpetually. Each week, there was a predictable tempo and rhythm to our encounters—she came to trust it and even depend on it. It was as close as she had come to being with an other peacefully.

For some, particularly those who carry a significant trauma history, learning to experience the other as safe, secure, and loving may be the first developmental prerequisite for experiencing the other as a "trauma which heals." Levinas has been critiqued many times before by Irigary (1991) and Alford (2002) for not allowing space in his thought for connection, dialogue, rhythm, participation, attachment, and relationship. Using Winnicott, Alford argues that Levinas overemphasizes the otherness of the other, the subject's responsibility to the other, and the infinite qualities of the other without properly balancing this with mutuality/reciprocity, sharing, and the play and needs of finite human-to-human relationship. Mitchell (2003) suggests that the dynamic presence of both ends of a continuum between safety/familiarity/predictability and adventure/otherness/novelty is needed for love to remain alive. McLaughlin (1995) also touches meaningfully upon this issue when he states, "We need to find in the other an affirming witness to the best that we hope we are, as well as an accepting and durable respondent to those worst aspects of ourselves that we fear we are. We seek to test and find ourselves in the intimacy of the therapeutic relationship, to become known to and accepted by the other" (434).

These nuances may capture something of the sensibilities being put forth here.

The other necessarily unsettles (which can be tremendously violent to one's narcissistic egoism) but can also invite and comfort. Indeed, for some trauma patients (like Jill), comfort and familiarity are experienced as violent. The totality of the I does not consist solely of selfish egoism. There may be parts ready to be awakened through caress.

Conclusion

The narrator of C. S. Lewis's allegorical tale notes that to walk on the grass of heaven is quite painful. It feels so solid, and he feels much like a phantom, having almost no substance. Accustomed to being asleep in the numbness of Hell, the vibrancy of experience (even grass beneath one's feet) was too much. It over activates the senses to the point of registering pain. The other is much the same in Levinas's thought. The excess of experience resident in the face-to-face encounter overloads and breaks the ego apart. However, it is a "trauma which heals" as it tears us free from the confines of small stories, sleepfulness, and ego imprisonment. This prison break has psychic casualties. In Levinas's (1986a) words, "The other haunts our ontological existence and keeps the psyche awake, in a state of vigilant insomnia" (28).

Levinas's words are shocking, radical, and even unsettling. They stand in diametrical opposition to the fortified and well-boundaried self out of which we live and its versions of freedom propagated in many Western philosophies, societies, and psychologies. His emphasis on violence done to the ego by the other is a necessary corrective to the complacency and safety-seeking of egoism. However, working with trauma victims in a clinical setting raises some difficult questions about his emphasis on the violence of otherness, alterity, and infinite separateness. These patients' identities, already traumatized and hemorrhaging, will respond differently to the alterity resident in face-to-face relation.

Sharing Levinas's sensibilities, my wish is that our patients will find themselves called forth from the narrow confines of the "sleep of ontology" (Stone 1998, 29) and the dissociative slumber of abuse and become increasingly open to the infinite and other. An insomnia made up of deep and unmodulated awareness, attunedness, and responsiveness to the other is understood as the greatest of freedoms. Alford (2002) reminds us that Levinas "also writes about insomnia as a type of 'ecstasy' that is utterly open to otherness because it neither knows nor categorizes, but just is, waiting for nothing...on the border between heaven and hell" (68).

CONCLUSION

The Demanded Self
Horizons More Vast Than History

> *Biblical religion is in a sense rebellion against the tyranny of things, a revolt against confinement in the world. Man is given the choice of being lost in the world or of being a partner in mastering and redeeming the world.* (Heschel 1963, 83)

> *One must keep one foot in the Eternal. A tough discipline of knowledge, exercises carried out every day in order to cling to the steep rock that juts out.... Only in this way is there fulfilled on earth and for men a privileged possibility: a free being who judges history instead of letting himself be judged by it.* (Levinas 1976/1990b, 227)

LEVINAS AS A PROPHETIC VOICE

It is not unusual to read the word "prophet" in many secondary texts describing Levinas's approach (Alford 2002; Ford 1999; Harold 2009). In his groundbreaking work *The Prophets*, Heschel (1962) provided an illuminating description of the characteristics of prophets. It provides a resonant picture of the prophetic dimension of Levinas's thought — particularly as it relates to his approach to rationality, the immanent and normative order, and the individual subject within psychological discourses.

First, Heschel writes, "The prophet is human, yet he employs notes one octave too high for our ears. He experiences moments that defy our understanding.... Often his words begin to burn where conscience ends" (10). Levinas describes the gaze of European philosophy and science as having an impaired conscience and urges philosophers to recognize that, to use Cohen's (1994) words, "there are more stringent demands than those of rigorous science" (xvii). He argues that where scientific discourse ends, there is more to be said and that we must "exceed the categories and structures which have thus far determined thought itself" (159); if we end with scientific discourse, we lose significant facets of human experience and identity. Of greatest concern for Levinas is the significant loss of the ethical relation to and responsibility for the other within the immanentizing and ontological constructs of modern social sciences. Without the *ought*, scientific definitions of the self remain merely procedural and instrumental, excluding any recognition of the other: "Without rejecting modernity, that is to say, without rejecting science, Levinas stands radically against these developments and the imperial inflation of psychology that is part and symptom of them. His countercriticism is precise: the problem is not with science, knowledge or truth, but rather with their hegemonic inflation, with the philosophy of science as totality. Levinas stands against the idea of the psyche reduced to immanent logic, to what science can know of it.... Levinas embraces science, but he embraces ethics more closely" (Cohen 2002, 37).

Levinas also challenges us to see that science's totalizing and constricting discourses are reflected, reinforced, and paralleled in the tendencies of egoist subjectivity. Levinas argues that the ontological and rationalist presuppositions that underlie the Western consciousness and the normative narcissism that characterizes the *self out of which we live* create cataracts that impair meaningful attention to the ethical imperative resident within the face of the other. Levinas thus defies conventional modes of understanding identity and ethics, his work challenging the monadic limits and self-entitled rights within which European-American persons function.

Furthermore, the pitch with which Levinas speaks ("one octave too high") makes him hard to listen to. That is, Levinas's sensibility makes his critique and constructions profoundly difficult to understand.[1] Speaking about Levinas's writings, Davis (1996) observes that "the text hovers on the edge of nonsense.... Similes are adopted but simultaneously undercut.... Levinas's text strains to describe something that it characterizes as lying beyond any experiential or cognitive measure" (121). The seduction and intoxication of certainty and universal truths are paralyzed in Levinas's literary and conceptual style. He intentionally undermines the reification and calcification process of conventional knowledge, almost taunting the constituting logic of modern (and 'Greek') thought.

In terms of modern psychologies, Levinas's critique of egology and depiction of the person as ethically constituted are discourses that are foreign and enigmatic (House 2005). In decentering the ego from its primacy, psychological theories and practices are without the resources to comprehend or assimilate a Levinasian framework. Modern psychologies' measurements offer only a depraved ability to listen to, recognize, and attend to Levinas's thought, which requires relinquishing normative measures for the self and their adjunctive discourses. Levinas's thought cannot be incorporated; he is a radical and reconstituting dialogue partner. This is the power of his translation project.

Heschel (1962) describes the prophet, secondly, as "an iconoclast, challenging the apparently holy, revered, and awesome. Beliefs cherished as certainties, institutions endowed with supreme sanctity, he exposes as scandalous pretensions" (10). In an interview, Levinas (2004) states, "Science...does not try to unsay itself, does not interrogate or challenge its own concepts, terms, or foundations; it forges ahead, progresses. In this respect, science attempts to ignore language by constructing its own abstract nonlanguage of calculable symbols and formulae....[I]t can never have the last word" (73). However, science, as a "metanarrative" (Lyotard 1984) and the epistemological headquarters within modern thought, has been given the last word; its "truths" have no means of calling themselves into question. As a fundamentally descriptive enterprise, it has no facilities to interrupt the present order and so the justice and goodness of the given order remains outside of its purview. Science's measurement of the immanent order provides only a dangerous reduction of the story. Modern psychology falls into what Levinas refers to as a philosophy of "presence" within Western history whereby what is visible becomes the basis of what is true. Levinas (1968/1994) critiques this epistemology and even describes the knowledge or data it generates as impeding our access to the truth. For Levinas, truth comes from lived, ethical relationship to the other, emerging out of a disruption of the self-evident truths out of which we commonly live.

The revered, cherished, and sanctified institution of science is shown to be pretentious in its assumption that it can function as a prescriptive determinant of being. I. F. Stone (1998) writes that Levinas fights for human beings to be "seen not as extensions of some impersonal self-in-being, but, rather, as approaching from outside any system I could devise to define them" (x). Williams (2007) has written, "There is a great liberation in this. It liberates the ethical — concern for what ought to be—from the ontological—concern for what is, and what it really is. Once we recognize that the answer to the question 'What is?' is bound to escape us in an ultimate sense, we are suddenly free to raise to prominence the question 'What ought to be?'" (691).

Furthermore, Levinas splinters the presumption of a self-interested and narcissistically oriented subject. Levinas (1961/1969) claims that the ego within the West has been valorized and endowed with a "sovereign," "imperial," and "heroic" status. The normative self is its own author of certainty, the final word of authority, an agentic and powerful subject. Levinas rejects this version of the self as a "certainty" and refers to the systems that emerged around it as unjust. He introduces the other as a "scandal" (Pitkin 2001) to these configurations of selfhood, upsetting its complacency. For Levinas, reverence is not given to the normal bell-shaped self, but rather to a self disturbed by an inexhaustible responsibility to the other.

Modern psychologies have often functioned as scientifically legitimated institutions under the auspices of benign measurement and secular assurances (see Levinas 1974/1998c, 58). These psychologies have become the source of commonsensical thought, defining and legitimating discourses about the self that emerge from within particular contexts. This social sanctioning, and its subsequent creation of the egoist subject, is questioned in Levinas's thought.

Thirdly, Heschel (1962) points out, "What seems to be exaggeration is often only a deeper penetration, for the prophets see the world from the point of view of God, as transcendent, not immanent truth" (14). The radical way Levinas describes the irreducibility of the other, the denucleating of the self in the other's presence, and the status of the self as hostage, accused, persecuted, and substitutionary has led some to describe Levinas's work as hyperbolistic.[2] Levinas, however, draws from revelation far less domesticated by empirical and positivistic measures.

Furthermore, throughout Levinas's works, there is a clear expression that immanent truth (history and systems) is banal and not meant to be the source of meaning and identity. Levinas wants to restore the interrupting power of the transcendent, which is absent within the given order. Levinas argues that immanence must be called into question and conditioned by the transcendent order. This conditioning and interruption requires a memory older than historical memory; a memory that witnesses more than what is illuminated in history (Levinas 1976/1990b). Brueggemann (1999) explains, "The prophets hold to a 'metahistory' voiced in Israel's liturgy and memory, but not otherwise visible in the world" (52).

Modern psychologies are inherently restricted to an immanentizing methodology. Thus, the meaning that these psychologies produce fits within the language games of the present order. Levinas hopes to introduce an order born from the infinite encounter with the other, not the sterile, observable, replicable, and predictable given. In this way, psychology's conversation with Levinas may allow a reorientation of its theories toward otherness, the transcendent, and the ethical interhuman relationship.

Fourth, Heschel (1962) describes Hebrew prophets as providing "a scream in the night…while the world is at ease and asleep," working to "conquer callousness, to change the inner man as well as to revolutionize history" (16). Levinas describes the Western ego as immune to others and fundamentally incognizant of its moral responsibility in its self-reflexive orientation. He critiques these egos, vying for themselves, at war with one another, with no responsibilities for the other person (Levinas 1961/1969, 1974/1998c). It is a picture of selfhood characterized by moral slumber.

The intention of Levinas's work is not merely to describe human experience and consciousness phenomenologically and descriptively.[3] Rather, there is a pervasive messianic eschatology throughout his texts (Gibbs 1992; Lesser 1996; Levinas 1976/1990b; Ward 1996). He states that "holiness demands it—to die for the other. In this attitude of holiness, there is a reversal of the normal order of things, the natural order of things, the persistence in being of the ontology of things and of the living. For me that is the moment where, through the human, the beyond being—God—comes to mind" (Levinas and Robbins 2001, 47–48). Particularly in *Difficult Freedom,* Levinas (1976/1990b) constantly challenges persons to relate in such a way as to bring about a peaceful world order and refuse to "accept the verdict of...History" (166).[4] Reflecting this sensibility, Heschel (1955) writes, "A demand such as 'love thy neighbor as thyself' is not at home in the self" (101). This demand must come from beyond history, from beyond essence, being, and ontology. This is the heart of Levinas's philosophy. Cohen (1994) states this beautifully: "Thus to care for one's neighbor more than oneself, to take on responsibility for the other, ethics, and to take on the other's responsibilities, justice, is to enter into a *sacred* rather than an ontological or epistemological history" (158).

Levinas focuses on how justice is made possible by our lived existence. He asserts that this question does not naturally or readily arise from the "anonymous unfolding" of history (1976/1990b, 226). To the contrary, in his chapter "The Meaning of History," Levinas argues that it "is wrong to expect justice from history" (226). Without moral attention and receptivity to the other, history becomes a "series of crimes" (226). Uninterrupted and left to its own trends, it leads to moral sterility and violence. The given order (history and nature) cannot be the determinant of identity, selfhood, and consciousness. Levinas's experiences as a Lithuanian Jew who survived the Holocaust makes this assertion especially poignant (see chapter 2).

Hence, to find our meaning in the tides of history is, ultimately, to be judged by history and its capricious platitudes bathed in the powerplays of time. Normality remains merely a reflection of the reigning zeitgeist and its derivative configurations of the self. Through methodology that generalizes historical patterns into principles of selfhood, modern psychological constructs of self are inevitably a reflection of the cultural milieu and dominant philosophical paradigms (Cushman 1995), which does not ensure justice, but rather has the potential of propagating and maintaining an unjust configuration of the self. Ford (1999) writes, "Individuals receive their meaning from the totality and lose confidence in any sense of identity or responsibility that appeals beyond the verdict of history in which the violent and unjust are often successful" (47).

For these reasons, the trends generated in history such as our "cancerous individualism" (Bellah et al. 1985) and self-interested orientations must be denounced as "counter-sense or madness" (Levinas 1976/1990b, 227). Levinas called for an "inversion of the apparent order" (xiv). He cried for us to "swim eternally against the filthy, criminal tide of man'" (144). There are, Levinas (1961/1969) writes, "horizons more vast than history, in which history itself is judged" (246).

Instead of locating the person within a historical system or naturalistic essence, Levinas calls for ethical relationship to the other to interrupt and constitute human identity, suggesting that within ethical relationship to the other, persons "refuse the summation of the historical record" (25). For Levinas, constructs of selfhood should be the product of a calling more fundamental and original than the capricious movements of history—a calling known only in the demand that comes in relationship to the other.[5]

Levinas (1968/1994) argues that universalizing and naturalistic claims about the self are means of forming detached measurements that ignore the more fundamental ethical relationship that conditions human identity (see chapters 2–5). The given or the natural is not cognizant of that which transcends it and precedes it. Rather, Levinas (1974/1998c) spoke of a "presynthetic, prelogical" (107) and immemorial past that is older than these concepts and that is both before and anachronistically within the sociality of beings. Before history, characteristics, and essentialist pictures of the self, Levinas asserts the question of the other, an alterity beyond our measures, an identity beyond our equations, and places its origin in a calling that demands our response. The self that history produces is without regard for this calling, which is a memory prior to history. Levinas (1961/1969) wrote, "The eschatological, as the 'beyond' of history, draws beings out of the jurisdiction of history and the future; it arouses them in and calls them forth to their full responsibility... beings have an identity 'before' eternity, before the accomplishment of history" (23). For this reason, history and the given order cannot appropriately be the determinant of identity, selfhood, and consciousness. The command upon the self must come from beyond history, from a place and time otherwise than within the realm of being. Levinas (1991/1998a) asserts that to live out of something "otherwise than being" is the "shattering of indifference—even if indifference is statistically dominant" (xii). Statistical dominance (i.e., normativity) should not lay the foundation for our definitions of selfhood.

Parting Statements: The Demanded Self

> *The good—the prescriptive—is the ground of the real and the true. The good is found neither in the sky nor in the mind, but in the transcendence of the face-to-face relation and, no less, then, in the plurality of social and interpersonal relations. That is to say, goodness is found—concretely lived—in moral kindness and just institutions.* (Cohen 2003b, 147)

At a metalevel, Levinas is suggesting that the West's preoccupation with reason, constricted domain of immanence, and egological subject were indicative of a disordered being, a being founded on a "will to truth" and undisturbed by goodness. This has become the "false consciousness" of the West and a "societal pathology" or "folie à millions" (Fromm 1955, 15) that functions as the basis of how persons understand themselves and others. It is a version of the self informed by our sociopolitical and economic ethos, a 'Greek' and Euro-American philosophical trajectory, and many psychological theories and practices. It falls squarely into the temptation of temptation of which Levinas warned, orienting consciousness toward itself and toward a being that constitutes a possessive knowledge. This narrative framework out of which we live remains only at the beginning of the story as it valorizes an ego that is defined and lived in such a way as to blind us to the ethical call of the other. It is a morally anemic self that is deafened to others.

This critique and espousing of a Levinasian-inspired demanded self chisles away at the metalinguistic infrastructure and home that surrounds us. Our fluent language, that which feels most like home—our normative way of being—is called into question. Cushman (2007) writes, "Readers, therapists, and patients fall into [the] textual gaps; engage with their interlocutors there, wrestle with God there. We live in those gaps; we are our best selves there" (79). The self is put into exile, sent away from the complacency of a language within which it has lived, a language through which it has experienced itself and others. We are homeless, particularly from the home of a narcissistic, monadic egology, an "ontological 'homelessness' of consciousness" (Levinas 1989, 238). In this way, Levinas charges us to allow infinity to condition our totalities.

NOTES

Notes to Chapter One

1. See Cushman's work on the "empty self" for a powerful illustration of how the language of how the self is configured both reflects and propagates a particular context. The implications of this upon relationships and culture are hauntingly described in his works (Cushman 1990, 1995, 2009).

2. Arthur Kleinman (1988) and many others argue that these cultural idioms—implicit constructs of the self—ultimately mediate our encounter with ourselves, the world, and others. Cushman (1995) poignantly adds, "Everyday social interaction calls upon us to develop a multitude of interpretations about the immediate social context, and philosophical hermeneutics challenges us to become more effective at noticing those daily interpretations, those we are aware of, and those that we are not aware of; those that help us open our awareness to new possibilities, and those that close off possibilities; those that help us see the forbidden, and those that shut off, or help us disown and avoid, the forbidden; those that reproduce an old, destructive terrain, and those that help us develop a world in which new possibilities have the opportunity to emerge" (353).

3. A system forms invisibly around this self, a symbiotic allegiance of the political, economic, and social status quo to the ways of perceiving, values, and experiences preponderant in a particular construction of the self. It is a co-constructing relationship, both sides reinforcing each other. As Taylor (1989) states, "The causal arrow runs in both directions" (206). A latent and covert self is the product, a version of the self out of which one lives but under the trance of exclusivity and givenness. It becomes an unmistakable yet diffuse power that shapes all perception and experience. It is assumed, unformulated, and commonsensical. The "self" becomes a "discourse"—a "discursive formation" that is "governed by rules, beyond those of grammar and logic, that operate beneath the consciousness of individual subjects and define a system of conceptual possibilities that determine the boundaries of thought in a given domain and period" (Gutting 2003, 3). Stern (2003) explains it as follows: "For Foucault, power is effective to the extent that it is not perceived. To just that extent, it shapes individual experience, and it does so while obviating the necessity to explain the exclusion of alternative. Alternatives are simply unformulated" (137; see Foucault 1977).

4. Modern psychology fits squarely into the "will to knowledge" tradition that has spanned from Plato's Ideas to the Kantian transcendental ego. This

trajectory represents a well-trodden lineage wherein philosophers have attempted to stand outside of history and society in order to gain a vantage point from which universal knowledge can be known ("logocentrism"). Modernity, the Enlightenment project, and its modern sciences mark a significant next step in this process whereby human beings believed themselves capable of disengaging from tradition, situadedness and even (at times) corporeality in order to ascertain universal principles, timeless truths, and certain "facts" (Critchley 2001; Taylor 1989; Toulmin 1990; Williams 2005). Modernity was a historical era wherein the West attempted to throw off the alleged hindrances to reason's progress. Tradition was deemed to be a prejudicing force; one prominent assumption in modernity was the forward progress of humanity. Unencumbered by the shackles of hereditary knowledge, the modern sciences marched onward into new territories of discovery, an entire world to place under objective observation. History, ala Hegel and others, was the unfolding of this enlightening process. Clarity, certainty, and fullness of knowledge were the intoxicating promises of modern science. History was to be trusted.

5. If the metaphor of a parentified child is appropriate for science in early modernity, then it is useful to think about modern psychology as being a foster child in this family system. This insight was arrived at in personal communication with Heather Macdonald.

6. Locke's use of the term "reformation" is an interesting word choice considering its close historical proximity to the Protestant Reformation that helped propell science into its esteemed status. The Protestant Reformation did not end with theological changes, but rather created the space for reformation across all domains of human function (e.g., political shifts, new economic systems, etc.). And, reciprocally, this religious Reformation was allowed to come about in the space of this changing world. The Protestant Reformation remains one of the largest markers in Western history for sociopolitical and ideological shifts. Reformation across the board was the ethos of the next few centuries.

7. Burston and Frie (2006) write that "in the German language a distinction is often made between the natural sciences (*Naturwissenschaften*) and the human sciences" (*Geisteswissenschaften*) (2). Modern psychology, from early on, worked to affiliate primarily with the natural sciences. Freud built his theoretical framework with a clear desire for it to be linked to purely physiological processes.

8. Hume (empiricist) and Kant (Enlightenment philosopher) were both opposed to the formation of a psychological science. Even in their emphasis upon rationality and staunch methodology, they recognized the inability of the human being to possess that degree of self-reflexivity (Burston and Frie, 2006).

9. It is important to point to the impossibility of dialoguing with any monolithic form of psychology. Psychology, despite a preponderant desire to legitimate itself as a branch of science, has many variegated forms. The discourses employed in defining the self range from Freud to Skinner to Rogers to Beck to Sullivan. They are qualitatively different means of understanding the human self.

However, significant modern trends undergird the majority of psychology's young lineage. Recognizing that the myriad theoretical systems (with their assumptions about the structure of the self and the derivative formulas of pathology, health, and treatment methods) are like different languages, I consider the metalinguistic parameters out of which most of these languages arise: the syntactual rules and ideological parameters that these languages share.

For instance, the majority of psychological paradigms are thoroughly modern and unabashedly Darwinian, empirical, and foundationalist epistemologies. This work does not focus on a particular school of thought within psychology, but on the encompassing, overarching system to which the majority of psychology tends to subscribe. As a rule, most modern psychological systems esteem functionality and adaptability (heavily influenced by evolutionary theory), employ naturalistic principles, found their depictions upon normative measures, and define freedom as self-creation and autonomous rationality. Though psychological orientations may vary in how this is manifest and the specific details may create antithetical frameworks, these attributes are central to the formation of constructs of the human self and the derivative understandings of human health, pathology, and treatment. Even with their vast differences in language, thinkers like Freud, Skinner, Beck, and Rogers still share these fundamental elements. It is what Wittgenstein (1953/2001) might refer to as a "family resemblance." I seek to consider the foundational structure of this metalinguistic framework whose diverse offspring both founded and currently maintains the *self out of which we live*.

For the remainder of this work, the terms "modern psychologies" or "psychology" are used to point to the linguistic trends and modernist influences that are shared across many psychological traditions. The terminology of "modern psychologies" is borrowed from Browning's (1987) recognition of the many forms that psychology has taken in the modern era. I recognize that to critique the whole of psychology as being derivative of the modern project is to neglect various movements within postmodern psychologies and less mainstream forms of psychology that are not susceptible to the same critiques. However, the majority of contemporary movements within modern psychology subscribe to the metaframework that is being critiqued in this book. With this clarification in place, a closer look at these psychologies' role in contemporary culture is possible.

10. See Gergen's (2000) chapter entitled "The Self Under Siege" for a helpful discussion about the role that modern psychologies have played in "scientizing" and providing a more expansive language for human deficits and pathology. He argues that this acquired vocabulary shapes people's self-definitions and perceptions in such a way as to then require a profession that can promise a cure (e.g., psychology). Gergen also discusses the significant effects of psychological vocabulary upon culture and the public at large as it is disseminated.

11. The exception to this is within the rich moral psychology literature that has burgeoned over the last half century. I am grateful to Linda Wagener for conversations and resources that have pointed in the direction of this otherwise fairly insulated branch of contemporary psychology.

12. Birrell (2006) has this to say to the clinical psychology profession: "[E]thics in our profession has largely come to mean a system giving us rules on

how to relate to our colleagues and clients, not a matter of how we are or are not present with the human being facing us" (98).

13. Brown (1997) argues against the patriarchal descriptions of the human person that dominate in society and have historically been unattended to by psychology's code of ethics. Birrell (2006) writes, "Mainstream ethics has emphasized the autonomous self and a system of ethical codes, an approach that has remained largely unquestioned. This mainstream ethics is largely an ethic of the 'Said,' emphasizing universality, control, and reason" (110).

14. Interestingly, recent research within the moral psychological community has found evidence that the relationship between moral behavior and moral consciousness (ability to formulate moral judgments and showing evidence of high moral reasoning) is not as strong as what was once thought (Blasi 1983, 1984, 1994). In the post-Kohlbergian moral psychological tradition, the focus on moral reasoning as the source of moral behavior "dead ended," unable to account for how people actually behaved. Recent scholarship on moral exemplars shows that instead of moral cognition and reasoning, the very shape of the self, a self constituted as a moral agent that evidences the presence of moral emotions (e.g., empathy), determines the extent to which one engages in moral actions. Morality is not merely a derivative function of executive processes, but is rather an outgrowth of the moral identity and orientation of the self in relationship to others. The shape of the self and its configuration in regards to others—its moral identity—is a more substantial predictor of one's moral behaviors. These insights were the result of conversation with Dr. Linda Wagener. In chapter six, I discuss what is meant by the "shape of the self."

15. It should be noted that despite its reductive methods for doing so, psychoanalysis has worked hard to understand (and continues to contend with) the issue of morality and selfhood (Fromm 1947; Marcus 2008; Meissner 2003). More recent psychological paradigms, emerging from cognitive and behavioral schools, have been almost wholly dismissive and neglectful of the moral dimension of selfhood.

16. Little work has been done exploring the appropriateness of applying Levinas in a variety of crosscultural contexts. The assertions about the "Western" or "modern" self are large blankets that intend to point to general trends and patterns within history. In the form presented here, the self is defined through its particular philosophical heritage and must be translated in a more local fashion when it is being applied elsewhere. The self's narcissism may apply in one context and have little bearing or significance in the next. Crosscultural sensitivity and/or a dialogue must take place using indigenous forms of discourse/ethics in order for this conversation to remain meaningful and nonviolent (Dueck 2002; Dueck and Reimer 2003, 2009; Enriquez 1993; Gergen et al. 1996). Some interesting work is being done applying Levinas's thought in a variety of different cultural settings (see Rivera 2007). Such work should be encouraged as ethical concern for the other can take a variety of forms, richly informed by other religious systems and cultural expressions.

17. This will require particular nuance as I concur with Taylor and others that the self is always situated in a moral horizon and is located within a particular

moral topography. It is not being argued that the self is without morality, but rather that the modern self is without a *particular* morality as understood from a Jewish philosophical system: an ethical disposition that orients it toward others and for others. It lives within the "ontological individualism" (Bellah et al. 1985) and "cultural narcissism" (Lasch 1979) that keeps it shut off from responsibility to others. I agree with Birrell (2006), when she states that "standard notions of ethics are not adequate in a quest to be truly ethical. These standard ways of thinking about ethics stand too far from the ethical moment and create a false clarity" (96).

18. For the remainder of this work, the terms "holiness," "goodness," and "ethics" will be used interchangeably to mark this alternate way of understanding the term "ethics."

19. Some have argued that psychologists, particularly early psychoanalytic thinkers (Freud, Jung, Adler), generated personality theories that were embedded in moral frameworks and were concerned about morality (Williams 2007). The philosophies and sciences of modernity have "accredited a cramped and truncated view of morality in a narrow sense" (Taylor 1989, 3). I argue that though there are implicit and explicit assumptions about what is "good," these still emerge from a secularized, immanent, and individualized depiction of the human person derived from Enlightenment ideology. Levinas offered a different path; he "[i]ntends by the 'ethical' something much more profound than what usually comes to mind in treatments of the topic in contemporary psychology, psychoanalysis, and philosophy. Most discussions of ethics and 'the ethical' in contemporary thought center on ethical principles, which, in turn, depend for their existence on rational arguments" (Williams 2007, 685).

20. Choosing the work of Levinas, means necessarily excluding a multitude of others whose prophetic voices have incredible potential for helping psychology move from guardian of the status quo to an ideology and practice oriented toward goodness and social responsibility. Numerous prophetic voices have recognized the deadening quality of the self out of which we live. Fromm (1955) suggests that we are living out of a shared, deluded construct of the self that is ultimately inauthentic to what it actually means to be human. R. D. Laing (1969) mirrors this concern as he describes how "our 'normal' 'adjusted' state is too often the abdication of ecstasy, the betrayal of our true potentialities, that many of us are only too successful in acquiring a false self to adapt to false realities" (12). These thinkers will be given short shrift throughout this work, in no way representing the level of significance they have in the equations being put forth.

21. Fromm (1955) argues that a preponderant "societal pathology" and "folie à millions" in the West rendered normality meaningless. Laing (1969) refers to normality as a "pervasive madness" and argues that all of our frames of reference were "ambiguous and equivocal" (11).

22. Referring to Huxley's *Brave New World* as an illustration, Fromm (1955) states, "This alienation and automatization leads to an ever-increasing insanity. Life has no meaning, there is no joy, no faith, no reality. Everybody is 'happy'—except that he does not feel, does not reason, does not love" (360). Consider Rieff's (1987) statement: " 'therapeutic,' with nothing at stake beyond

a manipulable sense of well-being. This is the unreligion of the age and its master science" (13). Heschel (1963) writes, "A life of manipulation is the death of transcendence" (82).

23. The choice to use the term "patients" rather than "clients" throughout this text was made after significant deliberation about the liabilities and merits of each. Though the term "patients" can quickly lend to a medicalized description with a built-in hierarchy of expertise (on the therapist's side), the term "client" remains too loaded with consumerist implications. Neither term is appropriate for putting words to the suffering other that comes to me in therapy.

24. Gergen (2000) states, "If we can comprehend the origins and changes in our Western beliefs about the person...we can soften the grip of what is currently taken for granted. If what we take to be solid facts about human beings turn out to be byproducts of a particular social condition, then such 'facts' are more appropriately considered opinions or myths. Thus...historical awareness might release us from the prisons of our current conventions of understanding" (10–11).

Notes to Chapter Two

Using James Joyce's idiom, Derrida (1978) characterizes Levinas as "Jewgreek.Greekjew" with "Levinas' project being the synthesis of two economies" (Ward 1996, 165). Some portions of this chapter incorporate material previously published in an encyclopedia entry "Emmanuel Levinas" in D. Leeming, K. Madden, and S. Marlan's *Encyclopedia of Psychology and Religion* (Goodman 2009) and the article "Psychology in Pursuit of Justice: The works and lives of Emmanuel Levinas and Ignacio Martin-Baro" in *Pastoral Psychology* (Goodman, Walling, and Ghali 2010). Both pieces are used with permission from the publishers.

1. Interview was a part of Wright, Hughes, and Ainsley's chapter in Bernasconi and Wood (1988). See also Levinas (1988/2007b).

2. See chapter five (75–87) in *The Levinas Reader*, entitled "Ethics as First Philosophy" for one of Levinas's (1989) first descriptions of this idea. A further development of what Levinas meant by this phrase can be found in *Totality and Infinity*, particularly in the sections entitled "Metaphysics Precedes Ontology" and "Ethics and the Face" (Levinas 1961/1969).

3. See Alford 2002, 2007; Douglas 2005; Dueck and Goodman 2007; Faulconer 2005; Gantt and Williams 2002; Kunz 1998; Marcus 2007, 2008; Orange 2009; Sayre 2005 for several examples. Levinas's work is also being recognized and applied in research (Clegg and and Slife 2005), developmental (Vandenberg 1999), theoretical (Williams and Gantt 1998), and social (Slife, Reber, and Richardson 2005) psychology.

4. Peperzak (1993) appropriately warns that reading Levinas as a conversation between Greek and Hebrew culture is to assume that there is such thing as a monolithic Greek culture and a monolithic Hebrew culture. Neither exists. Both have variegated histories with many strands and strains of thought and practice.

It is, undoubtedly, an oversimplification to pose it in such terms. But, this simplification, though providing us only a partial picture, is helpful nonetheless (8).

5. This quote oversimplifies both Greek and Hebrew sensibilities, linking prophecy with Judaism and philosophy with Greek. Judaism has its own forms of philosophy, propositions, and doctrines and is not merely a prophetic stance. Likewise, Greek thought has its own prophetic markers (e.g., Blaise Pascal, Soren Kierkegaard). That said, this chapter will retain some of this oversimplification by suggesting that Judaic sensibilities are a prophetic corrective to conventional theory, which is largely derived from a Greek heritage. This is not to say that Judaism is only this prophetic corrective or that Greek thought is without its own sources for correction.

6. One wonders if this is, in part, a product of the liberal democratic and secularizing forces that work hard to "purify" scholarship for the sake of universal accessibility. Or, it is possible that the lack of biblical literacy in contemporary culture (Lindbeck 2006) immediately excludes the Jerusalem pole from receiving its necessary and due attention.

7. For instance, a recent *Psychoanalytic Review* in August 2007, dedicated to scholarship on Levinas as his work pertains to psychoanalytic theory and practice, makes little mention of Levinas's Judaism. While Husserl and Heidegger are named as part of his intellectual lineage, Rosenzweig, Chouchani, Scripture, Talmud, and Jewish ethics are excluded. This is odd considering that Levinas himself writes that Rosenzweig so impacted his work that footnoting him would be ludicrous (Cohen 1994; Levinas 1961/1969), and he attributes a significant amount of his intellectual development to his "great master" (Levinas, qtd. in Malka 2002/2006, 127). Gibbs (1992) admonishes Levinas scholars, "The significance of his long years at the Normal School, of his own Lithuanian heritage, and most of all the learning with Chouchani are not used to interpret his philosophical insights" (10).

8. Many of these terms are shared between the Christian and Jewish tradition (and other faith traditions as well). Their meaning is pregnant with millennia of development within both traditions. Caution must be exacted in understanding their meaning in Levinas's texts.

9. See Beavers's (1993) lecture "Emmanuel Levinas and the Prophetic Voice of Postmodernity" for a compelling comparison of the Greek state and the Jewish state. Ultimately, Beavers makes the argument that Greek states enforce "abstract and impersonal juridical act[s]" by which its citizens are meant to comply (4), whereas Jewish states begin "with humans facing humans," then build into just communities. He contended that contemporary society retains a Greek state model where, to use Levinas' words, "men find themselves side by side rather than face to face," leaving all men "anonymous" to one another (Levinas 1989, 212).

10. Burggraeve (2007) provides an incisive look into the "bipolarities" in Levinas's work by pointing out the influences from the "Jerusalem Pole" (e.g. talmudic studies) and from the "Athens Pole" (e.g. Russian literature, Husserl). Again, Peperzak (1993) is highly critical of viewing Levinas's work as a bipolarity. He states, "Levinas is not only heir to (a certain) Greece and (a certain) Israel

but also to the Roman Empire with the medieval and modern transformations of its law, to the Slavic and Germanic elements that entered into his formation, and even to a certain form of Christianity that has marked and impregnated two thousand years of European history" (8). Moyn (2005) even argues for a reading of Levinas that recognizes a largely Protestant version of ethics.

11. Judaism, as all cultural and religious institutions, takes on a variety of forms and traditions. There is incredible diversity within the Jewish tradition. This caveat is important for two reasons. First, it situates this work and helps the reader to recognize that this Jewish critique of the Western self is *a* Jewish critique, not *the* Jewish critique. Second, part of the process of unpacking Levinas's work requires a consideration of the form of Judaism out of which he spoke.

12. A significantly larger list could be easily compiled that would include his favorite Russian novelists, his itinerant talmudist teacher, Chouchani, his close friendship with Maurice Blanchot, his incredibly intimate relationship with his wife (Raissa), his dialogues with Derrida (George 2007), his readings of Rosenzweig and Buber, and his intrigue with Bergson's theories on temporality, to list only a few.

13. There is some contention over whether it is appropriate to describe Levinas's family (and Levinas himself) as assimilated. Burggraeve (2007) used this term (22), but others like Gibbs (1992) described it as going too far. The important thing to note is the dynamic exposure to a variety of traditions and their continuous interplay throughout his heritage. Levinas describes his family as being engaged with surrounding culture (Russian literature, etc.) while also valuing their Jewish heritage. His family remained kosher, observed Shabbat and the Jewish holidays, and Levinas received a traditional Hebrew education (Malka 2002/2006, 6).

14. This insight was gained in conversation with Dr. Susannah Heschel.

15. The united opposition against Hasidism, initially under Vilna Gaon in Lithuania, was called the "*misnagdim*" which meant "those who oppose" (Malka 2002/2006). Burggraeve (2007) described Levinas's Judaism as a "Mitnagged Judaism," leading to "exaggerated and obsessional...reservations about mystical enthusiasm" (22, 24) in Levinas's thought. This can be seen, in part, in the relationship between Levinas and Buber. Some have argued that neither one really worked to understand the other (Lipari 2004). Lipari states that their communications were "marked by miscommunication and misrecognition" (122). Furthermore, Levinas—who referred to himself as a materialist—was uncomfortable with language that appeared too "otherworldly," spiritual, or mystical. One can see much of this throughout his critiques of Buber (see chapter 4 in Levinas 1989) and throughout the confessional writings in *Difficult Freedom* (Levinas 1976/1990b).

16. Consider, for instance, the occasional reference in Levinas's work to the term "Jew" or "Hebrew" as inclusive of all persons. However, Levinas also challenged Jewish communities toward a remembrance of their particularity. This was a constant tension in Levinas's work. See an excellent article by Cohen (2003b) entitled, "The Universal in Jewish Particularism: Benamozegh and Levinas."

17. See Cushman's (2007) *A Burning World, An Absent God: Midrash, Hermeneutics, and Relational Psychoanalysis* for a helpful discussion of this topic within psychoanalytic and hermeneutical thought.

18. See also chapters one through three (by Catherine Chalier, Robert Gibbs, and Charles E. Scott, respectively) in Adriann Peperzak's (1995) *Ethics as First Philosophy: The Significance of Emmanuel Levinas for Philosophy, Literature, and Religion,* for varying perspectives on how Levinas's Judaism influenced his philosophical system (and vice versa). Alfred Tauber (1998) writes a compelling description of how Levinas's perspective on time carried forward his Jewish heritage as well.

19. Levinas retained strong feelings of reverence throughout his lifetime for Heidegger's thought and equally strong feelings of anger over his continued political affiliation with the National Socialist party. Levinas's (1968/1994) words are clear: "One can forgive many Germans, but there are some Germans it is difficult to forgive. It is difficult to forgive Heidegger" (25).

20. Levinas was also invited into frequent conversation with John Paul II, who was an avid reader of Levinas's work (Malka 2002/2006). Marion (2000, 2003/2006) has provided a powerful translation of Levinas's work into the Catholic tradition. Westphal (2004) and J. K. Smith (2004) have popularized Levinas within the Reformed Christian tradition. Peperzak (2000) describes the immense popularity of Levinas's work in Christian intellectual circles.

21. Gibbs (1992) argued that "the intellectual atmosphere of Paris has more than a little to do with the segregation. Levinas wants his philosophic works to be received as such. The regnant postreligious consciousness, combined with a never completely absent anti-Semitic scent, makes the reception of boldly Jewish thought by the philosophical community difficult" (22). Furthermore, Levinas hoped to be recognized as actually engaging in philosophical work, not mere theology.

22. See Herzog's (2005) "Benny Levy versus Emmanuel Levinas on 'Being Jewish'" for a helpful article on Levinas's own developmental journey in terms of how he understood the relationship between his Judaism and philosophy. She points to contradictory stances between Levinas's early work, "Etre juif," and his most mature philosophical work, *Otherwise than Being, or Beyond Essence.* See also Ford (1999) for a helpful discussion about Levinas's dismissive stance about the conventional use of theological discourse. Purcell's (2006) *Levinas and Theology* provides an indepth assessment of this issue as well.

23. Some refer to Levinas as postmodern (Westphal 2004) and others as an alternative to modernism and postmodernism (Gantt and Williams 2002), both viable positions. This book describes him as postsecular, which can be interpreted as a part of the postmodern movement. Blond's (1998) book entitled *Post-Secular Philosophy: Between Philosophy and Theology* is a careful look at continental thought and its post-secular turn.

24. Walzer's work on the concept of "thick" and "thin" is helpful in understanding what is meant here. See Walzer (1994) and Dueck and Reimer (2003).

25. One example is the Jewish Midrash, described by Robbins (1991) in the following way: "Midrash, from the root word *darash*, 'to seek or search out...is primarily an attitude toward scripture, rather than a genre: its basic impulse is searching out the Bible for its present relevance, 'actualization,' 'projecting the biblical past onto the present.'" Robbins refers to this as a "biblicization of the present." She states, "Midrash privileges neither a controlling interpretive self, nor is it necessarily oriented toward the (hermeneutic) task of understanding" (16). This book suggests the midrashic dialogical style as a viable alternative heuristic device, one means of relinking reason and identity.

26. This universalizing practice within Levinas can be understood as emerging from a Western, Jewish ethical monotheism, prominent within liberal Jewish circles of European Jewry. This observation was gained in conversation with Dr. Susannah Heschel.

27. A variety of perspectives on Levinas's translation project can be found in the introduction to Levinas's *Nine Talmudic Readings* by Aronowicz (1994); chapter 4 of Robbins (1991) entitled "Alterity and the Judaic: Reading Levinas"; chapters 1 and 7 in Gibbs (1992); chapter 5 of Cohen (1994); Cohen's (2003b) article on Jewish particularism; H. Putnam's (2002) chapter two in the *Cambridge Companion to Levinas*; and Burggraeve (2007).

28. From Plato to Rosenzweig, translation within the Jewish tradition has taken on a variety of forms (Seidman 2006). Cushman (2007) points to poignant parallels between current trends in postmodern hermeneutical theory and the millennia old practices of midrashic methodology and discourse: "intertextuality," "interpersonal engagement," "the absence-presence dialectic," and "prohibitions against idolatry" (47). The notion that truth is born out of relationship is not a recent philosophical innovation or discovery, but rather ancient Jewish wisdom increasingly recognized in the present.

29. Levinas preferred the term "Hebrew" over "Jewish" in order to avoid (as much as possible) pietistic and creedal connotations (Gibbs 1992, 156). However, he readily sanctioned the description of his Hebrew thought as being "the language of the Bible," "biblical Thought," and "above all, always ethical" (157). Greek language and thought is not meant to point at a particular historical or ethnic group. For Levinas, "Greek represents the style...which is universal, conceptual, antimetaphorical, and philosophical. Greek is the language of the university; it is the common language of the West" (157). Over the course of Levinas's career, there was a significant movement in his relationship to the Greek tradition. Early on, Greek thought was the monolithic source of our conceptual and societal ills. However, as his writing gained nuance, he recognized the essential place that Greek thought had as a conversation partner and disseminator of wisdom.

30. Gibbs (1992) takes great pain to avoid reducing Levinas's work to a sterile, unidirectional translation project. He prefers the term "correlation" to capture something of the way in which Judaism "comes to meet philosophy, demanding a different perspective and offering new resources for a thus altered philosophy" (5). According to Gibbs, "We will see not only how philosophy

becomes Jewish, but also how philosophy and its other come into correlation and how the fall of one philosophical vision through criticism by its other creates a new philosophy" (5). Though the term "translation" will continue to be employed throughout this work, its meaning should engender Gibbs's more dynamic "correlational" description.

31. The risk, of course, is that the original meaning from the tradition will be lost in translation or mutate to such a degree that it is no longer recognizable (Gibbs 1992, 2000). Cohen (2003b), Gibbs (2000), and Robbins (1991) provide examples of how this has taken place. Levy accused Levinas of becoming a philosophical convert and being lost on his "return to Judaism" in the mires of Western philosophical thought (Herzog 2005).

32. Foucault's work is analogous in this way. He was particularly interested in the "evocation of 'limit-experiences,' which push us to extremes where conventional categories of intelligibility begin to break down" (Bergo 2007, 2).

Notes to Chapter Three

1. It is unfair to wholly attribute to Greek thought this conception of truth as synonymous with detached reason. Critchley (2001) reminds readers, "For Socrates, and for nearly all ancient philosophers that came after him, the wisdom that philosophy teaches concerns what it might mean to lead a good human life.... Philosophy should form human beings and not just inform them" (1). The Good is an essential part of the World of Ideas that underlies all of rational thought, according to Plato. Socrates was concerned with the good life and Aristotle with the virtues and wisdom. Levinas also reminds his readers of the exceptions throughout Western philosophical history where the Good (Plato), the idea of the Infinite (Descartes' third meditation), and duty/responsibility (Kant) make their appearances. However, it is fair to attribute the foundations and origins of that which became exaggerated and disproportionately emphasized within modernity to its Greek forebears.

2. A large percentage of psychologists understand their theoretical orientation to be cognitive-behavioral. This perspective, the fastest growing within clinical psychology, focuses on the formation of a less distorted rationality, a purer reason with which one can approach the world. Pathology is seen in terms of cognitive distortions and maladaptive cognitions.

3. This chapter's specific focus on the divorce between ethics and reason is not meant to continue subordinating beauty to a lesser quality or dimension. With its particular focus on ethics and justice, Jewish philosophy is often critiqued for its neglect of aesthetics. These critiques are worthy of continued consideration.

4. Levinas references the myth of Gyges throughout many of his works (Levinas 1961/1969, 61, 90, 170, 173, 221–22; 1974/1998c, 113, 118, 145, 149). Kunz (1998) playfully engages this topic and fleshes out what a "Gyges Complex" might look like clinically (111–14).

5. Derrida is referring to the "Greek" as Levinas did—per Western philosophical thought. Regarding his use of the term "autism," it is helpful to look at a

definition of this disposition. Kanner first described autism in 1943 as an "obsessive desire for the maintenance of sameness" (as ctd. in Sarason and Sarason 2005, 516).

6. Alterity and the irreducible otherness of the other become a more and more radical theme throughout Levinas's work, from *On Escape* to "Diachrony and Representation." Cohen (1994) writes, "The movement of Levinas's thought is like that of waves, as Derrida was the first to say, but we must think of the waves as those of an approaching tide, each wave pushing a bit further than the last, each venturing a more radical interpretation of alterity" (135). Hansel, Levinas's son-in-law, suggests that in Levinas's earlier work, he was still functioning from within the sameness of egology as he described the "there is" (*il y a*) and had yet to conceptualize the inbreaking of the other. This can be seen in works such as *Existence & Existents* (Levinas 1947/2001). By the time of *Totality and Infinity*, the face of the other had deeply disturbed any prior egology within Levinas's thought (Hansel 2007).

7. Danziger (1990) points to the origins of this definition of individual differences in the work of Francis Galton and in Walter Dill Scott. Scott assists in operationalizing personality in such a way as to assist in Army personnel selection (and testing) in World War I. This model was also applied, in early forms, to personnel selection for various business operations. See a more thorough history on the development of measurements of individual differences in Leahey's (2004) chapter four "The Rise of Applied Psychology."

8. See Birrell's (2006) article severely critiquing the discourse of a generalized other and showing it to be abstracted from concrete, lived experience. She suggests that such ethical theory as Kohlberg's emerged from a "liberal moral theory" derivative of such thinkers as Rawls and Kant (98).

9. Application of terms like "bipolar" or "schizophrenia" may seem inherently reductive and an epitomization of sameness. However, for some people who struggle with the whiplashing effects of bipolar disorder or the fragmenting effects of schizophrenia, there can be a sense of relief, connection, and meaning that assists in the organization and normalization of their lived experience. Diagnostic categories are not inherently problematic. They are tremendously thoughtful human enterprises to create a sophisticated and helpful language to make sense of human suffering and allow research to parse out particulars in treatment approaches. Regrettably, it is not always used or experienced this way.

10. Levinas (1991/1998a) is wary of using the word "love" due to its thinned out meaning within contemporary life. To him, love is not feelings, fusion, reciprocity, and "care." So, instead of using the word love, he often uses the more poignant words, ethics or responsibilities. Atterton (2007) clarifies this point: "If Levinas...doesn't use the word *love*, it is because for him love is an ambiguous relation, compromised by egotistical need and satisfaction" (254–55). Only ethics, as Levinas (1974/1998c) conceives it, is capable of "evoking...gratuitous personal sacrifices" (573–74). However, when Marion asked Levinas whether his work could be properly understood as that of "love," Levinas accepted and affirmed it (2004, 54). Levinas was not opposed to the word "love" as long as

it was couched in ethical terms instead of that of fulfillment, self-reflexivity, feelings, and romance. Levinas (1991/1998a) writes, "Subjection to the order that orders man, the *I*, to answer for the other is, perhaps, the harsh name of love. Love that is no longer what this compromised word of our literature and our hypocrisies expresses, but the very fact of the approach to the unique, and, consequently, to the absolutely *other*, piercing what merely shows itself—that is, what remains the 'individual of a genus' " (174). The word "love" increasingly appears in Levinas's later works. See his *Entre Nous* (1991/1998a). See also Beals (2007) chapter 3 for a treatment of Levinas's use of the term.

Notes to Chapter Four

Some portions of this chapter incorporate material adapted from my "The great divorce: Ethics and identity" published in *Pastoral Psychology;* "The 'heroic I': A Levinasian critique of modern narcissism" in *Theory and Psychology* (Goodman, Dueck, and Langdal 2010); and "Psychology in pursuit of justice: The works and lives of Emmanuel Levinas and Ignacio Martin-Baro" in *Pastoral Psychology* (Goodman, Walling, and Ghali 2010). Material is used with publisher's permission.

1. See chapter 2 of Heschel's (1963) *Who is Man?* for a creative discussion of how "Know thyself" has functioned within Western history.

2. See Kunz (1998) for a description of the paradox between power and weakness. His example of Vanier and the L'Arche communities in his prologue provides a poignant illustration. Malka (2002/2006) speaks to Levinas's attraction to an inverted power when he states, "Where Nietzsche would have seen an inversion of the powerlessness of the Other, the cunning whereby herd mentality is able to appropriate for itself the power of the wild beasts via myths of guilt, Levinas describes the original inversion as happening the other way. Original 'power,' which is something ego-less, resides with the weak and vulnerable, and it is only through the cunning and atheistic myths told by the ego to itself that the divine forces of illeity, making their demands out of the vulnerable face of the Other, are pushed into oblivion in favor of discourses that signify without remainder and without trace and consolidate their totalitarian rule" (xxiii).

3. See also Baird (2007) for excellent scholarship regarding the meaning of kenosis in Levinas's work.

4. Gantt and Williams (2002) write, "As a discipline, psychology developed well after the defining features of Enlightenment rationality (i.e., objectivism, determinism, mechanism, and individualism) were firmly in place" (3).

5. Foucault describes how language shifted from "punishment" to "normalization" as a "vehicle of more effective control" (Gutting 2003, 4; see also Foucault (2002).

6. However, in making this statement Levinas does not deny the person as a sensate being. Levinas understands material existence to be of significant importance. One of the failures of the modern project is its locating of identity in the rational faculties of the human person, to the exclusion of corporeality,

the body. The material, the body, is essential to Levinas's thought. He hopes to restore the sensate subject. "In *Otherwise than Being* Levinas describes ethical obligation in terms of the subject's corporeal sensibility and proximity, vulnerability, and passivity toward the other. The ethical subject is subject to the other as 'sensibility on the surface of the skin, at the edge of the nerves'.... Since the human person is susceptible to wounding and pain, ethics is a lived, bodily relation to the other. 'Only a subject that eats can be-for-the-other'" (Olthuis 1996, 141). There is not enough space in these pages to attend to the sensate focus of Levinas's thought. A helpful source on this topic is Critchley's (2002) introductory chapter to *The Cambridge Companion to Levinas* (1–32).

7. Both hermeneutical and social constructivist camps argue that for science to have value or meaning, its findings must always be located in a larger narrative. All scientific inquiry is first funded by theoretical assumptions. Hypotheses are generated from assumed philosophical frameworks (e.g., Piaget's Kantian paradigms, etc.). This is the nature of situated consciousness; the inevitability that reason is conditioned, lived, embodied, and historical. There is no philosophy or ideology from "no where" (Nagel 1986). All of science is paradigm-based and a part of a particular research program (with specific philosophical assumptions) (Kuhn 1996).

8. An important caveat is needed here. It is not that empiricism is an inappropriate methodology for the psychological sciences. Empiricism, when localized to an object of study, can be an incredibly powerful and transformative tool, allowing research to be done on schizophrenia, depression, bipolar disorders, trauma, and a myriad of other essential objects of study. It is its application to definitions of the self and the use of the normative order to determine a human nature that overextends the boundaries of a healthy empiricism. It cannot venture into this territory without violating itself and reducing the self.

9. Heschel (1963) writes, "Empirical intemperance, the desire to be exact, to attend to 'hard' facts which are subject to measurement, may defeat its own end. It makes us blind to the fact behind the facts—that what makes a human being human is not just mechanical, biological, and psychological functioning" (9).

10. The concern over this issue fueled the "third force" psychology in the 1960s and 1970s. Humanistic and existential psychologies challenged the field over its reductive descriptions of the human person (May, Angel, and Ellenberger 1994).

11. Richardson, et al. (1999) write that "the psychological science, when conceived mainly along the lines of a natural science, is untenable." They continue by describing three "premises of naturalistic psychology." They are as follows: "First, we found that it relies on an unnecessary and ultimately implausible division of the world into objective facts ordered by causal laws that are what they are independent of our interpretations, and subjective experiences that are either epiphenomena of this 'objective reality' or the results of objectively specifiable causal processes. Second, we saw that its attempt to treat humans as natural objects and to use the methods of the natural sciences to study them is dehumanizing and distortive. Third, we found that the effort to maintain a sharp

distinction between fact and value has been entirely unsuccessful, resulting in an ostensibly objective scientific endeavor that in fact perpetuates a disguised ideology. These notable failures of the naturalistic aspirations for psychology cut to the very core of the attempt to fully objectify psychology, and any remedies that are offered must be similarly thoroughgoing" (277).

12. Furthermore, Cushman and Gilford (2000) show how (particularly with managed care at the helm), psychotherapy's "defining characteristic" is its "normalizing function" (994).

13. Burston and Frie (2006), quoted here, represent a compelling postmodern perspective within psychology that they refer to as a "human science perspective." They summarize the perspective as follows: "For psychotherapists who embrace a human science perspective, the self is never an isolated, sovereign entity, but a product of history, culture, and language as well as personal agency or choice. And in direct contrast to Descartes, postmodernism also rejects any concept of the self or subjectivity that is not understood as culturally, linguistically, or socially constructed" (31). Though the majority of the human science perspective is conducive to the work presented here, there are some critical differences between Levinas's philosophy and this approach. For instance, believing that every concept of the self or subjectivity is constructed denies revelation that comes from beyond our constructional abilities. Levinas contends that there is a self beyond ourselves that shapes our subjectivity. We are not the sovereign determiners of our concepts, even corporately.

Notes to Chapter Five

Some portions of this chapter incorporate material adapted from my "The Great Divorce: Ethics and Identity," "The 'heroic I': A Levinasian Critique of Modern Narcissism," and "Psychology in pursuit of justice: The works and lives of Emmanuel Levinas and Ignacio Martin-Baro." Material is used with publisher's permission.

1. How the self is defined in relationship to that which is other than itself has become one of the most fundamental (though often neglected) questions within contemporary Western thought (Atkins 2005; Burston and Frie 2006; Cohen 2002). How one defines the self has significant implications concerning how the self is understood to relate to other selves (Poland 2000). What questions are asked about the human self often determine the definitions that emerge (Levinas 1985). The question of selfhood has been asked throughout history in a variety of ways. Likewise, the answers to these questions have been manifold. Siegel (2005) suggests that whether explicitly or implicitly, "the nature and meaning of selfhood have been recurring questions...in practically every known human time and place" (3).

2. Levinas (1989) writes that "within a society whose boundaries have become, in a sense, planetary: a society, in which, due to the ease of modern communications and transport, and the worldwide scale of its industrial economy, each person feels simultaneously that he is related to humanity as a whole,

and equally that he is alone and lost. With each radio broadcast and each day's papers one may well feel caught up in the most distant events, and connected to mankind everywhere; but one also understands that one's personal destiny, freedom or happiness is subject to causes which operate with inhumane force. One understands that the very progress of technology—and here I am taking up a commonplace—which relates everyone in the world to everyone else, is inseparable from a necessity which leaves all men anonymous. Impersonal forms of relationship come to replace the more direct forms...in an excessively programmed world" (212). Levinas was even critical of "cafes," which he deemed to be locations of anonymity.

3. Rieff (1987) explains, "Psychoanalysis is yet another method of learning how to endure the loneliness produced by culture...the meaningfulness of social existence no longer grants an inner life at peace with itself" (32).

4. Romanticism was a strong counterresponse to the mechanizing and categorizing of human identity. However, it lacked any meaningful interconnection between identity and goodness. Consider, for instance, the "romantic" response of Rogers and the humanists and existentialists within the "third force" psychologies of the latter part of the twentieth century. They reject the stimulus-response notions of behaviorism and the drive theories of psychoanalysis for their reductions of the human subject and its implicit determinism. However, in their place they suggest a version of human freedom and actualization that almost utterly lacks any form of responsibility to one's neighbor.

5. This example came from a helpful conversation with Derek George around the implications of Levinas's thought.

6. The work of Buber had a profound impact on Levinas. A significant amount of overlap can be seen in their emphasis upon relationality, the ethical encounter, and critiques of the Western self. For a more detailed account of the similarities (and differences), see Atterton, Calarco, and Friedman's (2004) *Levinas and Buber: Dialogue and Difference;* chapter 4 of Levinas's (1989) *The Levinas Reader* entitled "Martin Buber and the Theory of Knowledge"; and Casey's (1999) article entitled, "Levinas and Buber: Transcendence and Society."

7. In Hebrew Scripture, the people of Israel are admonished to care for the poor and the needy. Liberation theology seeks to place this sensibility at the center of theological foci. For this reason, liberation theologians frequently cite Levinas; see the work of Rivera (2007) for an example.

8. Some postmodern writers and critics of postmodernity would disagree with this statement. For some, postmodernity actually radicalizes and intensifies the individual subject. That is, within particular forms of postmodernism, individual subjectivity is deemed to be the only source of knowledge and its own authority. If there are no overarching frameworks with which to adjudicate truth, then each subject provides its own interpretation that has equal merit. Each text has an infinite amount of interpretations. See Siegel (2005) for an alternate and critical perspective on postmodern depictions of the individual subject.

9. Levinas has been described as a posthumanist instead of an antihumanist. Lacan would be an example of an antihumanist (Roberts 2007).

10. Welsh and Dueck (2007) have written, "One of the consequences of such a fundamental cultural shift towards the objectification of all knowledge has been the impoverishment of human psychic life through a gradual depletion of the moral and ethical frameworks in which human identity had been deeply steeped prior to the scientific revolution" (1).

11. It is impressive to consider how closely this mirrors the colonialistic imperialism of Western modernity, the insular quality of nation-states within the modern era, and the foreign policy of the Western powers over the last 500 years. See Toulmin's (1990) *Cosmopolis: The Hidden Agenda of Modernity* (1990). The works of Walzer, Foucault, and Dueck point to the ways in which the political world/ethos shapes the language of self-understanding propagated in any given society.

12. Cohen (2002) states this clearly: "Psychology's logic is inexorable: all meaning comes from the psyche, hence is immanent, psychological.... All other explanations that claim to exceed the immanence of the psychological or sociological are *merely* mythological.... Each psyche becomes a world, the world" (39). This is what Levinas (1985) refers to as the "sovereign I" (101).

13. Cushman (1995) challenges psychologists to move beyond merely maintaining the status quo. If social responsibility is not inherent in our practice as "healers", then we are merely "mechanics" of the machinery of a society, with all of its values—however just or unjust.

14. Are they part of a general system of what Rieff (2006) refers to as "deathworks"—"an assault, a blow, a battle against something vital to the established culture" (xxiii), which we become blind to because of its status as commonsensical? Rieff (1987, 2006) refers to "moral demands" as one of the vital elements that is omitted by cultures caught in the "deathworks" and critiques contemporary constructs of the self as being products of the "triumph of the therapeutic culture," where commitments to authority, sacral order, and any sense of demandedness and covenant have been lost. The emphasis upon individual fulfillment and expressiveness as the "goods" of the modern self trumps the formation of any "hypergoods" that emerge from outside of this self (Taylor 1989). See also Brueggemann (1999).

15. The issue of being "subject to" is fundamental to demandedness. Persons struggle against being subject to anyone beyond themselves. When subjection does take place, it is commonly a subjection to the cultural status quo, authoritative structures (government, etc.), and various forms of self-interest. In religious contexts, subjection to commonly comes in the forms of being subject to a reified and rigid set of behavioral proscriptions (mistaken for morality) or types of experience (emotional experiences of God, etc.). We are hampered, within our language and context, in our desire and ability to be subject to glorious and painful relationship to another wherein God moves, speaks, and conditions. A giving of ourselves—in covenant—to loving relationship, sacrificial relationship, other-centered relationship is the beginning of a monumental shift, a countercultural practice, a prophetic inflow into our lives. It is the beginning of justice.

Notes to Chapter Six

An earlier and briefer version of this chapter, "*Hineni* and transference: The remembering and forgetting of the other," was published in *Pastoral Psychology*. Also incorporated into this chapter is material adapted from "Hearing 'Thou shall not kill' when all the evidence is to the contrary: Psychoanalysis, enactment, and Jewish ethics" published in Lewis Aron and Libby Henik's edited work, *Answering a Question with a Question: Judaism and Contemporary Psychoanalysis*. Incorporated and adapted material was reused with permission from the publishers.

1. See, for instance, the work of Blasi. He argues that the very structure of the self, one's identity, is a more robust predictor of moral action than cognition. Though cognition (moral judgment and consciousness) is important, it is not sufficient in explaining moral behavior. This marks a significant shift in emphasis within moral psychological theory that had previously maintained a model driven primarily by Kohlbergian stages that focus primarily on moral attributes and rationality.

2. Levinas (1976/1990b) articulates, "Moral consciousness is not an experience of values, but an access to exterior being: external being is, *par excellence,* the Other" (293). Levinas, quoting Scripture, continues, "Be merciful like Him." In the same paragraph he writes, "The attributes of God are given not in the indicative, but in the imperative. The knowledge of God comes to us like a commandment, like a *Mitzvah*. To know God is to know what must be done" (17).

3. This represents a complicated issue as the shape of the self is a consequence of a variety of variables and levels (intrapsychic, biological, interpersonal, historical, sociopolitical, etc.), though this work ultimately contends that it is within the context of one's relational history that this shape takes form more fully. It is in relationship to others that our orientation to others finds its shape. It is, in this way, highly reciprocal. See Aron (1996); Balswick, King, and Reimer (2005); Lerner (2001); Mitchell (1988).

4. Putnam (2002) argues, "When Levinas speaks of saying *me voici* what he means is virtually unintelligible if one is not aware of the Biblical resonance" (38). This is another example of the way in which Levinas's work can only be properly understood with a certain degree of theological and biblical literacy (see chapter 2). Putnam further argues that this is another example of the universalization of a Jewish theme: "[J]ust as the traditional Jew finds his dignity in obeying the divine command, so Levinas thinks that every human being should find his or her dignity in the obeying of the fundamental ethical command...the command to say *hineni* to the other, to say *hineni* with what Levinas calls 'infinite' responsibility" (39).

5. It represents a "We will do and we will hear" that characterizes the receiving of the Torah at the foot of Sinai. In "The Temptation of Temptation," Levinas (1968/1994) describes how the Israelites obey and act before being reassured by knowledge and rationality. He states, "We will do *in order* to understand...reveals the deep structure of subjectivity....Thus, the concern to show,

in the first place, that the apparently upside-down order is, on the contrary, fundamental" (42). Doing precedes hearing.

6. See also Levinas's description of the *à-Dieu* throughout *Of God Who Comes to Mind* (1998b, 172–77).

7. Derrida (2007) writes about Abraham's response, "Here I am," as an inevitable facet of our relation to the other. Even when we denounce or repel the other, we are still functioning out of responsiveness. Even when we say "No" to the other, it means that there was first a question and call upon us to which we are compelled to respond.

8. Levinas (1974/1998c) uses the analogy of maternity as a picture of the human psyche lived for the other (see also Cohen 1994; 2002; Olthuis 1996, 144). He describes the feminine in highly passive terms, receptive and obligated. These statements have brought on considerable criticism from feminist critiques such as de Beauvoir, Irigaray, Chanter, Chalier, Katz, and Heschel. Derrida, too, is critical of Levinas on this issue. See Cohen's (1994) chapter entitled "The Metaphysics of Gender" (195–219) for a defense of Levinas on this subject.

9. In *Otherwise than Being*, Levinas wrote, "The fact that the other, my neighbor, is also a third party with respect to another, who is also a neighbor, is the birth of thought, consciousness, justice and philosophy. The unlimited initial responsibility, which justifies this concern for justice, for oneself, and for philosophy can be forgotten. In this forgetting consciousness is a pure egoism. But egoism is neither first nor last" (128).

10. Lynne Layton (2009) points her readers to Judith Butler's (2004) work that is "indebted to Levinas" and "develops a relational view of subjectivity that revalues vulnerability, dependency, and suffering, and makes them the ground of a politics that would differ significantly from a politics based in rights and an autonomous self" (118).

11. Levinas was critical of Freudian depictions of the unconscious (See chapter 4 in Levinas 1974/1998c). However, Levinas might have been more receptive to some of the more recent descriptions of the unconscious coming out of the relational psychoanalytic school of thought. There has been a significant amount of increased interest in the interchange between Levinas and psychoanalytic theory in recent years. See, for instance, Donnel Stern (2003). Particular psychoanalytic thinkers have argued that Levinas's critiques of the Freudian unconscious were misguided and based upon an unsophisticated reading of Freudian theory (Hutchens 2007). In recent literature, there have been some serious critiques concerning Levinas's depth of understanding of Freud and psychoanalysis. Still others have worked to draw strong parallels between Freud and Levinas (Atterton 2007; Gans 1996; Tallon 2007).

12. By "forgotten" here, one's repressed or disowned history is being spoken about, not the forgotten dyad referred to earlier.

13. Levinas used the term "light" synonymously with a Husserlian depiction of consciousness. For Husserl, the "light" of one's constitutional abilities illuminates what is being seen, allowing it to be seen. For an example of Levinas's critique, see *Time and the Other* (1987, 64–66).

14. Freud was careful to distinguish two types of transference: obstructive vs. facilitating transference.

15. Relationality is a fairly popular trend within contemporary theory. It is a counter-response to the monadic descriptions of the person preponderant throughout much twentieth century literature. The individual subject is not as viable as it was previously. In place of *cogito*, an emphasis upon relationality has emerged, with theories beginning to shift to the interhuman. A prime example within psychology has been the emergence of the relational psychoanalytic and intersubjective schools of thoughts. Relational psychoanalysis—a response to the drive models of Freudian psychoanalysis—works to translate much psychoanalytic theory into a more relational and intersubjective language to better reflect contemporary shifts in philosophy and epistemological findings. See Mitchell and Aron 1999; Mitchell 1988; Aron 1996; Stolorow, Atwood, and Brandchaft 1994). However, Levinas did not suggest relationship as a remedy for the egology of Western thought. Ethical, asymmetrical relationship is significantly different from mere emphasis upon the interhuman. It is a radical relationality where the other constitutes the self. Coming from a Jewish perspective, he asked about the ethics within the relationship. Relationship, in general, is less important than responsibility, which is only possible within relationship. Overall, current epistemological shifts are a beneficial corrective that might allow more space for inclusion of Levinas's thought, providing an opportunity for positive translation.

16. Language, conversation, and speaking hold enormous power in Levinas's thought. He spoke about the face not as physiology, but as language (Levinas 1974/1998c). The following quote further expresses this point: "Consciousness is the impossibility of invading reality like a wild vegetation that absorbs or breaks or pushes back everything around it. The turning back on oneself of consciousness is the equivalent not of self-contemplation but of the fact of not existing violently and naturally, of speaking to the Other" (Levinas 1976/1990b, 9). For a helpful article that links Levinas's concept of conversation and psychoanalysis as a "talking cure," see Atterton (2007).

17. Levinas took seriously the bounds of history. Levinas's work is a cousin to the hermeneutical tradition, as well as a staunch alternative to the Heideggerian tradition. It is a reframe of the story, allowing for a different ending. He recognized the situatedness of experience and the concreteness of the ego. Corporeality and experience, significant emphases in Levinas's thought, are within history. In a conversation with Marion, Levinas affirms the hermeneutic notion of horizons as fundamental to phenomenology (Horner 2005). However, Ricoeur (1992) critiques Levinas for not adequately recognizing the historicity of being and the situatedness of human consciousness, even in relationship to an infinite other.

Notes to Chapter Seven

Incorporated into this chapter is material adapted from "Hearing 'thou shall not kill' when all the evidence is to the contrary: Psychoanalysis, enactment, and Jewish ethics" published in *Answering a Question with a Question: Judaism and*

Contemporary Psychoanalysis (2010). Material is reused with permission from the publishers.

1. In a recent *Psychoanalytic Dialogues*, Lynne Layton (2009) addresses the issue of empathy, complicity in sociopolitical origins of suffering, and the experience of patient's suffering. It is a helpful exploration that shares a great deal with a Levinasian sensibility as it redefines terms in order to reconnect analysts with a more substantive sense of recognition of the issues of justice resident in our definitions and meanings.

Notes to Chapter Eight

1. People living in these residences are caught in the web of memories and regrets, living and reliving experiences without escape from their claustrophobic circuit. For instance, out of curiosity, two characters ventured out to find the home of Napoleon and upon looking at him through one of the windows discovered him "walking up and down—up and down all the time—left-right, left-right—never stopping for a moment…he never rested. And muttering to himself all the time. 'It was Soult's fault. It was Ney's fault. It was Josephine's fault. It was the fault of the Russians. It was the fault of the English.' Like that all the time. Never stopped for a moment. A little, fat man and he looked kind of tired. But he didn't seem able to stop it" (Lewis 1946, 12).

2. Levinas writes about two different forms of insomnia. First, the vacuousness of being and its brutal lack of subjectivity (see Alford 2002 and Marcus 2008 for a clearer picture of this), what Levinas terms the "there is" (*il y a*), generates a terror that keeps one from sleep. This terror dominated Levinas's early works, particularly *On Escape* and *Existence and Existents*. Some have argued that this early emphasis was informed by Levinas's experience of imprisonment and catastrophic familial losses during World War II (Alford 2002; Cohen 1994). The second form of insomnia described by Levinas gives an account of the violent awakening that the self experiences when its egoist slumber is disrupted in proximity to the other. It is this second account that will be the focus of this piece.

3. Mitchell (2003) states, "It is the very otherness of the other that defines the limits to one's own omnipotence and creates the vulnerability, often the experience of helplessness, that accompanies desire. Thus romantic longing skates always on the edge of humiliation" (141).

4. Critchley (1999) writes, "Trauma is a 'non-intentional affectivity,' it tears into my subjectivity like an explosion, like a bomb that detonates without warning, like a bullet that hits me in the dark, fired from an unseen guy and by an unknown assailant" (190).

5. One issue that is not given an appropriate amount of attention throughout this work is the applicability of Levinas's thought to persons who are already powerless or selfless. A significant question posed by feminist scholars is whether Levinas's ethical discourse of sacrifice, substitution, kenosis, and subjection is appropriate for particular groups that bear a history of being in the one-down position. Levinas's thought may challenge the egoist fantasies of dominant

cultures, but does it empower the powerless? Feminists, for instance, have argued against Levinas's language regarding the feminine and the facets of his discourse that implicitly call women to remain in a trodden upon and selfless position (Chanter 2001; Olthuis 1996). See Cohen's (1994) chapter "The Metaphysics of Gender" for a powerful defense of Levinas on this topic. See also the works of Irigaray (1991) and Chanter (2001) for some of the well-formulated feminist critiques of Levinas's thought. The lack of attention to this critique in this work is merely due to the lack of space. A healthy dialogue between feminist thinkers and Levinas's thought allows for rich social critique and balance, which should also be applied to the situation of particular ethnic minorities that have been oppressively subjected historically.

Another poignant example of this critique is the question of how a person who has never been allowed to develop a sense of self (e.g., trauma victim) can understand and apply Levinas's framework. Is it fair to state that one needs to have a self in order to sacrifice this self to the other? However, this retains the baggage of egological depictions of the self as a possession or object. Is it fair to consider what type of self is a prerequisite for kenosis to be made possible? The difficulty with this is that it further maintains a language for selfhood that is tied to attributes and characteristics. The issues of challenging the very syntax of our constructs of the self can be seen in this example, but they need considerable more attention and nuance.

6. Laing (1969) and Fromm (1955), among many other social theorists, consider the sociopolitical forces that entrap the self in alienation. Cushman (1995) explains how economic infrastructures exert significant influence on the configuring of consumptive and inward-facing selves. Becker (1973) views the narcissism inherent in being organisms as contributing to the formation of self-centering myths we tell ourselves. Social context provides much of the terrain and landscape upon which we build our residences in Hell. This is rarely attended to adequately in psychotherapeutic theories and practices.

Notes to Conclusion

1. Much has been written on the opaqueness of Levinas's writing and whether it is an essential facet of what he is working to accomplish or an unnecessarily obtuse and frustrating corpus. Beals (2007) provides a thorough summary of varying opinions on this point in his second chapter entitled, "Levinasian Terminology."

2. Derrida, Caputo, and Ricoeur have each written considerably on the topic of Levinas's use of hyperbolic terms and whether his overall vision is an impossible ideal. Both Derrida (1978) and Caputo (1993) hold that he is speaking about an impossible ethic, but one that inspires and calls us forward. Levinas (2004) responds to charges of utopianism in his interview with Kearney. Ricoeur (1992) understands Levinas's hyperbolistic expressions and the impossibility of his ethic as philosophically irresponsible and inapplicable in its current form (Beals 2007) and "overkill" (Ford 1999, 84).

3. There is a contentious debate within secondary texts on Levinas concerning whether his ethics are descriptive or prescriptive. Some scholars understand Levinas as remaining strictly adherent to the phenomenological method and thus finding ethics to be a sensate description of human experience. Others understand Levinas as prescriptively calling for ethics to be a part of human experience. In this work, this opposition—descriptive versus prescriptive—is considered misleading because, from a Jewish perspective, the descriptive and prescriptive are inextricably interwoven. As a Jew, Levinas cannot describe human experience without a deeper sensibility about prescriptive function.

4. This is not to deny the extraordinary richness of historical identity. Gadamer's "historically situated" consciousness need not stand in opposition to what is being stated. Rather, Levinas's radicality is that history, situatedness, embodiment, and events are not the original and most primary processes. Levinas is not dichotomizing between ethics and history. Rather, he shows that history must be conditioned by what precedes and lives within it, ethics. History, consciousness, and our situatedness are ultimately derivative of an ethical relationship to the other.

5. Gibbs (1992) writes, "The function of eternity is characteristically ethical and as such fractures the totality which a historicist immanentism presupposes" (26).

REFERENCES

Adler, A. 1979. *Superiority and social interest: A collection of later writings*. New York: W. W. Norton and Company.

Alford, C. F. 2002. *Levinas, the Frankfurt school, and psychoanalysis*. Middletown, CT: Wesleyan University Press.

———. 2007. Levinas, Winnicott, and therapy. *Psychoanalytic Review* 94: 529–51.

American Psychological Association. 1992. Ethical principles of psychologists and code of conduct. *American Psychological Association*. Accessed May 12, 2006. http://www.apa.org/ethics/code1992.html.

Aron, L. 1996. *A meeting of minds: Mutuality in psychoanalysis*. Hillsdale, NJ: The Analytic Press.

———. 2003. The paradoxical place of enactment in psychoanalysis: Introduction. *Psychoanalytic Dialogues,* 13(5): 623–32.

Aronowicz, A. 1994. Translator's introduction to *Nine talmudic readings* by E. Levinas. Bloomington: Indiana University Press.

Atkins, K., ed. 2005. *Self and subjectivity*. Malden, MA: Blackwell Publishing.

Atterton, P. 2007. "The talking cure": The ethics of psychoanalysis. *Psychoanalytic Review,* 94:553–76.

Atterton, P., M. Calarco, and M. Friedman, eds. 2004. *Levinas and Buber: Dialogue and difference*. Pittsburgh: Duquesne University Press.

Badiou, A. 2002. *Ethics: An essay on the understanding of evil*. New York: Verso.

Baird, M. 2007. Whose kenosis? An analysis of Levinas, Derrida, and Vattimo on God's self-emptying and the secularization of the west. *The Heythrop Journal* 48:423–37.

Balswick, J., P. King, and K. Reimer. 2005. *The reciprocating self: Human development in a theological perspective.* Downers Grove, IL: InterVarsity Press.

Barrett, W. 1958. *Irrational man: A study in existential philosophy.* New York: Anchor Books.

Beals, C. 2007. *Levinas and the wisdom of love: The question of invisibility.* Waco, TX: Baylor University Press.

Beavers, A. F. 1993. *Emmanuel Levinas and the prophetic voice of postmodernity.* Retrieved September 16, 2007. http://faculty.evansville.edu/tb2/trip/prophet_print.htm.

Becker, E. 1973. *The denial of death.* New York: The Free Press.

Bellah, R. N., R. Madsen, W. M. Sullivan, A. Swidler, and S. M. Tipton. 1985. *Habits of the heart: Individualism and commitment in American life.* Berkeley: University of California Press.

Benjamin, J. 1998. *Shadow of the other: Intersubjectivity and gender in psychoanalysis.* New York: Routledge.

Berger, P. 1970. *A rumor of angels: Modern society and the rediscovery of the supernatural.* New York: Anchor Books.

Bergo, B. 2007. Emmanuel Levinas. *Stanford encyclopedia of philosophy.* Retrieved April 30, 2007. http://plato.stanford.edu/entries/levinas/

Bernasconi, R., and D. Wood, eds. 1988. *The provocation of Levinas: Rethinking the other.* London: Routledge.

Bernstein, R. 1976. *The restructuring of social and political theory.* Philadelphia: University of Pennsylvania Press.

———. 1983. *Beyond objectivism and relativism: Science, hermeneutics, and praxis.* Philadelphia: University of Pennsylvania Press.

Birrell, P. J. 2006. An ethic of possibility: Relationship, risk, and presence. *Ethics and Behavior* 16:95–115.

Blasi, A. 1983. Moral cognition and moral action: A theoretical perspective. *Developmental Review* 3:178–210.

———. 1984. Moral identity: Its role in moral functioning. In *Morality, moral behavior and moral development,* ed. W. M. Kurtines and J. L. Gewirtz. New York: Wiley.

———. 1994. Bridging moral cognition and moral action: A critical review of the literature. Vol. 2 of *Fundamental research in moral development,* ed. B. Puka. New York: Garland Publishing.

Bloechl, J., ed. 2000. *The face of the other and the trace of God: Essays on the philosophy of Emmanuel Levinas.* New York: Fordham University Press.

Blond, P. 1998. Emmanuel Levinas: God and phenomenology. In *Postsecular philosophy: Between philosophy and theology,* ed. P. Blond. London: Routledge.

Bloom, A. 1987. *The closing of the American mind.* New York: Simon and Schuster.

Boesky, D. 1982. Acting out: A reconsideration of the concept. *International Journal of Psychoanalysis* 63:39–55.

Bromberg, P. 1998. *Standing in the spaces: Essays on clinical process, trauma, and dissociation.* Hillsdale, NJ: Analytic Press.

———. 2003. Something wicked this way comes. Trauma, dissociation, and conflict: The space where psychoanalysis, cognitive science, and neuroscience overlap. *Psychoanalytic Psychology* 20:558–74.

———. 2006. *Awakening the dreamer: Clinical journeys.* New York: Routledge.

Brown, L. 1997. Ethics in psychology: *Cui Bono?* In *Critical psychology: An introduction,* ed. D. Fox and I. Prilleltensky. Thousand Oaks, CA: Sage Publications.

———. 2004. *Subversive dialogues: Theory in feminist therapy.* New York: Basic Books.

Browning, D. S. 1987. *Religious thought and the modern psychologies: A critical conversation in the theology of culture.* Philadelphia: Fortress Press.

Brueggemann, W. 1999. *The covenanted self: Explorations in law and covenant.* Minneapolis: Fortress Press.

Buber, M. 1958. *I and thou.* New York: Charles Scribner's Sons.

Burggraeve, R. 2000. The Bible gives to thought: Levinas on the possibility and proper nature of biblical thinking. In *The face of the other and the trace of God,* ed. J. Bloechl. New York: Fordham University Press.

———. 2007. *The wisdom of love in the service of love: Emmanuel Levinas on justice, peace, and human rights.* Milwaukee: Marquette University Press.

Burston, D., and R. Frie. 2006. *Psychotherapy as a human science.* Pittsburgh: Duquesne University Press.

Butler, J. 2004. *Precarious life: The powers of mourning and violence.* New York: Verso.

———. 2005. *Giving an account of oneself.* New York: Fordham University Press.

Caper, R. 2000. *Immaterial facts: Freud's discovery of psychic reality and Klein's development of his work.* New York: Routledge.

Caputo, J. 1993. *Demythologizing Heidegger.* Bloomington: Indiana University Press.

Casey, D. 1999. Levinas and Buber: Transcendence and Society. *Sophia* 38: 69–92.

Century of the self. Curtis, A., dir. 2002. United Kingdom: BBC Documentary.

Chanter, T. 2001. *Feminist interpretations of Emmanuel Levinas re-reading the canon.* University Park: Pennsylvania State University Press.

Chused, J. F. 1991. The evocative power of enactments. *Journal of the American Psychoanalytic Association* 39:615–40.

Clapp, R. 1993. *Families at the crossroads: Beyond traditional and modern options.* Downers Grove, IL: Intervarsity Press.

Clegg, J. W., and B. D. Slife. 2005. Epistemology and the hither side: A Levinasian account of relational knowing. *European Journal of Psychotherapy, Counseling, and Health* 7:65–76.

Clouser, R. A. 2005. *The myth of religious neutrality: An essay on the hidden role of religious belief in theories.* Rev. ed. South Bend: University of Notre Dame Press.

Cohen, R. 1985. Translator's introduction to *Ethics and identity: Conversations with Philippe Nemo* by E. Levinas. Pittsburgh: Duquesne University Press.

———. 1994. *Elevations: The height of the good in Rosenzweig and Levinas.* Chicago: The University of Chicago Press.

———. 2002. Maternal psyche. In *Psychology for the other: Levinas, ethics, and the practice of psychology,* ed. E. Gantt and R. Williams. Pittsburgh: Duquesne University Press.

———. 2003a. Translator's introduction to *Humanism of the other* by E. Levinas. Chicago: University of Illinois.

———. 2003b. The universal in Jewish particularism: Benamozegh and Levinas. In *Religious experience and the end of metaphysics,* ed. J. Bloechl. Bloomington: Indiana University Press.

———. 2005. Review of "On escape." *European Journal of Psychotherapy, Counselling, and Health* 7:109–15.

———, ed. 1986. *Face to face with Levinas*. Albany, NY: SUNY Press.

Critchley, S. 1999. *Ethics-politics-subjectivity: Essays on Derrida, Levinas, and contemporary French thought*. Brooklyn: Verso.

———. 2001. *Continental philosophy: A very short introduction*. New York: Oxford University Press.

———. 2002. Introduction. In *The Cambridge companion to Levinas*, ed. C. Critchley and B. Bernasconi. New York: Cambridge University Press.

———. 2007. *Infinitely demanding: Ethics of commitment, politics of resistance*. New York: Verso.

Cushman, P. 1990. Why the self is empty: Toward a historically situated psychology. *American Psychologist* 45:599–611.

———. 1995. *Constructing the self, constructing America: A cultural history of psychotherapy*. Garden City, NY: DaCapo Press.

———. 2007. A burning world, an absent God: Midrash, hermeneutics, and relational psychoanalysis. *Contemporary Psychoanalysis* 43:47–87.

———. 2009. Empathy—what one hand giveth, the other taketh away: Commentary on paper by Lynne Layton. *Psychoanalytic Dialogues* 19:121–37.

Cushman, P., and P. Gilford. 2000. Will managed care change our way of being? *American Psychologist* 55:985–96.

Danziger, K. 1990. *Constructing the subject: Historical origins of psychological research*. Cambridge: Cambridge University Press.

———. 1997. *Naming the mind: How psychology found its language*. Thousand Oaks, CA: Sage Publications Inc.

Davis, C. 1996. *Levinas: An introduction*. South Bend: University of Notre Dame Press.

Davies, J. M., and M. G. Frawley. 1991. Dissociative processes and transference-countertransference paradigms in the psychoanalytically oriented treatment of adult survivors of childhood sexual abuse. In *Relational Psychoanalysis: The Emergence of A Tradition*, ed. S. Mitchell and L. Aron. New York: The Analytic Press.

Derrida, J. 1978. *Writing and difference*, trans. A. Bass. Chicago: The University of Chicago Press.

———. 2007. Abraham, the Other. In *Judeities: Questions for Jacques Derrida* by B. Bergo, J. Cohen, and R. Zagury-Orly. New York: Fordham University Press.

De Tocqueville, A. [1835] 1969. *Democracy in America*, trans. G. Lawrence. Garden City, NY: Doubleday and Company, Inc.

Doherty, W. A. 1995. *Soul searching: Why psychotherapy must promote moral responsibility.* New York: Basic Books.

Dostoyevsky, F. [1880] 2004. *The Brothers Karamazov*, trans. Constance Garnett. New York: Farrar, Straus, and Giroux.

———. [1866] 2008. *Crime and punishment.* London: Oxford University Press.

Douglas, H. 2005. The idea of a possibility. *European Journal of Psychotherapy, Counseling, and Health* 7:89–95.

Dudiak, J. 2007. 'God' and 'Beyond': Reading Kierkegaard and Levinas with Professor Westphal. Paper presented at annual meeting, North American Levinas Society, June 10–12, 2007, Purdue University, West Lafayette, IN.

Dueck, A. 1995. *Between Jerusalem and Athens: Ethical perspectives on culture, religion, and psychotherapy.* Grand Rapids, MI: Baker Books.

———. 2002. Babel, Esperanto, shibboleths, and Pentecost: Can we talk? *Journal of Psychology and Christianity* 21:72–80.

Dueck, A., and D. Goodman. 2007. Expiation, substitution, and surrender: Levinasian implications for psychotherapy. *Pastoral Psychology* 55:601–17.

Dueck, A., and T. Parsons. 2007. Religion, Levinas, and psychotherapy. *Pastoral Psychology* 55:271–82.

Dueck, A., and K. Reimer. 2003. Retrieving the virtues in psychotherapy: Thick and thin discourse. *American Behavioral Scientist* 46:1–15.

———. 2009. A *Peaceable Psychology: Christian therapy in a world of many cultures.* Grand Rapids, MI: Brazos Press.

Ellis, A., and S. Blau, eds. 1998. *Albert Ellis reader: A guide to well-being using rationale motive behavior therapy.* New York: Kensington Publishing Corp.

Engel, F. 1941. *Ludwig Feuerbach and the outcome of classical German philosophy.* New York: International.

Enriquez, V. 1993. *From colonial to liberation psychology: The Philippine experience.* Manila: University of Philippines Press.

Ericksen, R., and S. Heschel, eds. 1999. *Betrayal: German churches and the Holocaust*. Minneapolis: Augsburg Fortress Publishers.

Faulconer, J. E. 2005. Knowledge of the other. *European Journal of Psychotherapy, Counseling, and Health* 7:49–63.

Faulconer, J. E., and R. Williams. 1985. Temporality in human action: An alternative to positivism and historicism. *American Psychologist* 40:1179–88.

———, eds. 1990. *Reconsidering psychology: Perspectives from contemporary continental philosophy*. Pittsburgh: Duquesne University Press.

Ford, D. 1999. *Self and salvation: Being transformed*. Cambridge: Cambridge University Press.

Foucault, M. 1970. *The order of things: An archaeology of the human sciences*. New York: Vintage Books.

———. 1977. *Power/knowledge: Selected interviews and other writings*. New York: Pantheon Books.

———. 1990. *The history of sexuality, Vol. 1: An introduction*. New York: Vintage.

———. 2003. *Abnormal: Lectures at the Collège De France 1974–1975*. New York: Picador.

Fox, D., and I. Prilleltensky, eds. 1997. *Critical psychology: An introduction*. Thousand Oaks, CA: Sage Publications.

Freud, S. [1905] 1958a. Fragment of an analysis of a case of hysteria. Vol. 7 of *The standard edition of the complete psychological works of Sigmund Freud*, ed. and trans. J. Strachey. London: Hogarth Press.

———. [1914] 1958b. Remembering, repeating, and working-through. Vol. 12 of *The standard edition of the complete psychological works of Sigmund Freud*, ed. and trans. J. Strachey. London: Hogarth Press.

———. [1927] 1961a. *The future of an illusion*. Trans. J. Strachey. New York: W. W. Norton and Company.

———. [1930] 1961b. *Civilization and its discontents*. Trans. J. Strachey. New York: W. W. Norton and Company.

Fromm, E. 1947. *Man for himself: An inquiry into the psychology of ethics*. New York: Henry Holt and Company.

———. 1955. *The sane society*. New York: Henry Holt and Company.

Fryer, D. R. 2007. What Levinas and psychoanalysis can teach each other, or how to be a mensch without going meshugah. *Psychoanalytic Review* 94:577–94.

Gabbard, G. O. 1995. Countertransference: The emerging common ground. *International Journal of Psychoanalysis* 76:475–85.

Gadamer, H. G. 1975. *Truth and method.* 2d rev. ed. New York: Continuum Publishing Company.

Gans, S. 1996. Levinas and Freud: Talmudic inflections in ethics and psychoanalysis. In *Facing the other: The ethics of Emmanuel Levinas,* ed. S. Hand. Richmond, England: Curzon Press.

Gantt, E. E., and R. N. Williams, eds. 2002. *Psychology for the other: Levinas, ethics, and the practice of psychology.* Pittsburgh: Duquesne University Press.

George, D. 2007. *Theo-logical hospitality: Every other as w(holy) other.* Unpublished ms.

Gergen, K. 2000. *The saturated self: Dilemma of identity in contemporary life.* New York: Basic Books.

———. 2001. Psychological science in a postmodern context. *American Psychologist* 56:803–13.

Gergen, K. J., A. Gulerce, A. Lock, and G. Misra. 1996. Psychological science in cultural context. *American Psychologist* 51:496–503.

Gibbs, R. 1992. *Correlations in Rosenzweig and Levinas.* Princeton: Princeton University Press.

———. 2000. *Why ethics? Signs of responsibilities.* Princeton: Princeton University Press.

Ginot, E. 2007. Intersubjectivity and neuroscience: Understanding enactments and their therapeutic significance within emerging paradigms. *Psychoanalytic Psychology* 24:317–32.

Goodman, D. 2009. Emmanuel Levinas. In *Encyclopedia of Psychology and Religion,* ed. D. Leeming, K. Madden, and S. Marlan. New York: Springer Reference.

———. 2010. Hearing "thou shall not kill" when all the evidence is to the contrary: Psychoanalysis, enactment, and Jewish ethics. In *Answering a Question with a Question: Judaism and Contemporary Psychoanalysis,* ed. L. Aron and L. Henik's. Brighton, MA: Academic Studies Press.

Goodman, D., A. Dueck, and J. Langdal. 2010. The 'heroic I': A Levinasian critique of modern narcissism. *Theory & Psychology* 20(5):1–19.

Goodman, D., and Grover, S. 2008. Hineni and transference: The remembering and forgetting of other. *Pastoral Psychology* 56(6):561–71.

Goodman, D., and Marcelli, A. 2010. The great divorce: Ethics and identity. *Pastoral Psychology* 59(5):563–83.

Goodman, D., S. Walling, and A. Ghali, 2010. Psychology in pursuit of justice: The works and lives of Emmanuel Levinas and Ignacio Martin-Baro. *Pastoral Psychology* 59(5):585–602.

Gutting, G. 2003. Michel Foucault. *Stanford encyclopedia of philosophy*. Accessed March 10, 2006. http://plato.stanford.edu/entries/foucault/.

Haidt, J. 2003. The moral emotions. In *Handbook of Affective Sciences*, ed. R. J. Davidson, K. R. Scherer, and H. H. Goldsmith. Oxford: Oxford University Press.

Hallie, P. 1994. *Lest innocent blood be shed: The story of the village of Le Chambon and how goodness happened there*. New York: HarperPerennial. Original edition, 1979. New York: Harper & Row.

Hansel, J. 2007. "Being otherwise" and "being Jewish" in Emmanuel Levinas's early work. Paper presented at annual meeting, North American Levinas Society, June 10–12, 2007, Purdue University, West Lafayette, IN.

Harold, P. 2009. *Prophetic politics: Emmanuel Levinas and the sanctification of suffering*. Athens: Ohio University Press.

Harrington, D. R. 2002. A Levinasian psychology, perhaps.... In *Psychology for the other: Levinas, ethics and the practice of psychology*, ed., E. E. Gantt and R. N. Williams. Pittsburgh: Duquesne University Press.

Heidegger, M. 1977. *The question concerning technology and other essays*. Trans. W. Lovitt. New York: Harper Colophon.

———. [1927] 1996. *Being and time*. Trans. J. Stambaugh. Albany: State University of New York.

Herzog, A. 2005. Benny Levy versus Emmanuel Levinas on "being Jewish" *Oxford Journals* 26:15–30.

Heschel, A. J. 1955. *God in search of man: A philosophy of Judaism*. New York: Farrar, Straus, and Giroux.

———. 1962. *The prophets.* New York: Harper and Row.

———. 1963. *Who is man?* Stanford: Stanford University Press.

———. 1996. *Moral grandeur and spiritual audacity,* ed. S. Heschel. New York: Farrar, Straus, and Giroux.

———. 2006. *Heavenly Torah: As refracted through the generations,* ed. and trans. G. Tucker. New York: The Continuum International Publishing Group Inc.

Hillman, J., and M. Ventura. 1992. *We've had a hundred years of psychotherapy and the world's getting worse.* San Francisco: HarperCollins Publishers.

Hirsch, I. 1994. Countertransference love and theoretical model. *Psychoanalytic Dialogues* 4(2): 171–92.

Horner, R. 2001. *Rethinking God as gift: Marion, Derrida, and the limits of phenomenology.* New York: Fordham University Press.

———. 2005. *Jean-Luc Marion: A Theo-logical introduction.* Burlington, VT: Ashgate Publishing.

House, R. 2005. Commentary: Taking therapy beyond modernity? The promise and limitations of a Levinasian understanding. *European Journal of Psychotherapy, Counseling, and Health* 7:97–108.

Huskinson, L. 2002. The self as violent other: The problem of defining the self. *Journal of Analytical Psychology* 47:437–58.

Husserl, E. [1901] 2001. *Logical investigations.* Trans. J. N. Findlay. New York: Routledge.

Hutchens, B. C. 2007. Is Levinas relevant to psychoanalysis? *Psychoanalytic Review* 94:595–616.

Irigaray, L. 1991. Questions to Emmanuel Levinas: On the divinity of love. In *Re-reading Levinas,* ed. R. Bernasconi and S. Critchley. Bloomington: Indiana University Press.

Joseph, B. 2001. Transference. In *Kleinian theory: A contemporary perspective,* ed. C. Bronstein. New York: Brunner-Routledge.

Kepnes, S., P. Ochs, and R. Gibbs. 1998. *Reasoning after revelation: Dialogues in postmodern Jewish philosophy.* Boulder: Westview Press.

Kirschner, S. R. 2005. Toward critical openness. In *Critical thinking about psychology: Hidden assumptions and plausible alternatives,* ed. B. D. Slife, J. S. Reber, and F. C. Richardson. Washington, DC: American Psychological Association.

Kleinman, A. 1988. *The illness narratives: Suffering, meaning, and the human condition.* New York: Basic Books.

Kosky, J. L. 2001. *Levinas and the philosophy of religion.* Bloomington: Indiana University Press.

Kuhn, T. 1996. *The structure of scientific revolutions.* 3d ed. Chicago: The University of Chicago Press.

Kunz, G. 1998. *The paradox of power and weakness: Levinas and an alternative paradigm for psychology.* New York: State University of New York Press.

———. 2006. *Levinas psychoanalysis.* Paper presented at the Psychology for the Other Seminar, October 21–23, 2006, Seattle University, Seattle, WA.

Laing, R. D. 1967. *The politics of experience.* New York: Ballantine Books.

———. 1969. *The divided self.* New York: Penguin Books.

Lasch, C. 1979. *The culture of narcissism: American life in an age of diminishing expectations.* New York: W. W. Norton and Company.

Layton, L. 2009. Who's responsible? Our mutual implication in each other's suffering. *Psychoanalytic Dialogues* 19:105–20.

Leahey, T. 2004. *A history of psychology: Main currents in psychological thought.* 6th ed. Upper Saddle River, NJ: Pearson Prentice Hall.

Lerner, R. 2001. *Concepts and theories of human development.* 3d ed. Mahweh, NJ: Lawrence Erlbaum.

Lesser, A. H. 1996. Levinas and the Jewish ideal of the sage. In *Facing the other: The ethics of Emmanuel Levinas,* ed. S. Hand. Cornwall, UK: Curzon Press.

Levinas, E. 1969. *Totality and infinity: An essay on exteriority.* Trans. A. Lingis. Pittsburgh: Duquesne University Press. (Original pub. French, 1961).

———. 1985. *Ethics and infinity.* Trans. R. Cohen. Pittsburgh: Duquesne University Press.

———. 1986a. Dialogue with Emmanuel Levinas. In *Face to face with Levinas,* ed. R. Cohen. Albany: SUNY Press.

———. 1986b. The trace of the other. Trans. A. Lingis. In *Deconstruction in context,* ed. M. C. Taylor. Chicago: University of Chicago Press.

———. 1987. *Time and the other.* Trans. R. Cohen. Pittsburgh: Duquesne University Press.

———. 1989. *The Levinas reader.* Ed. and trans. S. Hand. Cambridge, MA: Blackwell Publishers.

———. [1934] 1990a. Reflections on the philosophy of Hitlerism. Trans. S. Hand. *Critical Inquiry* 17:63–71.

———. 1990b. *Difficult freedom: Essays on Judaism* Trans. S. Hand. Baltimore: The Johns Hopkins University Press. (Original pub. French, 1976).

———. 1994. *Nine talmudic readings.* A. Aronowicz, Trans. Bloomington: Indiana University Press. (Original pub. French, 1968).

———. 1996. *Emmanuel Levinas: Basic philosophical writings,* ed. A. T. Peperzak, S. Critchley, and R. Bernasconi. Bloomington: Indiana University Press.

———. 1998a. *Entre nous: On thinking-of-the-other.* Trans. M. B. Smith and B. Harshav. New York: Columbia University Press. (Original pub. French. 1991).

———. 1998b. *Of God who comes to mind.* Trans. B. Bergo. Stanford, CA: Meridian Press. (Original pub. French, 1982).

———. 1998c. *Otherwise than being: Or, beyond essence.* Trans. A. Lingis. Pittsburgh: Duquesne University Press. (Original pub. French, 1974).

———. 1999. *Alterity and transcendence.* Trans. M. B. Smith. New York: Columbia University Press. (Original pub. French, 1995).

———. 2000. *God, death, and time.* Trans. B. Bergo. Stanford: Stanford University Press. (Original pub. French, 1993).

———. 2001. *Existence and existents.* Trans. A. Lingis. Pittsburgh: Duquesne University Press. (Original pub. French, 1947).

———. 2004. Emmanuel Levinas: Ethics of the Infinite. In *Debates in continental philosophy: Conversations with contemporary thinkers,* ed. R. Kearney. New York: Fordham University Press.

———. 2007a. *Beyond the verse: Talmudic readings and lectures.* Trans. G. Mole. New York: Continuum. (Original pub. French, 1982).

———. 2007b. *In the time of the nations.* Trans. M. B. Smith. New York: Continuum. (Original pub. French, 1988).

Levinas, E., and J. Robbins, 2001. *Is it righteous to be? Interviews with Emmanuel Levinas.* Stanford: Stanford University Press.

Lewis, C. S. 1946. *The great divorce.* New York: HarperCollins Publishers.

Lindbeck, G. 2006. The church's mission to a postmodern culture. *Postmodern theology: Christian faith in a pluralist world,* ed. F. Burnham. Eugene, OR: Wipf and Stock Publishers.

Lipari, L. 2004. Listening for the other: Ethical implications of the Buber-Levinas encounter. *Communication Theory* 14:122–41.

Long, W. J. 2006. Quantum theory and neuroplasticity: Implications for social theory. *Journal of Theoretical and Philosophical Psychology* 26:78–94.

Lyotard, J. F. 1984. *The postmodern condition: A report on knowledge.* Trans. G. Bennington and B. Massumi. Minneapolis: University of Minnesota Press. (Original pub. French, 1979).

MacIntyre, A. 1984. *After virtue.* 2d ed. South Bend: University of Notre Dame Press.

———. 1989. *Whose justice? Which rationality?* South Bend: University of Notre Dame Press.

———. 1990. *Three rival versions of moral enquiry: Encyclopaedia, genealogy, and tradition.* South Bend: University of Notre Dame Press.

———. 1998. *A short history of ethics. A history of moral philosophy from the Homeric age to the twentieth century* 2d ed. South Bend: University of Notre Dame Press.

———. 1999. *Dependent rational animals.* Chicago: Open Court Publishing Company.

Malka, S. 2006. *Emmanuel Levinas: His life and legacy.* Trans. M. Kigel and S. Embree. Pittsburgh: Duquesne University Press. (Original pub. French, 2002).

Marcus, P. 2007. "You are, therefore I am." Emmanuel Levinas and psychoanalysis. *Psychoanalytic Review* 94:515–27.

———. 2008. *Being for the Other: Emmanuel Levinas, ethical living, and psychoanalysis.* Milwaukee: Marquette University Press.

Margulies, A. 2000. Commentaries. *Journal of the American Psychoanalytic Association* 48:72–79.

Marion, J.-L. 2000. The voice without name: Homage to Levinas. In *The face of the other and the trace of God,* ed. J. Bloechl. New York: Fordham University Press.

———. 2004. From the other to the individual. In *Transcendence: Philosophy, literature, and theology approach the beyond,* ed. R. Schwartz. New York: Routledge.

———. 2005. "Mihi magna quaestio factus sum": The privilege of unknowing. *The Journal of Religion.* 85:1–23.

———. 2006. *The erotic phenomenon.* Trans. S. Lewis. Chicago: University of Chicago Press. (Original pub. French, 2003).

Maroda, K. 1998. Enactment: When the patient's and analyst's past converge. *Psychoanalytic Psychology* 15:517–36.

Matrix. 1999. Dir. A. Wachowski and L. Wachowski. Warner Brothers and Village Roadshow Productions.

May, R., E. Angel, and H. F. Ellenberger, eds. 1994. *Existence.* Lanham, MD: Rowman and Littlefield Publishers.

McClendon, J. W., and J. M. Smith. 1994. *Convictions: Defusing religious relativism.* Rev. ed. Eugene: Wipf and Stock Publishers.

McLaughlin, J. T. 1991. Clinical and theoretical aspects of enactment. *Journal of the American Psychoanalytic Association* 39:595–615.

———. 1995. Touching limits in the analytic dyad. *Psychoanalytic Quarterly* 64:433–65.

McWilliams, N. 2008, August. *Conversation Hour: Rediscovering the Common Ground of Psychoanalysis and Humanistic Psychology.* Paper presented at the annual meeting of the American Psychological Association, August 7–10, 2008, Boston Convention Center, Boston, MA.

Meador, K. 2003. "My own salvation:" The *Christian Century* and psychology's secularizing of American Protestantism. In *The secular revolution: Power, interests, and conflict in the secularization of American public life,* ed. C. Smith. Los Angeles: University of California Press.

Meissner, W. W. 2003. *The ethical dimension of psychoanalysis: A dialogue.* Albany: State University of Albany Press.

Merleau-Ponty, M. 2002. *Phenomenology of perception.* Trans. F. Williams. London: Routledge and Kegan Paul. (Original pub. French, 1945).

Milbank, J. 2006. *Theology and social theory: Beyond secular reason.* 2d ed. Cambridge, MA: Blackwell Publishing Limited.

Mitchell, S. A. 1988. *Relational concepts in psychoanalysis: An integration.* Cambridge: Harvard University Press.

Mitchell, S. 2003. *Can love last? The fate of romance over time.* New York: W. W. Norton and Company.

Mitchell, S. A., and L. Aron. 1999. *Relational psychoanalysis: The emergence of a tradition.* Hillsdale, NJ: Taylor and Francis Group.

Moyn, S. 2005. *Origins of the other: Emmanuel Levinas between revelation and ethics.* New York: Cornell University Press.

Murphy, N. 2003. Theology in a postmodern age. *The Nordenhaug Lectures 2003.* Czech Republic: International Baptist Theological Seminary.

———. 2005. Constructing a radical-reformation research program in psychology. In *Why psychology needs theology: A radical-reformation perspective,* ed. A. Dueck and C. Lee. Grand Rapids, MI: Williams B. Eerdmanns Publishing Company.

Nadler, A. 1997. *The faith of the mithnagdim: Rabbinic responses to Hasidic rupture.* Baltimore: The Johns Hopkins University Press.

Nagel, T. 1986. *The view from nowhere.* Cambridge: Oxford University Press.

Ogden, T. 1994. *Subjects of analysis.* Northvale, NJ: Jason Aronson.

Olthuis, J. H. 1996. Face-to-face: Ethical asymmetry or the symmetry of mutuality? In *The hermeneutics of charity: Interpretation, selfhood, and postmodern faith,* ed. J. K. Smith and H. I. Venema. Grand Rapids, MI: Brazos Press.

———. 2001. *The beautiful risk: A new psychology of loving and being loved.* Grand Rapids, MI: Zondervan.

Oppenheim, M. 2006. *Jewish philosophy and psychoanalysis: Narrating the interhuman.* New York: Lexington Books.

Orange, D. *Thinking for clinicians: Philosophical resources for contemporary psychoanalysis and the humanistic psychotherapies.* New York: Routledge.

Ornstein, A. in press. Do words still matter? Further comments on the interpretative process and the theory of change. *International Journal for Progress in Self Psychology.*

Peperzak, A. T. 1993. *To the other: An introduction to the philosophy of Emmanuel Levinas.* West Lafayette: Purdue University Press.

———, ed. 1995. *Ethics as first philosophy: The significance of Emmanuel Levinas for philosophy, literature, and religion.* London: Routledge.

———. 2000. The significance of Levinas's work for Christian thought. In *The face of the other and the trace of God: Essays on the philosophy of Emmanuel Levinas,* ed. J. Bloechl. New York: Fordham University Press.

Perls, F. 1969. *Gestalt therapy verbatim.* Lafayette, CA: Real People Press.

Pitkin, A. 2001. Scandalous ethics: Infinite presence with suffering. *Journal of Consciousness Studies* 8:231–46.

Poland, W. 2000. The analyst's witnessing and otherness. *Journal of the American Psychoanalytic Association* 48:17–34.

Potok, C. 1975. *In the beginning.* New York: Alfred A. Knopf.

Prilleltensky, I. 1994. *The morals and politics of psychology: Psychological discourse and the status quo.* Albany: State University of New York Press.

Purcell, M. 2006. *Levinas and theology.* New York: Cambridge University Press.

Putnam, H. 2002. Levinas and Judaism. In *The Cambridge companion to Levinas,* ed. S. Critchley and R. Bernasconi. New York: Cambridge University Press.

Putnam, R. D. 2000. *Bowling alone: The collapse and revival of American community.* New York: Simon and Schuster.

Rabinowitz, A. 1999. *Judaism and psychology: Meeting points.* Northvale, NJ: Jason Aronson.

Richardson, F. 2006. *Power and strong relationality.* Paper presented at the annual meeting of the American Psychological Association, August 3–6, 2006, New Orleans Convention Center, New Orleans, LA.

Richardson, F. C., B. J. Fowers, and C. B. Guignon. 1999. *Re-envisioning psychology: Moral dimensions of theory and practice.* San Francisco: Jossey-Bass Publishers.

Ricoeur, P. 1992. *Oneself as another.* Trans. K. Blamey. Chicago: University of Chicago Press.

Rieff, P. 1987. *The triumph of the therapeutic: Uses of faith after Freud.* Chicago: University of Chicago Press.

———. 2006. *My life among the deathworks: Illustrations of the aesthetics of authority.* Charlottesville: University of Virginia Press.

Rivera, M. 2007. *The touch of transcendence: A postcolonial theology of God.* Louisville: Westminster John Knox Press.

Robbins, J. 1991. *Prodigal son / elder brother: Interpretation and alterity in Augustine, Petrarch, Kafka, Levinas.* Chicago: University of Chicago Press.

Roberts, J. 2007. *Lacan and Levinas on subjectivity and alterity.* Paper presented at annual meeting of the American Psychological Association, August 2–5, San Francisco, CA.

Rubenstein, R. L. 1992. *After Auschwitz: History, theology, and contemporary Judaism.* 2d ed. Baltimore: The Johns Hopkins University Press.

Santner, E. L. 2001. *On the psychotheology of everyday life: Reflections on Freud and Rosenszweig.* Chicago: University of Chicago Press.

Sarason, I. G., and B. R. Sarason. 2005. *Abnormal psychology: The problem of maladaptive behavior* 11th ed. Upper Saddle River, NJ: Pearson Prentice Hall.

Sartre, J.-P. 1948. *No exit and three other plays* S. Gilbert, Trans. New York: Knopf. (Original pub. French, 1944).

———. [1943] 2001. *Being and nothingness.* Trans. H. E. Barnes. New York: Citadel Press.

Sayre, G. 2005. Toward a therapy for the other. *European Journal of Psychotherapy, Counseling, and Health* 7:37–47.

Seidman, N. 2006. *Faithful renderings: Jewish-Christian difference and the politics of translation.* Chicago: University of Chicago Press.

Shuman, J. J., and K. G. Meador. 2003. *Heal thyself: Spirituality, medicine, and the distortion of Christianity.* New York: Oxford University Press.

Siegel, J. 2005. *The idea of the self: Thought and experience in Western Europe since the seventeenth century.* New York: Cambridge University Press.

Siegel, R. 2009. *This Very Moment: Mindfulness in Psychotherapy.* Grand Rounds presentation, September 2009, Cambridge Health Alliance/Harvard Medical School, Cambridge, MA.

Slife, B. D., J. S. Reber, and F. C. Richardson. 2005. *Critical thinking about psychology: Hidden assumptions and plausible alternatives.* Washington, D.C.: American Psychological Association.

Slife, B. D., and D. C. Wendt. 2006. *The next step in the evidence-based practice movement.* Unpublished manuscript, Brigham Young University.

Smith, J. K. 2004. *Introducing radical orthodoxy: Mapping a postsecular theology.* Grand Rapids, MI: Baker Academic.

———. 2006a. *Who's afraid of postmodernism? Taking Derrida, Lyotard, and Foucault to church.* Grand Rapids, MI: Baker Academic.

———. 2006b. Postmodern theologies: Continental thought. Lecture notes, course taught at Fuller Theological Seminary, Pasadena, CA.

Smith, M. B. 2005. *Toward the outside: Concepts and themes in Emmanuel Levinas.* Pittsburgh: Duquesne University Press.

Sorenson, R. L. 2004. *Minding spirituality.* Hillsdale, NJ: The Analytic Press.

Stern, D. 2003. *Unformulated experience: From dissociation to imagination in psychoanalysis.* Hillsdale, NJ: The Analytic Press.

Stolorow, R. D., G. E. Atwood, and B. Brandchaft. 1994. *The intersubjective perspective.* Northvale, NJ: Jason Aronson.

Stone, I. F. 1998. *Reading Levinas / reading talmud: An introduction.* Philadelphia: The Jewish Publication Society.

Stone, L. 1984. *Transference and its context.* New York: Jason Aronson.

Tallon, A. 2007. Can Levinas's ethical metaphysics contribute to psychoanalysis? The case for and against. *Psychoanalytic Review* 94:657–80.

Tauber, A. 1998.Outside the subject: Levinas's Jewish perspective on time. *Graduate Faculty Philosophy Journal* 20/21:439–59.

Taylor, C. 1989. *Sources of the self: The making of the modern identity.* Cambridge: Harvard University Press.

———. 2007. *A secular age.* Cambridge, MA: The Belknap Press.

Thorndike, E. 1918. The nature, purposes, and general methods of measurement of educational products. *The measurement of educational products.* Seventeenth Yearbook of the National Society for the Study of Education. Bloomington, IL: Public School Publishing.

Toulmin, S. 1990. *Cosmopolis: The hidden agenda of modernity.* Chicago: University of Chicago Press.

Vandenberg, B. 1999. Levinas and the ethical context of human development. *Human Development* 42:31–44.

Visker, R. 2000. The price of being dispossessed: Levinas's God and Freud's trauma. In *The face of the other and the trace of God: Essays on the philosophy of Emmanuel Levinas,* ed. J. Bloechl. New York: Fordham University Press.

Vitz, P. 1994. *Psychology as religion: The cult of self-worship.* 2d ed. Grand Rapids, MI: William B. Eerdmanns Publishing Company.

Walzer, M. 1994. *Thick and thin: Moral argument at home and abroad.* South Bend: Notre Dame University Press.

Ward, G. 1996. On time and salvation: The eschatology of Emmanuel Levinas. In *Facing the other: The ethics of Emmanuel Levinas,* ed. S. Hand. Cornwall, UK: Curzon Press.

Weber, M. 1994. *Weber: Political writings.* Ed. P. Lassman and trans. Speirs. Cambridge: Cambridge University Press.

Welsh, E., and A. Dueck. 2007. *An unfolding of love in the works of Kristeva and Levinas: Implications for psychotherapy.* Paper presented at the Psychology for the Other conference, October 26–28, 2007, Seattle University, Seattle, WA.

Westphal, M. 2000. Commanded love and divine transcendence in Levinas and Kierkegaard. In *The face of the other and the trace of the Divine,* ed. J. Bloechl. New York: Fordham University Press.

———. 2004. *Transcendence and self-transcendence: On God and the soul.* Bloomington: Indiana University Press.

Wiesel, E. [1960] 1990. *The night trilogy.* New York: Hill and Wang.

Wiesel, E., L. Dawidowicz, D. Rabinowicz, and R. Brown. 1990. *Dimensions of the holocaust.* Chicago: Northwestern University Press.

Williams, R. N. 2005. The language and methods of science: Common assumptions and uncommon conclusions. In *Critical thinking about psychology: Hidden assumptions and plausible alternatives,* ed. B. D. Slife, J. S. Reber, and F. C. Richardson. Washington, DC: American Psychological Association.

———. 2007. Levinas and psychoanalysis: The radical turn outward and upward. *Psychoanalytic Review* 94:681–701.

Williams, R. N., and E. E. Gantt. 1998. Intimacy and heteronomy: On grounding psychology in the ethical. *Theory and Psychology* 8:255–70.

Wittgenstein, L. [1953] 2001. *Philosophical investigations.* Trans. G. Anscombe. Malden, MA: Blackwell Publishing Ltd.

Wright, T., P. Hughes, and A. Ainsley. 1988. The paradox of morality: An interview with Emmanuel Levinas. In *The provocation of Levinas: Rethinking the other,* ed. R. Bernasconi and D. Wood. London: Routledge.

Yalom, I. 2000. *Love's executioner and other tales of psychotherapy.* New York: Perennial Classics.

INDEX

Abraham, 76, 123, 199n7
Adam and Eve, 59
Alford, C. F., 51–52, 108–09, 163, 168, 170–72
alienation, 97, 108–09, 202n6
alterity, 27, 58, 63–64, 78. *See also* other, the; transference
American Psychological Association, 12–13
anarchic self. *See* demanded self
anonymity, 195–96n2
anxiety, 166
Arendt, Hannah, 65
Aron, Lewis, 151
Aronowicz, A., 39, 100
Atkins, K., 70
Augustine, 98
avoidance, 161
awakening of the self, 160–64, 168–70, 201n2
Awakening the Dreamer (Bromberg), 161

Barrett, W., 59
Beals, C., 59, 202n1
beauty, 55–56
Becker, Ernest, 74, 85, 87, 202n6
being, 200n17
Being and Time (Heidegger), 30–31
bell-shaped self, 82–84, 91
Bernstein, R., 83
Bible. *See* Torah
Birrell, P., 66, 183–84n12, 184n13
Blanchot, Maurice, 31, 188n12
Bloom, A., 110
Bromberg, P., 161
Brown, I., 13, 184n13
Browning, D., 182–83n9
Brueggeman, Walter, 10, 114, 143, 177

Buber, Martin, 10, 102, 188n15, 196n6
Burggraeve, R., 33, 56, 187–88n10
Burston, Daniel, 182n7, 195n13

Century of the Self, The (TV series), 95
Chouchani (Rabbi and teacher), 187n7, 188n12
Chused, J. F., 155
cogito, 58, 70, 96, 99–100, 123, 135, 200n15. *See also* Descartes, René
Cohen, R.: on being human, 81; on ethics, 78–79; on goodness, 121; on Greek philosophy, 47; on Judaism, 27, 34–37, 48; on knowledge, 71; on Levinas's response to the Holocaust, 34; on modern psychology, 110, 197n12; on my brother's keeper, 122; on reason, 57; on responsibility, 102, 178; on science, 6–10, 174; and self-alienation, 97; on subjection, 201–02n5; on suicidal inclinations, 112; on translation, 49–50
colonial imperialism, 197n11
communication, 149. *See also* conversation
conatus amandi, 100–03
conatus essendi, 100–02
consciousness: commands on self prior to, 79–80; complacency-in-being, 77; and construction of knowledge, 99; and desire for immortality, 74–75; and ethics, 120, 130–31; Heidegger on, 60; Husserl on, 199–200n14; non-intentional, 122, 140–41; and the psyche, 105–06. *See also* ego; psyche
conversation, 138–39, 200n16. *See also* communication
counter-intentionality, 61
counter-transference, 147–48

Crime and Punishment (Dostoyevsky), 63
Critchley, S., 8–9, 25–26, 93, 123, 129, 201n4
Curtis, Adam, 95
Cushman, Philip: on God, 41; on the good, 15–16; and Jewish thought, 40, 42, 190n28; on modern psychology, 195n12, 197n13; on questioning, 51; on the self, 5, 21, 77, 95, 180, 202n6; on social interactions, 181n2

Danziger, K., 82
Dasein, 101
Davis, C, 174
death, 74, 101, 197n14
demanded self: commands from outside itself, 105–06, 121; defined, 4; ethically constructed, 105–06; and psychotherapy, 113–15, 142. *See also* ethics; responsibility
democracy, 97
Denial of Death, The (Becker), 74
Dependent Rational Animals (MacIntyre), 100
Derrida, Jacques: on Abraham, 199n7; on Greek language, 48; and Levinas, 31, 186, 188n12, 202n2; on the self, 20, 103–04; on translation, 50
Descartes, René, 8, 45, 81. *See also cogito*
De Tocqueville, Alexis, 96
dialogical ethics, 21, 40
Difficult Freedom (Levinas), 120, 177
dissociation, 166
Divine, 55, 78. *See also* God; Other, the
Doherty, W. A., 15, 19
Dostoyevsky, Fyodor, 63
Dueck, Alvin, 39, 65, 108, 152, 197n10

Ebner, Mark, 10
ego: concreteness of egoism, 75; ennui of, 75; and existence for its own sake, 101; in modern philosophy, 57–58; and morality, 14; and the Other, 108; and the other, 60–61, 76–79; prehistory of, 124–25; and the primordial dyad, 130–31; and rupture of immanence, 86; sovereignty of, 57–58, 64, 73–74, 77, 176, 197n12; super, 14; Taylor on, 14; yearning for immortality, 85. *See also* consciousness; organic narcissism
egology, 80, 87, 108–11
empiricism, 60, 194n8
enactments, 147–51, 152–57
Enlightenment, 96
ethics: codes of, 184n13; Cohen on, 78–79; and consciousness, 120, 130–31; descriptive *vs.* prescriptive, 203n3; and dis-interested knowing, 64–65; essencelessness of, 78–79; ethical codes, 12–13; ethical optics, 20–21, 65, 80, 102–03; as first philosophy, 26, 64, 85–86; Gibbs on, 203n5; hyperbolistic expressions of, 202n2; and identity, 179; and justice, 29; meaning of, 16–18; and modern philosophy, 32–34; and the other, 36, 142, 174; preceding cognition, 65; and primordial responsibilities, 130–31; and the psyche, 12; and the self, 1–3, 13–18, 46, 100–06, 109–10, 185n19; and submission to Torah, 30; subservient to reason, 55–57; Taylor on, 18; and transcendence, 100. *See also* demanded self; justice; morality; responsibility
"Etre juif" (Levinas), 189n22
expiation, 153, 156

face, the: commands of, 140; and facelessness of generalities, 68; as language, 200n16; of the Other, 81; of the other, 61, 77–79, 86, 140; primordial calling of, 154; and the sovereignty of the ego, 73–74; and trace of the Divine, 78; transcendence of, 78; as the widow, orphan, and stranger, 102–03. *See also* intersubjective space; Other, the
fascism, 13
feminist thought, 201–02n5
Ferenczi, Sándor, 151
Ford, D., 34, 178, 189n22
for-the-other, 61
Foucault, M., 4, 66, 103–04, 191n32, 193n5
Fowers, B. J., 19
freedom, 56, 61, 115, 143
Freud, Sigmund: critiques of, 97–98; and intersubjective space, 147; and morality, 14; and self-knowledge, 51; and transference, 132–33, 137, 200n14; on the unconscious, 199n11
Frie, Roger, 182n7, 195n13
Fromm, Erich, 19–20, 97, 107–08, 185n21, 185–86n22, 202n6
Fryer, D. R., 161

Gadamer, H. G., 89, 139, 203n4
Galileo, 81
Gantt, E., 13, 51, 193n4
Gergen, K., 82, 111, 183n10, 186n24
Gibbs, Robert: on ethics, 203n5; and history, 139; on Jewish influence on Levinas, 27, 187n7, 189n21; on Levinas's translation project, 190–91n30; and transference, 133; on translation of Torah, 45–46
God, 41, 123, 129, 198n2. *See also* Divine; *hineni*; Other, the

goodness, 15–16, 55–56, 106, 120–21, 143
Great Divorce, The (Lewis), 159–60
Greek language, 40–50
Greek philosophy, 26–31, 49–52, 55, 57–59, 187n5, 187n9. *See also* philosophy, modern
Guignon, C. B., 19
Gyges, myth of, 58–59, 61–62

Haidt, J., 161
Halperin, David, 35
Hasidic Judaism, 28–29, 188n15
healing, 164–65
Hebrew language, 40–50
Hegel, G. W. F., 99
Heidegger, Martin: and death, 101; on detached reason, 60; and inner space, 98; and the intentional I, 58; and Levinas, 30–31, 189n19; and Nazism, 31; on science, 88–89
Heinz dilemma, 120
Hell, 159–60, 164
hermeneutical philosophy, 12
Herodotus, 59
Heschel, Abraham Joshua, 2–3, 87, 100, 173, 175, 185–86n22, 194n9
hineni, 120–29, 131–37, 143, 198n4. *See also* God; Other, the
Histories (Herodotus), 59
history, 123–25, 131–39, 177–79, 181–82n4, 200n17, 203n4
holiness, 16, 103, 177
Holocaust, 25, 31–34
hostage, the self as, 60, 104, 114, 122, 128, 153, 162
human corporeality, 193–94n6
human nature, 13–14
Huskinson, L., 99
Husserl, Edmund, 30, 58, 60, 135, 199–200n14

identity, 80, 90–91, 97–98, 178–79, 193–94n6
idolatry, 29, 38
immanence, 86, 177
immemorial past, 123–25
immortality, desire for, 74–75, 85
individualism, 184–85n17, 196n8
inner space, 98
insomnia, 114, 161, 168–72, 201n2. *See also* sleep
intentional I, 58
intersubjective space, 11–12, 147. *See also* face, the; other, the
In the Beginning (Potok), 47
invisibility, 58–59, 61
Irigaray, Luce, 170

Jacob, 123
Jewgreek.Greekjew, 186
Jewish people, 65
Jewish philosophy, 26–31, 32–34, 40, 42, 190n28. *See also* philosophy, modern
Jill (patient), 165–70
Joseph, B., 132
Judaism: diversity within, 188n11; eternal dialogue of, 48; Levinas and, 34–37, 92; Lithuanian, 27–29, 188n15; Litvak, 28–29; and obedience, 198–99n5; principles of, 44–50; and prophecy, 187n5; terminology of, 27, 46; and Torah, 143; and the widow, orphan, and stranger, 102–03; and the yearning for the other, 76. *See also* Hebrew language; *hineni*
justice, 4–5, 29, 32–34, 120, 125, 130–31, 178–79. *See also* ethics; morality; responsibility

Kant, Immanuel, 16, 45, 96, 182n8
kenosis, 3, 80, 113, 201–02n5
Klein, Melanie, 136
knowledge, 64–65, 67, 71, 99, 125, 198n2

Kohlberg, Lawrence, 120, 198n1
Kunz, George, 85, 109–10, 193n2

Laing, R. D., 97, 107, 185n20, 202n6
Layton, Lynn, 199n10, 201n1
Le Chambon, France, 119–20, 143
Levinas, Emmanuel: biographical information, 27–28, 30–31; works of: *Difficult Freedom*, 120, 177; "Etre juif," 189n22; "The Meaning of History," 178; *Nine Talmudic Readings*, 39, 62; *Otherwise than Being*, 32–33, 189n22; "Reflections on the Philosophy of Hitlerism," 33; *Totality and Infinity*, 31, 75, 106
Lewis, C. S., 159
liberation theology, 196n7
Lithuanian Judaism, 27–29, 188n15
Litvak Judaism, 28–29
Locke, John, 7, 20, 110, 182n6
Long, W. J., 109
love, 103
Love's Executioner (Yalom), 61
Lyotard, J. F., 8, 31, 38

MacIntyre, Alasdair, 25–26, 38, 99
Malka, Salomon, 32, 44, 193n2
Marcus, P., 165
Marion, Jean-Luc, 61, 67, 78, 189n20
Maroda, K., 148
maternity, 199n8
Matrix (movie), 168
Mauriac, François, 25
McLaughlin, J. T., 171
McWilliams, Nancy, 148
"Meaning of History, The" (Levinas), 178
memory. *See* remembering
Merleau-Ponty, Maurice, 30–31
messianic eschatology, 177
metaphysical desire, 75–76
Midrash, 41, 190n25

Mill, John Stuart, 96
mineness, 101, 134. *See also* other, the
misnagdim, 188n15
Mitchell, S. A., 133, 148, 161, 171, 201n3
mitzvot, 37
modern philosophy. *See* philosophy, modern
morality, 1–3, 13–14, 31–34, 177, 184n14, 198nn1–2. *See also* ethics; justice; responsibility
Moses, 123
Murphy, N., 93, 98–99
my brother's keeper, 121–22
mystery, 134
mysticism, 28

nature and morality, 14
Nazism, 13, 30–34, 65, 119–20, 189n19
Nietzsche, Friedrich, 193n2
Nine Talmudic Readings (Levinas), 39, 62
non-intentional consciousness, 122, 140–41
normality, 82–85, 91–92

ontology, 33, 65
Oppenheim, M., 46
optics, ethical, 20–21, 65, 80, 102–03
organic narcissism, 74, 87. *See also* ego; self, the
original traumatism, 163
Ornstein, Anna, 149
Orthodox Judaism, 28–29
Other, the, 79, 81, 108, 126, 162, 193n2. *See also* Divine
other, the: asymmetrical needs of, 102; avoidance of, 161; calling or commands of, 122, 129, 140; and comfort, 171; death of, 101; and the ego, 60–61, 76–79; ethical relationships to, 203n4; face of, 61, 77–79, 86, 140; and goodness, 121; and guilt, 101–02; and identity, 179; longing for, 201n3; in modern psychology, 66–69, 139; as my brother's keeper, 121–22; responsibility for, 16–17, 36, 61, 102–05, 114–15, 174, 178; revelation of, 42–44; and the self, 76, 79, 122, 125–26, 129, 140, 168–70; and third parties, 130–31; and transference, 134; and violence, 162–63, 171–72; vulnerability of, 101–03. *See also* alterity; face, the; God; *hineni;* intersubjective space; mineness
Otherwise than Being or Beyond Essence (Levinas), 32–33, 189n22

paranoid-schizoid position, 136
Parsons, T., 39, 65, 108
Pascal, Blaise, 45
patients, rational, 69–70
Peperzak, A., 59, 186–87n4, 189n20
phenomenology, 30
philosophy, modern: and the ego, 57–58; as egology, 80, 87, 108–11; and engagement with history, 181–82n4; and freedom of the self, 61; and idolatry, 38; and intersubjective space between persons, 11–12; moral failure of, 25–26; and the other, 66–69, 139; postmodern, 15, 36–38, 93, 103–04, 195n13, 196n8; postsecular, 37, 189n23; of presence, 175; and reason, 55–57; and responsibility, 32–34, 61; and science, 38, 194n7; Taylor on, 10. *See also* Greek philosophy; Jewish philosophy
Pitkin, A., 44
Plato, 45
Potok, Chaim, 47
primordial dyad, 130–31, 139
Prophets, The (Heschel), 173
prophesy, 173, 175–78, 187n5
Protestant Reformation, 182n6

psyche, 43, 53, 81, 105–06, 126–27, 152–54. *See also* consciousness; self, the
psychoanalysis, 20, 86, 140, 148–49, 184n15, 196n3, 200n15
psychology, modern: about, 182–83n9; challenges to mainstream thought, 11–12, 197n13; Cohen on, 110, 197n12; criticism of, 18–20; Cushman on, 195n12, 197n13; as egology, 108–11; on ego's yearning for immortality, 85; and empiricism, 194n8; and ethical condition of the self, 1–3, 13–16, 46, 109–10, 185n19; and freedom of the self, 61; and generalization of the other, 66–69; and Greek philosophy, 50–52; Hume and Kant on, 182n8; and Levinas's influence, 141–43, 186n3; and loss of communal identity, 97–98; moral failure of, 25–26; and philosophy of presence, 175; postmodern perspective, 195n13; postsecular approach, 39; and relationality, 200n15; and sameness, 87; and scientific epistemology, 7–8, 82–84, 89–92, 194–95n11; and selfhood, 51–52; terminology of, 9–11, 15, 69, 107, 111, 186n24, 193n5; and transference, 132–33, 137; and translation, 47
psychotherapy, 110, 112–15, 137–42, 147–54, 168–70, 195n12
Putnam, H., 37, 101, 198n4

radical passivity, 128
radical transcendence, 27
Rawls, John, 16
reality, 37–38
reason, 55–65, 125
redemption, 43–44
"Reflections on the Philosophy of Hitlerism" (Levinas), 33

remembering, 43, 137–41, 150–51, 177
respect, 150
responsibility: before consciousness, 120; and the ethical "I," 80; and *hineni*, 123–29; Levinas on, 2–3; and modern philosophy, 32–34, 61; for the other, 16–17, 36, 61, 102–05, 114–15, 174, 178; primordial, 130–31; subservient to reason, 56; taught by Torah and Midrash, 41; of therapists, 152–54; and transcendence, 112; for the widow, orphan, and stranger, 36, 102, 126. *See also* demanded self; *hineni*; justice; morality
revelation, 42–44, 195n13
Richardson, Frank, 19, 89, 110, 194–95n11
Ricoeur, P., 31, 200n17, 202n2
Rieff, Philip, 8–9, 96–98, 185–86n22, 196n3, 197n14
risk, 161
Robbins, J., 49, 190n25
Rosenzweig, Mark, 10, 87, 187n7, 188n12
Rubenstein, R. I., 65

sameness, 87, 91–92, 108–11, 150–51, 159–60, 165
Samuel, 123
Samuel (patient), 145–46, 150–51, 152–56
Sartre, Jean-Paul, 30–31, 61, 63, 75
schizoid self-alienation, 97
science, philosophical framework of, 38, 194n7
scientific epistemology: critiques of, 65, 174–76; emergence and dominance of, 6–10, 182n6; and modern psychology, 82–84, 194–95n11; and moral failure of, 25–26; and morality, 15; strengths and weaknesses of, 88–92
Secular Age, A (Taylor), 59

secular reason, 38
self, the: alienation of, 97, 108–09, 202n6; as an ethical optics, 20–21; and anonymity, 195–96n2; awakening of, 160–64, 168–70, 201n2; bell-shaped, 82–84; commands on prior to consciousness, 79–80, 179; and construction of knowledge, 99; constructs of, 4–5, 51, 181nn2–3, 198n3; definitions of, 5–6, 9, 195n1; disengagement of, 57–59, 63, 99, 125; egoist, 1–2; ethical condition of, 1–3, 13–18, 46, 100–06, 109–10, 185n19; and freedom, 56, 61; and *hineni*, 122–29, 143; and history, 123–25; as hostage, 60, 104, 114, 122, 128, 153, 162; and kenosis, 3, 80, 113, 201–02n5; as masterfully bounded, 107–08; and modern psychology, 13–16, 51–52; and morality, 1–3, 177; narcissism of, 174–76; and ontological individualism, 184–85n17; and the other, 76, 79, 122, 125–26, 129, 140, 168–70; outward orientation *vs.* interiority, 128–29; passive *vs.* agentic, 127; religiosity of, 79; and relinquishing of being, 127; self-assertion, 134; self-reflexivity of, 95–100, 136; and the sovereign I, 19, 197n12; statistical constructs of normality, 82–85, 91–92; and subjection, 197n15; transcendence of, 39; and trauma victims, 201–02n5; uniqueness and responsibility, 103–07; and violence, 161–64; vulnerability of, 128. *See also hineni*; organic narcissism; psyche
self-emptying. *See* kenosis
separation, 135
Shoah. *See* Holocaust
sleep, 164–65, 172. *See also* insomnia

Smith, J. K., 38, 189n20
social constructivist philosophy, 12
Spinoza, Baruch, 86, 100
Stern, Donnel, 5, 181n3, 199n11
Stone, I. F., 176
stories, societal, 5–6
subjectivity. *See* self, the
substitution, 153, 156, 163
suicidal inclinations, 112

Talmud, 40–50
Taylor, C.: on ego and morality, 14; on ethics, 18; on the good, 16; and inner space, 98; on modern philosophy, 10; on moral failure, 25–26; *A Secular Age*, 59; on the self, 96, 181n3
temptation of temptation, 62–65, 77
thinking otherwise, 33–34
third parties, 130–31, 137–38, 142, 199n9
Thorndike, E., 82
"Thou shalt not kill," 146, 153, 156
time, 124, 147
Torah, 30, 43, 44–50, 123, 143
totalitarianism, 56
Totality and Infinity (Levinas), 31, 75, 106
tragic heroes, 87–88
transcendence: and being human, 87; epistemic, 36–37; and ethics, 100; of the face, 78; and immanence, 177; radical, 27; and responsibility, 112; of the self, 39
transference, 131–37, 147–48, 200n14. *See also* alterity
translation, 37–38, 40–50, 190n28
trauma, 163–65, 201n4, 201–02n5. *See also* violence

Ulysses, 73, 76
unconscious, 147–48, 199n11
uniqueness, 103–07

Vichy government, 31
violence, 56, 137, 146, 152–57, 161–64, 171–72, 201n2. *See also* trauma
visibility, 58–59
Visker, R., 162–64
vulnerability, 101–03, 128, 149–50, 151

Westphal, M., 36, 189n20
widow, orphan, and stranger, 36, 102–03, 126

Wiesel, Elie, 1
Williams, R. N., 13, 18, 51, 112, 141, 176, 193n4
Winnicott, 170–71
wisdom, love of, 55, 71
World War II, 31–32, 119–20
wounding, 164–65

Yalom, I., 61
Yeshiva learning, 28

Goodman, David M.
The demanded self

MAY 3 0 2012